Teaching the Severely Handicapped Child

Teaching the Severely Handicapped Child

Basic Skills for the Developmentally Disabled

Robert M. Browning

Director, Child Psychology Clinic and School
Middleton, Wisconsin

Allyn and Bacon, Inc.
Boston   London   Sydney   Toronto

Dedicated to
Ellen Rose Browning
my wife
whose courage, nurture, and collaboration
made this possible

Library of Congress Cataloging in Publication Data

Browning, Robert Mitchell, 1938–
Teaching the severely handicapped child.

"This book follows as a sequel to Behavior modifica-
tion and child treatment: an experimental clinical
approach."
Bibliography: p.
Includes index.
1. Behavior therapy. 2. Handicapped children—
Care and treatment. 3. Child psychotherapy—Residen-
tial treatment. 4. Exceptional children—Education.
I. Title.
RJ505.B4B762   362.7′8′1968   79–23619
ISBN 0–205–06877–4

Printed in the United States of America

Contents

Preface

This book is most relevant to those who must teach and treat severely handicapped children who may be diversely diagnosed as psychotic, autistic, multiply handicapped (blind or deaf and psychotic), mute and undifferentiated brain-damaged with specific learning disabilities, particularly with respect to language disabilities. The curriculum was initially developed in a residential program, which made it possible to have the controlled conditions necessary to test out the treatment steps and to accumulate more precise data. However, the program is quite relevant to a diversity of settings where the school and/or home is willing to provide the appropriate structure. Over the last few years it has been implemented in public schools, out-patient day care centers, homes, foster homes, group homes, as well as continued studies in a residential program. The treatment curriculum was devised for children whose generalization of training is extremely restricted and whose limited adaptations will require a continuously supportive environment to sustain them.

The primary message of this book is how to train such children to adapt maximally to their environment, utilizing specialized training techniques. A concurrent objective is to train parents, school, and other relevant persons in the home environment of the child, to understand the child's limited abilities, and to maintain the child's achievement level. To the extent that adaptation between child, family, and community cannot be achieved, one must decide on a treatment-based prognosis for alternate placement of the child in some place other than the home environment. Alternative placements outside the child's home may be seen on a scale from least to most restrictive, ranging from foster care, to a professionally trained foster home, to group home care, to a treatment-oriented residential center, or to a state-operated residential program.

Many of the treatment procedures presented here are not recommended for the normal child, the neurotic child, or for the youngster with minor behavioral disabilities. This book follows as a sequel to *Behavior Modification and Child Treatment: An Experimental Clinical Approach* (Browning and Stover 1971). It applies to the specialized clinical population for whom the treatment curriculum has been tested. In many respects, the book has an aura of mechanism in the manner in which the treatment programs are performed which is an unfortunate fact.

To counter an oversimplified notion of the treatment aims of this book, I would like to explain a few basic assumptions relevant to child treatment which have been gathered from our experience, some of which are supported by other investigators. These children are variously diagnosed as autistic, schizophrenic, symbiotic, brain-damaged retarded, retarded, and emotionally disturbed. They represent an etiologic enigma and seem to accumulate these diagnoses in direct proportion to the number of professionals who provide a diagnostic evaluation of the child. Regardless of the presumed heterogeneity of deficits of these children as implied by various reports in the literature (c.f. DeMyer Churchill, Pontius, and Gilkey 1971), we found common handicaps which resulted in their failure to acquire socially appropriate behaviors, caused their rejection from public school enrollment, and prompted the family to seek professional assistance for their child. These handicaps, which appear to run consistently through this admittedly varied group of handicapped children, were: inattention to tasks, lack of compliance, dominance of asocial operant language behaviors (for example, tantrums, aggression), bizarre behaviors, language deficits, failure to imitate, eating problems, incomplete toileting, social aloofness, and a lack of effectual reinforcers. The etiology of these handicaps, particularly for the psychotic and autistic child, is likely organic, with an environmental interaction (Darby 1976; Mulcahy 1973; Prior et al. 1976; Sullivan 1975; Tanquay et al. 1976). The treatment curriculum presented in this book is designed around these handicaps.

1
Prerequisites to Developing a Behavior Modification Program

The recurrent retort of the antagonists to behavior modification procedures is: "We tried that, and it did not work." Typically, that is an accurate description of their experiences, but closer examination often reveals that, unfortunately, they committed all the errors that guarantee that behavior modification approaches with this clinical population will not work. Successful implementation of the treatment curriculum outlined in this book is dependent upon satisfying several prerequisite criteria. These criteria may appear no different than what is normally assumed in directing a public school, an effective social-welfare agency, or a corporation. These necessary conditions are usually omitted in journal articles reporting on specific behavior modification techniques. The reader who attempts to perform such techniques is often confronted with failure, which is blamed upon a presumed inadequacy of the procedure as described in the journal article, when, in fact, the failure could be attributed to not providing program prerequisites. It has been my experience that failure to satisfy criteria, such as consistency and perseverence, would assume failure of any treatment program. These criteria represent the administrative priorities that must be established before initiating a multiple-response behavior modification program.

In performing the case studies cited later in the book, it was determined that 16 percent of staff time was involved in communication relevant to treatment programs for the children. The majority of that communication time was devoted to meeting these program prerequisites. The treatment programs themselves were already established. Staff knew how to perform them; but to assure that they were implemented satisfactorily meant that these prerequisites be monitored constantly. These prerequisites criteria are not justified by data, although for some there is a learning theory rationale which will be presented for their support.

FIRST PREREQUISITE: SIMPLE PROGRAMS

The case studies and the various treatment programs employed are deliberately designed to be simplistic. Such programs make it possible for the child to learn the response, and make it feasible for the staff, family, and teacher instructing the child to actually perform the programs.

Simple programs are an advantage because they take into consideration the nature of the deficits of profoundly disturbed children. These children adapt best to a program in which the cues, expectancies, rewards, and punishments are exceptionally clear and readily distinguishable from other competing stimuli. The complexity of the program should not exceed the extent of adaptive or operant behavior that is minimally expected for each child. When these children are immersed in a complex discrimination learning task, their confusion will assure either the acquisition of, or the reinstatement of, undesirable avoidance habits in reaction to the frustration engendered by a learning task to which they cannot adapt.

When a program is too complex, you may predict from the children's communication handicap that they will be unable to explain their frustration by telling you that they do not understand; you may expect that the children will perform with less attention and more errors. The children's responses to a confusing learning task will be evidenced by an acceleration of the many deviant behaviors which prompted the original diagnosis (retrieval). Thus, the complex programs to which the children readily adapt will subvert your treatment energies by increasing the likelihood of deviant responses. This will render the learning situation more noxious for the child, and diminish the reinforcing effects of the training staff and family. Often, the clinician's teaching these children find themselves ascribing this behavioral retrieval to negativism in the child, rather than recognizing the learning handicaps which characterize these children. Churchill (1972) explains this clinical error quite clearly. The habit acquired most rapidly and trained in a variety of circumstances is suggested to be the preferred treatment regimen for these concrete children, which is the justification for simplified techniques.

Staff, Parents, School Personnel

Simplified programs not only benefit the child, but also the staff, parents, and school personnel who will be responsible for the child following discharge. Programs that are simple in their cues and response expectancies, and performed in a graduated sequence of difficulty, will facilitate communication among staff and families. The families cited in this book have been exposed to a short and intense course in learning theory, behavior modification techniques, and most specifically to the programs performed with their youngsters. It has been observed that the amount of material retained was considerably less than what was actually instructed. We have not formally tested this hypothesis, but have found that parents require retraining at least every six months for optimal effects. Unfortunately, this was only performed when the child had retrieved so many behaviors that it necessitated our intervention to retain him or her in the home and community. Furthermore, with increasing time from discharge, the family seemed less informed and skilled in the materials they had been taught. It became apparent that the complexity of a treatment program had to be at a level the parents could comprehend, generalize from, and remember for several months. This same rationale applied to training school personnel, or other professionals, regardless of where the child resided.

Training school personnel and professionals from other facilities will, at best, be a short-term effort. The more simplified the concepts and language used to explain the training programs, the more likely it is that these persons will recall and implement the programs. The longer the management order, the more questions will be raised, but not asked, and the greater the variance among staff performing the programs. This will be observed by diminished consistency in the child's program, and the inevitable reduction in learning rates.

The design of behavior modification programs is relatively easy; it is their administration which is problematic. Several problems have been identified which interfere with maintaining simple programs. These problems are usually generated by the child treatment orientation of the professional. One such problem arises when professionals assign complex meaning to a child's behaviors and begins to make expectancies of the child that far exceed his or her capabilities. Again, it will be of help to refer to Churchill's (1969) discussion of this dilemma. This problem is likely to occur when confronted with a child who demonstrates a relative "high spot" in language, the content of which is very titillating to analytically-oriented individuals and leads to the exasperating conclusion that the child is *purposely* demonstrating the psychotic or maladaptive behavior that eventuated his or her referral. The child's learning problems are then explained away by some diffuse notion of "negativism." We have been snared by this misinterpretation repeatedly; namely, of maintaining expectancies for a child based on clinical hunches derived from the content of the child's sparse language. With such overinterpretation, one is liable to design programs which would be more plausible for the higher-level child, but such complex programs will prove to be futile to the psychotic child. Unfortunately, this leads to the trap of becoming more convinced that the child is purposefully not complying, or is being negativistic, the only justification for which is your hunch that the child is more intelligent than initially thought because of the content you assigned to delimit his or her language.

Another problem that interferes with maintenance of simple programs is that some professionals and families will want you to respond to the child as if he or she were normal and capable of progressing in a normal developmental sequence. This seems only fair, since it pacifies the parental hopes that their "sick" child may be made well. Operating on this premise would mean establishing more complex demands for the child, which would have the unfortunate consequences of failure. One should be aware that when children are referred at school age, they have already accumulated the evidence that they are unable to adapt to their environment as normal children.

I am speaking about the kinds of children referred to in the introduction, which is exclusive of the simply emotionally disturbed, disadvantaged, or emotionally deprived child. However, when you suggest a simple mechanical-like program, it will offend many professionals and parents who consider the psychotic child to be biologically intact, with deficits functional in nature. It may be explained to these individuals that those cases cited in journals in which an autistic child eventually becomes a college professor are unique and questionable in terms of original diagnoses.

The error of designing complex programs for the intellectually limited child is certain to fail, but at the same time there is likely to be pressure for you to construct such treatment regimens. If one is using exceptionally simple programs, with considerable positive reinforcement, the child may flourish and would then be able to advance to more complex programs. This error of underestimating the child's abilities can be tolerated and rectified. Yet, if one takes the opposite course of establishing programs in which a normal child would be likely to adapt, most psychotic children would demonstrate minimal, if any, progress. At best, they would have an ostensibly comfortable custodial environment, not so useful to testing their learning potential, but having a pleasant and delusional appearance to parents and professionals. The error incurred here is that the child would not be progressed to the level of his or her capability, which is an intolerable error.

← Even when parents prefer to think of their child as more complex than your development assessment suggests, if you allow complex programs, you will sabotage the parent training program. One cannot expect parents to perform intricate programs at home and still retain what may be called a "family." Your contract is with the entire family unit, including the child. To place excessive demands upon that family may be destructive, not only in the failure of the child to adapt to those programs and the resultant parental depression, but also in the time detracted from the needs of other siblings in the home.

←Another reason for using simple programs arises when the disposition of the child is decided to be institutional. In institutional facilities where custodial care is maintained, there is a scarcity of supervising professionals. Most work is performed by aids whose education and pay are correspondingly low, who do not always have a professional dedication, and who receive little supervision. This is not to discredit the concerted efforts characteristic of so many aids, nurses, and paraprofessionals in such facilities, but rather is recognition of the budget and costs they have to deal with, the administrative overstructures, and the limited amount of supervision allocated to each child. Cognizant of these circumstances, one should attempt to train the child to adapt to that minimally supervised environment with programs that the personnel will be able to comprehend and implement with a minimum of training. They will not perform intricate treatment programs; in fact, difficulty will be encountered in transferring the most simplistic procedures to many custodial facilities. This may, in part, be attributed to the diversity of opinion on child care among staff working in custodial care programs, which means your coordination will require not only the usual staff training but even greater diplomacy. It should be recognized that behavior modification is not taught pervasively on the graduate level in training psychologists, psychiatrists, or social workers. Examination of the texts used reveals an emphasis on single-case, single-response application, but an absence of information about devising and implementing multiple-response programs for a diversity of children.

SECOND PREREQUISITE: THE DOMINANTLY POSITIVE ENVIRONMENT

← A basic assumption of learning theory applied to the development of treatment programs is that known positive reinforcement is responsible for the acquisition of new behavior and maintenance of those responses in the home and community. This assumption is easily demonstrable with normal children; and with the learning impairments evident in psychotic, autistic, retarded, and neurologically impaired children, one is unlikely to see impressive gains with reinforcement systems in teaching new behaviors. This does not exclude positive reinforcement as a primary tenet in learning theory applicable to teaching handicapped children, but rather, these children are not as reliably responsive to the complex stimuli in their environment as are normal children. This means that acquisition of any response will require a more efficient learning condition. Failure to produce appreciable treatment gains in behavior modification programs with severely disturbed children is often attributable to failure to maintain sufficient trials with a known and clearly discernible positive reinforcement. Failure to preserve the treatment gains is often a result of being unable to sustain the reinforcers that were originally responsible for acquiring the response. The following discussion pertains to the conditions that will negate your attempts to continue a positive and contingent environment for a child.

← One error is to generalize from a journal article study in which positive reinforcement was used to train a child a particular response and conclude from that "thoroughbred scientific demonstration" that it is a clinically feasible technique. Another error is in failing to anticipate the massive number of trials required to teach a response. It is of methodological interest to demonstrate that a profoundly disturbed child can learn behaviors which were previously considered beyond his or her ability. It is another administrative problem to arrange a clinical regimen to teach and maintain that behavior for a lifetime. Problems arise of manpower and of monitoring the staff responsible for teaching the behavior to determine if they habituate to lower levels of performance and thereby fail to train the criterion level of the response. The training staff may fail to provide the necessary reinforcement because of the minimal gains and rewards they receive in working with the child. Fatigue, habituation, the noxious behaviors of the child, all combine to deter training efforts which require thousands of trials for even minimal gains, and which are dependent upon continuous and heavy reinforcement schedules to preserve the response.

Thinning Schedules

In the controlled and contrived setting of the laboratory, demonstration of thinning reinforcement schedules and maintenance of behaviors for short intervals of time is very plausible. When one is dealing with the child's natural environment, that laboratory control is absent; the child is as likely to train his or her environment as the environment is to train the child. The interaction is often one in which the parents may have been trained to tolerate extremely deviant behaviors in their child, and with slow, yet minimal gains, it becomes gradually less annoying, indeed reinforcing, to tolerate a lower-level approximation of the deviant behavior and to be content with that much gain. The child then trains the parent or staff to "thin the schedule," but much too quickly, so that extinction effects begin to occur before the response is reliably controlled. This can instill a steady downward spiral, with one finally concluding that the treatment regimen was ineffectual, or that the child was incapable of responding to the program.

The implication pervades some behavior modification literature that states a properly graded shaping program with the appropriate reinforcers will permit severely handicapped children to be almost unlimited in what they may learn. The implied assumption is that these children are not asymptotic in their growth potential. I maintain that response complexity will be limited by the extent of the child's retardation, which is more obvious in predicting academic achievement. These childrens' slow learning rates, their discrimination deficits, their tendency to retrieve recently controlled behaviors, and their dependency upon a continuous and highly visible reinforcement system, hardly render them to be responsive children in any training program. Furthermore, generalization seems to be achieved only if the child is trained in all situations. What the child learns in the treatment setting will not necessarily generalize to his or her home environment. In fact, the contrary is to be expected. This points to the reality of the manpower problem in constructing a positively reinforcing program, i.e., someone has to perform the arduous task of teaching the behavior with the child, everywhere.

Program Treatment by Parents

←Another error is to place excessive responsibility upon the parents for performing a program. It becomes an understandably difficult chore for parents to maintain a dominantly positive and contingent environment for the child who demonstrates symptoms of retardation and psychoses. For the parent to maintain such a positive environment presumes a strong and affirmative parent-child relationship. The growth of such a relationship with a psychotic child is immensely difficult; it is surprising how positive these parents usually are with their children. Many of us professionals are insensitive to what it would be like to raise an autistic child, who as an infant when picked up, would be placid and alternately rigid and rejecting of parental affection, which means that the child would be a confusing and non-rewarding youngster. Eventually, such a child may discourage and extinguish the parents displaying affectionate behavior toward him or her, simply because it has always been ineffectual since birth.

Many professionals have performed a lamentable disservice to parents of the severely handicapped child, particularly to those of the autistic child, by making generalized statements describing the parents as cold, aloof, and distant, which perpetrated the illogical conclusion that this relationship made the child deviant in behavior. More recent scientifically-oriented research has indicated that a biological condition is more likely accountable for the child's handicap (Gold 1967; Hutt et al. 1964; Hutt et al. 1965; Seller and Gold 1964; White, DeMeyer, and DeMeyer 1964; Ornity et al. 1969; Ornitz and Ritvo 1968a; Ornity and Ritvo 1968b). When one considers what it would be like to live with such a child, perhaps some empathy will be displayed to the parents and an understanding reached as to how the child may have trained them to remain aloof, if that is the case. A parent-child relation is determined in two ways, and even the autistic child contributes significantly to that interaction. Unfortunately, the psychotic child is more distressing to live with, since he or she is less capable of responding to the normal child-rearing practices and expectancies, which have been observed in these families, and which other investigators have shown are characteristic of these homes (DeMeyer et al. 1972).

It may be grossly unfair to demand parents to assume treatment responsibility for a child whose gains are so limited. To provide an exceptionally positive and contingent environment may be a behavioral expectancy far in excess of what may be reasonably demanded from the parents, considering their history with the child and their goals in life. It is amazing how these parents persist with their children despite all the disappointments they have received over the years. This is a laudable attitude, in fact, mandatory for parents who are going to subscribe to the parent-teaching approach. Yet, such persistence must be tempered in terms of the expectancies which can be made of the child's growth, and weighed against the effort the parents will have to exert in achieving limited gains. It should be routinely examined during the course of treatment if it is satisfactory, or destructive, for the family to retain their child. Our three-month evaluation with the parents centers around these problems, which usually have not been confronted before with the family.

Families now have more options with Public Law 94–142 that varies with the extent that the respective states have implemented their own laws to accommodate the federal mandate. This law requires that all special needs children receive appropriate instruction within their community school system, which is relevant to the feasibility of the child remaining at home and attending a public school. But one still has to be realistic in helping a family decide if remaining in the home and community school is a long-term and preferred disposition. Not only does the school have to uphold their end of the bargain, namely providing a relevant daily curriculum for the child, but the family must support the school by treating the child in a like manner. Educators are well versed in this debacle, where the child's participation in the school program fails because there has been no follow through in the child's home. Of course, the school does have the option of simply trying to do the best they can during the school day, requiring little or no follow through with the home, and hoping that the child will adapt to the two environments. This is not a preferred disposition, but in many instances it is the one which must be settled for.

The spirit of Public Law 94–142 is to provide the child with the least restrictive environment. Perhaps it is useful to look at that concept in the long run of a child's life. Parents usually need to be counseled in respect to the possible placement of their child when he or she becomes an adult. The least restrictive environments for the handicapped youngster may be sheltered apartment living, a group home, or professional foster care. But achieving that semi-independent living is going to be a function of the child accumulating some very well-controlled socialized behaviors. If a child is allowed to continue to develop with bizarre mannerisms, aggression, noncompliance, selfstimulatory behavior, and failure to attend, he or she will not be retained in community settings, with placement in sheltered workshop environments. These long-range predictions, which have a great deal to do with how restrictive an environment the child will develop into, may be predicted very well if one simply surveys the behavioral repertoire of the child, and considers not doing anything about those behaviors. Inattention and noncompliance are tolerable to adults for the young child, but these kinds of behaviors are not tolerated in the adult community. Thus, the child in the least restrictive home and school environment may end up as an adult in the most restrictive residential setting.

There are exceptions among family awareness of a child's disabilities and the feasibility of their performing the necessary programs.

To illustrate, we worked with one youngster whose profound retardation was obvious early in the program. However, his obsession with twirling strings, failure to attend, and obliviousness to people caused referring professionals to question if he was an autistic child with all the hope that accompanies the mystique of that diagnosis. His parents were cognizant of his retardation and did not have unbounded expectancies derived from the diagnosis of autism, although they had been subjected to that impression from past evaluations. Since their expectancies were consistent with the ability of their child, they were not unduly disappointed by the treatment-documented prognosis that their child's primary handicap was one of severe retardation, and although he could learn a few, limited behaviors, with massive trials and reinforcers, these responses would be so simple that one may seriously question if it would be a satisfactory experience for the family to endure. The treatment planning was altered to establish a home environment within which the child was taught rudimentary compliance, appropriate eating, and simple routines around sleep and restructuring the home so that he would not wander away. The family was able to tolerate this level of behavior, and were content to retain him in the home under such conditions until they were of an age where they would need the assistance of custodial or foster care for their son.

Documenting the necessary kind of positive environment to train and maintain a child's behavior is a first step, but its success is dependent upon the family's ability to perform such a program. It is demoralizing for a staff to work with a child only to see the child's parents unable, for whatever reasons, to adopt the programs they have established to be effective. Under such conditions, a counter-aggressive mood emerges within the staff directed toward the family, which is unjustified simply because the family cannot be behavior therapists for their child. When such a reaction is identified, it may be recommended to prepare an alternative disposition for the child, providing the parent-staff interaction cannot be rectified. It seems unwarranted to force a family through a program that they do not wish to follow, or may be incapable of comprehending, and will predictably fail to sustain at a later date. Yet, the alternative of not accepting the child for treatment because of such problems appears to be shirking the clinical responsibility that the parents originally requested of you.

If you are able to predict that your efforts will not succeed, it is a waste of everyone's time and money to continue pursuing treatment. It may be that those families will be more satisfied with other treatment approaches. As with all therapies, those patients motivated to change seem to effect that change, regardless of the theoretical bias of the clinician. In fact, motivation is a necessary precondition for any therapy to be maximally utilized. Before inception of any therapeutic endeavor, it should be assured that the family is motivated for change in their child.

THIRD PREREQUISITE:
REALISTIC EXPECTANCIES

←Seldom are the long-range treatment goals known at the inception of a child's residential program; the reality of those expectancies are generated during the course of treatment. The goal of the intake evaluation is to localize some point on a developmental scale to suggest at what age treatment may begin. The reliability from such a short contact is clouded by variables ranging from fear to fatigue, partially elicited by the unusual environment where the exam occurs. Seldom can one lend valid credence to initial diagnostic impressions of the child or parental report of the child's assets and limitations. Treatment plans are constructed around the child's abilities as they are observed during the first few weeks of residence. These expectancies will always be held in flux; they are not considered static until proven so. Some of the originally formulated treatment goals will remain valid during treatment. This is more likely the case when the extent of retardation is so profound that only a few simple skills such as dressing, self-feeding, and toileting are all that can be expected and maintained with the child. If the child's growth potential blossoms, as it may if there is a gainful language acquisition, expectancies will change more rapidly during the course of treatment.

With some children, it may be learned that the initial treatment expectancies are too high. It then becomes necessary to "back-up" in the program and be satisfied with lower-level responses. The recognition of such failure to move the child consistently along some growth continuum, even when it is at variance with the original hypothesis about the child, should be considered a success and not a failure. It would be disastrous if you had overlooked your failure with the child, and had the parents convinced that your expectancies were valid. That error is less tolerable than one of establishing treatment expectancies which are too easy for the child. Realization of the second error is a satisfying one to parents, where the former is debilitating.

Realistic expectancies for a child may change over the years, which is why follow-up should be maintained between the family and the original treatment team. It is often unsatisfactory to rely upon the home to maintain realistic behavioral expectancies for their child over the years for a variety of reasons. Some of the more common reasons are as follows:

1. Parents may assume they must handle all child problems by themselves without assistance, although they are likely to become less sensitive to their presence. Parents' objectivity is weakened by the fact that the child is always teaching them to adapt to his or her behavior, which may become stationary and less than what he or she is capable of performing. Parents may need to be monitored to determine if they are inadvertently allowing their child to retrieve the referral behaviors, or semblances of them, at such a gradual rate that they are unaware of their habituation.

2. The excessive demands of maintaining a child's treatment program may discourage the parents. Correspondingly, their expectancies may gradually decay to levels of behavior which are more easy to maintain. Parents are usually unaware of this gradual shift.

3. It is not uncommon for some parents to suffer an understandable degree of depression since the child's behavioral expectancies are at such a variance with those they have achieved with their other children. This depression may be maintained by their harboring hopes that their child will eventually "grow out of it," which implies that they do not have to be responsible for his or her change. With this attitude, they may begin to surrender their behavioral expectancies to "hope," rather than planning for them. In such instances, one would have to deal directly with their reactive depression to the child's limited growth.

4. New disabilities will emerge over the years with these children. To illustrate, a five-year-old child may be unable to read, and when she is fifteen years of age, she cannot be taught the responsibility of taking the city bus alone because of that reading deficit. The parents, as well as the professional, may not have anticipated this kind of problem when their child was young, at which time it was easy to accept nonreading because it did not interfere greatly with a five-year-old's existence.

Treatment expectancies established for a child must reflect the natural variance among families who are functioning as intact homes, both emotionally and socially. Traditionally, when families did not agree with the recommendations of professionals, that disagreement was discounted to psychologically abnormal implications, such as resistance, defensiveness, reaction formations, *ad infinitum*. It may be more fruitful to recognize the integrity of the family as it exists, and the privilege of the parents to demonstrate choice (Akerley 1975). It is with this orientation that we have tried to stipulate our expectancies in the homes, of which families have a choice of accepting or rejecting without a stigmata of being abnormal for choosing not to cooperate. This has not been a panacea as an approach in working with parents who may retract their child because they disagree with your recommendations. However, it will help professionals and families to stop fighting. A straightforward approach should be used with the parents, explaining all expectancies prior to initiation of treatment, the kinds of training materials for which they are responsible, the duration of involvement with the family, and money. It is with this information that families may decide to become invested in the treatment program. Still, this is not an entirely fair approach with families, since with the severely handicapped child the parents are usually at a loss in locating a treatment curriculum for their youngster. Because of the limitations in treatment resources, by default they are coerced into joining yours, with the effect of their being unable to honestly display their disagreements and perfunctorily doing what is expected of them. In those circumstances, the family may not be expected to profit as satisfactorily as others who have a choice and a more affirmative attitude to begin with.

Some families are never identified as being able to profit from a didactic approach. Perhaps other investigators have had similar experiences in which a family will collaborate apparently quite successfully, but after discharge the child will retrieve his or her referral behaviors quite rapidly. It is discouraging to find such parents focusing on one grand excuse such as the difficulties being entirely "medical," which erradicates their responsibilities for maintaining the growth which was evident in the child prior to discharge. I do not know if it is possible to anticipate such an eventuality, but to do so would be helpful.

Islands of Intact Behavior

The issue of "islands of intact behavior" still prevails amongst professionals working with psychotic and handicapped children, particularly those designated as autistic (Cain 1970). This notion is very destructive to establishing realistic expectancies. For reasons generated by hope, parents thrive on this hypothesis that their psychotic or autistic child may have an area of genius, or perhaps just above average intelligence, which, with proper training, may be capitalized into a career such as being a concert pianist. I have yet to identify a research report stipulating a group of children diagnosed as autistic, or with other obviously severe psychotic disorders, in which there were areas of behavior unusually elevated in reference to their chronological age. Considering the child's social age, it is not unusual for any child to demonstrate "high" and "low" spots in his or her response repertoire (Bartak and Rutter 1976; Ritvo et al. 1976).

To illustrate, we had one autistic child who was able to read prior to five years of age, with no known evidence of tutorial instruction in the home. In his first psychiatric examination, he picked up the *American Journal of Psychiatry* and read from it perfectly, but with no comprehension. At that time, he could not spontaneously tell someone his own name upon inquiry. This reading phenomenon was referred to as an "island of highly intact behavior," and is referenced in the literature as hyperlexia (Mehegan 1969). However, this youngster's spontaneous speech with meaningful language was limited to one- and two-word phrases. The reading skill was not intact; only the aspect of sight reading was acquired, which rendered it entirely useless as an adaptive behavior. Even with special instruction, this child did not progress at a rapid rate in reading comprehension skills as one might expect to be facilitated by this "island of intact behavior" of sight reading. It has been our experience that these children are depressed in most spheres of behavior, and that the few elevated responses which stand out in relative contrast deceive the investigator to presume that a greater potential lies in the child. Closer examination has revealed that these presumed areas of elevated behaviors are still below the expectancy for the child's chronological age. Furthermore, the deficit is often compounded by the fact that these elevated behaviors are not integrated with the entire response repertoire of the child. For example, there was another youngster who could ride a bicycle very skillfully. However, this behavior was not integrated with the comprehension of verbal commands, so that he was in a very dangerous position when riding the bicycle in traffic, avoiding other persons, and even traveling about the parking lot. That "island of intact behavior" was a physical skill that he was trained to use, but unfortunately was not integrated with the remainder of the skills necessary for bicycle riding. In other words, most children who can ride a bicycle well can also comprehend safety rules. This youngster was too retarded to verbally comprehend such social rules, so he was a danger to himself when on a bicycle.

Assessment

Initially, only limited statements can justifiably be given to the family regarding their child's disposition. These statements may be derived from so simple and obvious an instrument as the Vineland Social Maturity Scale. It samples typical and necessary living skills expected of a child at various ages, against which that child is compared. It is useful to convey to the parents the reality of their child's limited skills by requiring them to demonstrate with their child the questions contained in the examination. We administer the Vineland Social Maturity Scale in the child's home with the mother required to demonstrate each item. Several questions are answered during parental demonstration. One is that the issue of compliance comes into focus when the parents explain that their child really can do that which was asked, but he or she repeatedly fails to comply to that request. After several occasions of this kind of encounter, with the intense anxiety generated by the parents vainly trying to make their child perform, you are often left with the fact of compliance as a deficit in the child's repertoire which hampers his or her optimal achievement. This may provide a useful starting place for treatment, and one which parents can easily comprehend. Furthermore, you are not in the position of denying the parents' claim of the child's social skills, but rather stating that the child's failure to comply impedes his or her social growth. It is a less threatening starting place for treatment.

Several months treatment may be required before one may offer the parents a realistic appraisal of a child's intellectual capabilities. But if the psychologist has to test and predict, be wary of becoming trapped into being pretentious about the assessment of the child's intellectual abilities by ignoring the results of an intellectual evaluation. The problem begins with the professional who observes some parents supporting and reinforcing infantile levels of behavior in the child. The observation may be accurate, but the unwarranted presumption follows that such infantilizing has sustained a lower level of intellectual functioning in the child. Hence, by altering those reinforcement conditions of the parents, and their expectancies, the child will be able to function more intelligently, or operantly. This may be holding out a very false hope to the parents. In fact, as you may learn later in the training program with the child, the parents accurately gear their demands of the child to be consistent with what he or she is actually capable of achieving. We observed this with a a handsome five-year-old deaf child whose parents made expectancies of him commensurate with what one would expect of a nine-month-old. Continued inpatient studies revealed that this nine-month level was indeed what he was capable of functioning at, due to his severe retardation. The child did not appear retarded, which deluded many professionals, including us, into believing that his hearing loss was masking his performance as a potentially bright child. Each case must be judged individually; some families will maintain infantile levels of behavior in their children which will impair intellectual functioning. Blanket statements cannot be made about families and their children, particularly in respect to learning potential.

I am not hesitant in using diagnostic terms consistent with the expectancies established earlier in treatment, so that the parents do not acquire misconceptions about the abilities of their child. Previously, I would not commit myself to any statements regarding their child's abilities (Browning and Stover 1971). This was intended to convey to the parents that I was making no presumptions about the effectiveness of treatment, but my reluctancy to make any statements left it up to the family to establish their own hopes, which were ofen idealistic. No longer am I reluctant to cite the literature on long-term follow-up studies with autistic and schizophrenic children, to point out the fact of retardation, and to discuss the probability that these children may require services outside of the home as they approach adulthood. If their child is functioning in the retarded level at the inception of treatment, one should not be afraid to use such a term as *retardation*, since that is descriptive of their child and sets the pace at what is likely to be the status of that youngster. As treatment progresses, one may be able to vary these labels from severe to moderate to mild, with the parents being able to accept these prognostic changes. But if you have begun treatment using labels that presume that the child is capable of functioning close to normal, with the likelihood that this is a "rare circumstance" for any psychotic child, you will be in the position of asking the family to downgrade their expectancies for their youngster, which will understandably elicit resistance.

School Environment

Maintenance of realistic expectancies for the child is similarly problematic in many schools. A prevalent problem is that children functioning in the retarded range, regardless of diagnosis, are provided academic curricula when social training and prevocational experiences would be much more appropriate. In one instance, I observed an eighteen-year-old mongoloid child still being trained in his first grade primer, having spent his academic career on that same text. Such an academic approach with a severely retarded individual in which one attempts to provide a normal academic experience fosters delusional hopes about the child's eventual disposition. Time and effort could have been more usefully spent on training skills consistent with the capabilities one may expect of such a youngster, which would be exclusive of academic material. A minimum of academic training for many of these children is suggested. Instead, focus should be more on household chores, personal hygiene, walking safely in the neighborhood, etc., and later acquiring low-level job skills such as stock clerking and lawn work. Recommending nonacademic training and deemphasizing arts and crafts is often disagreeable to teachers and parents alike because it obviously depicts the child as abnormal, and contradicts the hopes they have mutually envisioned. Many parents want the teacher to maintain the expectancies that one would have for normal children, which may be socially myopic considering the adjustment that child will have to make after school is no longer available. Pre-primer reading and mathematics and skill in cutting pictures contribute little to the social demands which retarded children will be confronted with when the public school is no longer able to care for them six hours a day.

Parental Participation

Theoretically, individual educational plans not only allow for, but require, some degree of parental participation, even if it is so much as tacit agreement with that plan. Educators should be sensitive to what it is like being a parent involved in such a meeting. Typically, the parents are anxious, ambivalent, hoping for something just shy of a miracle to occur in the school, and seldom feel comfortable or knowledgeable enough to contribute. It is a humbling experience to have a neutral, third party, interview the parents after involvement in such a meeting, and ask them to explain what transpired in that meeting.

For many families, your asking them to be a comfortable participant in a multidisciplinary team is comparable to asking a flight passenger to be the co-pilot of a 747. Obviously, one would expect a lot of confusion on the flight deck in that example, and with the families we work with, we likewise see a lot of confusion in their performing programs in home as they are performed in the school. Parental participation in educational plans for the exceptional child is a preferred goal. It is unlikely that goal will be achieved unless time is taken to educate the parents. If you are having difficulty educating the parents, perhaps it would be useful to train parents of handicapped children who have already been in the curriculum to be the trainers for other parents.

FOURTH PREREQUISITE: REINFORCERS AND PROGNOSIS AS RELATED TO TREATMENT EXPECTANCIES

←The variety and the stability of the effective reinforcers a child has prior to treatment will provide some predictions of how responsive the child is liable to be to treatment. The more primitive the effective reinforcement systems are with a child, the more restricted is the prognostic statement concerning the child's likely progress in treatment. With a child whose reinforcers are so primitive that even food is variable and weakly reinforcing, it becomes very improbable that autonomous operant behavior will be acquired. I have worked with children for whom food was of minimal effect; its absence or presence as a reinforcer did not seem to assist in discriminating correct responses. This was even true when numerous meals were missed because the child did not approach the food. In such circumstances, one begins designing ingenious programs, such as using so primitive a reinforcer as rocking for training the child to eat a variety of foods, which would then, in turn, be used as rewards for training attention, etc. When one has to resort to such primitive reinforcing stimuli, such as self-stimulatory rocking responses with a five-year-old, it must be recognized that such a reinforcement represents a sample of the entire response repertoire of the child. The more primitive the available reinforcers for the child, so will be the level of responses demonstrated by that child in reference to chronological age. Rocking, for example, represents an infant level of reinforcement. With youngsters for whom food, social reinforcers, or play activities do not qualify as a reinforcing effect, or may not be quickly acquired as such, the probability is very great that you are dealing with a child with static limitations and the compensatory training attempted will have limited value. Such deficits in reinforcers relative to a child's age should be assessed at the beginning of treatment and carefully explained to the parents.

If you are not cognizant of such deficits, you may find yourself in the position of designing very complex experimental studies dependent upon unusual reinforcers, which would never be available to maintain the acquired behavior in the natural environment. Furthermore, it is most probable that you would also be training some extremely simple responses, at a very high cost, the overall effect of which may be to raise the hopes of the parents to a level far in excess of reality. It may be more humanitarian for the parents to accept the child at the retarded level, rather than perpetrate an illusion. I have been able to teach some exceptionally primitive youngsters how to handle puzzles, perform menial self-help skills, and eat acceptably by use of an intense and carefully controlled, 100 percent reinforcement schedule with one or two unusual rewards, all of which prove to be effective for that one response. The rewards may be a certain kind of candy, a particular sound, rocking, or even a light. The results prove that the child was not taught a complex and heuristic response; they demonstrated that he or she could learn a very simple response under a highly contrived and unusual training condition, which had to be closely monitored, was highly expensive, and whose effect was greatest in deluding the parents and ourselves about the capabilities of their child. Part of this difficulty again stems from a myth that has been perpetrated in the field that with sufficient trials, perfectly graduated shaping steps, and a closely monitored program, one can teach any child any response. This then leads to the presumption that if the child can learn something, he or she can learn anything. This ignores the reality that the simplistic response taught will remain dependent upon the streamlined learning situation which was responsible for its acquisition. As with all persons, there are static limitations or learning abilities, be it memory, generalization, or complexity of a discrimination response. The sooner the reality of these limitations are realized by a family of a retarded or psychotic child, the more realistic the expectancies are liable to be.

Prognosis is determined by the child's responsiveness to the treatment regimen presented in this book. This means that tests unrelated to the treatment curriculum are not used to make a prediction about the child. Rather, predictions about the eventual disposition of the youngster are based upon how rapidly he or she learns under circumscribed conditions. With such information, one may make limited predictions about the prognosis of the child, but at least they are factual. It is intended that the short-term treatment interval will either return the child to the home, or to some other facility outside of the home. A time-limited treatment interval not only generates a prognosis based upon data, but it also prevents the professional and the family from relentlessly pushing the child. This is the kind of difficulty we found ourselves in when we would have psychotic and autistic children in residence for two to three years. With such children who require such constant care, our recommendations at the conclusion of treatment may have been to remove the child from the home. But by this time, the parents have been so trained by us to maintain hope, to continue working, to remain unrealistic in their support of the intense programs we had devised, that they simply could not recognize the limitations of their child. An intense, short-term, six-month treatment interval is sufficient to ascertain whether the child can adapt to a home setting without being destructive to the family, and if the family could be satisfactorily trained to maintain the child in the home. If obvious progress is not performed in that period of time, one can seriously question if the child and family are adaptable to each other. This premise is based upon conducting the treatment hierarchy described later in this book.

FIFTH PREREQUISITE: CONSISTENCY

← Consistency is a necessary and essential ingredient to a successful treatment program, particularly with the severely handicapped child (Dullaart-Pruyser 1977; Kehrer 1974). One theoretical reason, as it applies to acquisition of new responses, is that the more smooth and consistent the learning conditions are, the more quickly the response will be acquired. Likewise, it would be predicted from the same theoretical orientation that more erratic training conditions would eventually lead to more stable behavioral rates, although this would require relatively greater numbers of trials to reach that level than in a smooth and consistent training condition. In actual clinical practice, one is at best erratic, and one strives for consistency in attempting to facilitate rapid response acquisition. The more consistent the presenting conditions of the stimuli and reinforcer, the more simplified is the discrimination, and the more rapid the learning, this being particularly relevant to psychotic, retarded, and brain-damaged children, who are characteristically handicapped in discriminating among stimuli (Lovaas et al. 1971).

A definition of *consistency in a learning situation* is that the condition surrounding the stimuli, the required response, and the reinforcement are repeated as identically as possible on successive trials. This would demand that staff and parents teaching the child a response would provide comparable teaching instructions and reinforcers for the same response at the same rate. It would mean that related behaviors surrounding the learning task would also be treated identically. It would mean, too, that for a response to be acquired in one situation and to facilitate generalization to another, it would require the same training conditions to be presented in the second situation. This consisent approach for assisting generalization is demanded by the very learning handicaps demonstrated by these children, since it is documented that they have difficulties in transferring what they have acquired in one situation to another. In order to maintain consistency across learning situations in a treatment program, several requirements must be fulfilled.

One requirement is that teachers and family perform identical programs, which requires greater effort than when raising normal children. This effort is represented partially in the time to train the staff and family to provide identical training conditions. A distinct advantage comes from this effort. When the child does retrieve some referral behaviors, which previously had been decelerated, and extinguishes some new behaviors for which he or she was trained, one has available documented training conditions that were successful during treatment, and which may be reinstated to retrain those behaviors. With an inconsistent program, particularly without documentation, one would be at a loss to determine the necessary and sufficient training conditions to reinstate the habits which the child lost.

Consistency represents agreement among staff and family on the programs that will be used continuously with the child. Achieving consistency in the special classroom in the public school, or the residential setting, is much different than it is for the family to achieve. In the school, it is an administrative and training problem. There, the teacher bargained for that kind of work, was specifically trained for it, is paid for it, has paid vacation, holidays, and sick leave. The family, however, did not bargain for their child's handicaps, they had to cope with it. They are not paid, there are no holidays, and there certainly are no sick days. Families have to cope with the problems of fatigue, depression, ambivalence, and must often learn to survive by tolerating the low-level responses. The teacher must understand that the child is training the teacher and the family as vigorously as the teacher is training the child. Families have often been albeit accidentally trained by the child to inadvertently reinforce or tolerate a lot of behavior, and those habits are going to be very strong. Thus, when you devise a program for the family to follow at home you have to take a hard look at the interaction between the child and the family on that behavior. Just because a family does not consistently follow your recommendations does not mean that they are pointedly subverting your efforts. It may simply mean they are so habituated to the child's behaviors, that they are unable to see the responses you are trying to teach them to attend to. Under those conditions, the ideal case would be to have someone in the home during critical times to help the family out in performing these kinds of programs. Obviously, the family is going to need nonthreatening feedback, in their efforts to achieve consistency in the home.

Compensatory Training

In reviewing the multitude of severely disturbed children who have been treated with a variety of techniques, regardless of approach, the prognosis is very limited. Lockyer and Rutter's (1969) review of outcome substantiates this overgeneralized statement. One does not conceptualize the treatment goals with these children as to make the "sick child well again." Those incidents in the literature in which presumed autistic children pursued a college education represents a minuscule percentage of the total number of children so diagnosed, and it may be questionable if that diagnosis was correct for those children who made such gains. The treatment approach offered here is a form of compensatory training in which one maximizes learning conditions to be most streamlined and efficient, and arranges environmental contingencies to facilitate and maintain that learning. The analogy of the victims of the polio seige during the 1940s whose atrophied limbs would never be rendered normal again, but rather with considerable training and effort could learn to "limp real good," illustrates the kind of compensatory training I am speaking about.

Compensatory training requires that you take into account the static deficits the child has, and then try to teach the child to compensate. For example, the discrimination deficit so characteristic of these children impairs generalization of training, and, as such, is a constant deficit for the child. Clinicians do not teach the child to overcome this basic discrimination handicap, but they may teach him or her some skills which, if maintained, will assist the child in discriminating better in later learning situations. Furthermore, clinicians must teach the people responsible for those learning situations how to maintain those skills they have taught the child to compensate for this handicap. To illustrate, we routinely teach the child to maintain very steady and prolonged eye contact during compliance and academic and language training. By maintaining a maximum of attention, they are likely to respond to the relevant components of the stimuli composing the learning task. Without being trained to attend sufficiently, we found that the learning rates are minimal, simply because the child misses the crucial stimuli embodied in the learning task due to his or her failure to attend specifically.

Retrievability

Retrievability of undesirable behaviors after treatment will be a function of how similar the child's environment compares to what it was prior to treatment. The child does not deliberately reinstate those conditions which maintained his or her habit patterns, but that reinstatement is understandable in terms of habit strengths and response hierarchies. To illustrate, if a child had been head banging for five years, and you succeeded in teaching her to decelerate this response in three months, little calculation is required to recognize the difference in response strength between banging and not banging her head. The techniques that effected the diminution of head banging would have to be maintained consistently, just as you would have to be extremely reliable in controlling the presence of those conditions which sustained head banging prior to treatment. This is simple to write about, and almost impossible to perform.

The reality of a treatment program is that everybody has to do the same thing: clinician, family, and school; and if they do not, those conditions which existed prior to treatment will gradually emerge to haunt the efficacy of behavior modification. Unfortunately, the young psychotic or neurologically handicapped child does not have years of appropriate behaviors acquired prior to the acquisition of the deviant behaviors. The majority of the child's treatment repertoire is composed of weak, recently acquired behaviors and strong, but temporarily deviant responses. Such a repertoire increases the likelihood of retrieving the old, more dominant and durable responses that have been maintained for years. It is hoped that as treatment progresses, erratic stimulus conditions and reinforcers will be introduced to make the newly acquired and appropriate behaviors more stable.

SIXTH PREREQUISITE: PERSEVERANCE

Colloquially speaking, perseverence is the quality of being repetitious, and maintaining the training programs regardless of the discouragement, numbers of trials, hours, and fatigue. Perseverance is obvious when one recognizes that profoundly disturbed and retarded children require thousands more trials than normal youngsters to learn less complex behaviors. This is not to recommend blind and stubborn perseveration; but rather, is an acceptance of the endurance required in working with these children while simultaneously monitoring the data to determine if acquisition is occurring, however slow. There are no tests that can be administered prior to treatment that will predict how the child will respond and how much effort will be required to obtain a particular treatment effect. Prognostic statements are based only upon the rate changes shown in the child's learning, and to show these effects may require weeks and thousands of trials of training the same response. Until such tests are available, the prognosis will continue to remain most reliably dependent upon the child's exposure to a circumscribed learning situation. Clinicians must persevere; they should not become discouraged after logging several thousand trials to teach a child some very simple compliance responses.

The children illustrated in this report are clinically described as *concrete*. In oversimplified terms, this means there is less generalization in their learning that results from a discrimination deficit which interferes with all learning. They are less sensitive to the subtle similarities and differences among stimuli in their environment. They are more likely to demonstrate greater error responses, and less predictable behavior for a trained response in new environmental circumstances. Part of their compensation for this handicap requires that we provide increased training trials in more diversified places to override these discrimination errors. So you must persevere; you must anticipate weeks of work with minimal progress with only your graphs to serve as your memory to recall if there is a predictive change occurring in the child's learning rate. The change is going to be so slight that one cannot rely upon clinical judgment to discern these gradual changes.

In attempting to persevere with a child, staff fatigue will be a primary factor to deal with. A daily schedule should be established so that neither the staff nor the child are exhausted. If fatigue is not recognized as a very real deterrent to persevering with these children, staff problems will accelerate, their job performance will decline, and the child's progress will deteriorate.

One alternative to offset this fatigue is to schedule training sessions during the day, the intervals between which staff may have breaks and work with different children in less strenuous activities. A value of session training is that it assures that the training will be performed with the child, that it will be performed by all staff which will assist generalization, and that it provides a daily routine to which the children can adapt. Perseverance is difficult to teach parents, since "holding out" and repeating trials under a multitude of conditions is an unnatural child-rearing requirement. This demand may be unrealistic for the family, and this should be appraised periodically to decide if such an expectancy is unreasonable, and if it is actually being performed by the family.

SEVENTH PREREQUISITE: CONTINUITY OF TREATMENT PROGRAM

In Kanner's (1971) follow-up study of his original eleven autistic children, from whom the descriptive label of autism became a popularized diagnostic entity, he concluded that those patients who spent the majority of their lives in state hospital environments did more poorly than those retained in homes. Lockyer and Rutter (1969) in their definitive follow-up study with a diversified group of psychotic children were able to specify in terms of intellectual and social quotients that children residing in institutional environments did not do as well, in terms of stability scores, as those retained in home environments. Loretta Bender (1969), whose experience with multiple handicapped children is probably unparalleled, similarly reports that children retained in institutional environments demonstrate both intellectual and physical declines during the course of their residence.

Such information raises two hypotheses. One hypothesis is that children diagnosed as psychotic will function optimally when retained in the natural environment of their home and community, regardless of the kind of treatment they receive there. An alternate hypothesis, which should be considered in fairness to those families who place their children in custodial care, is that these children were impossible to retain in the home, and by such natural selection the group of children who are in institutions represent a sample who would decline intellectually and socially regardless of the environment in which they were placed. In other words, it may likely be the case that many youngsters placed in institutional settings for long-term care were so severely impaired that it was unreasonable to retain these children in the home without being destructive to the integrity of the family. This hypothesis does not indicate that institutional environments have a beneficial effect on the children. It is very likely the case that custodial environments would not foster social or intellectual growth in any children, regardless of the prognosis.

We have had numerous cases for which a treatment-determined prognosis was established where the eventual disposition suggested to the family was residential care for the child. This is ultimately the family's decision, but the recommendation for it is based upon the demand the child will make upon that home, and the possible gains expected in that home environment. The minimum time in which we are usually able to formulate such an opinion is three months of intensive treatment. That opinion is based upon learning rates of the child in the programs performed, as well as assessing if the parents are able to acquire the instructional skills necessary to maintain the behavior in the home, and if it indeed would be feasible for them to maintain such an intense maintenance curriculum for a child. With some children we found it impossible to make that decision with certainty until after close to a year of extended treatment, simply because we were never really sure. A primary goal of short-term residential treatment is to predict the extent to which the child may adapt to the home environment, and to the extent the home may adapt to the child. If a reasonable compromise cannot be established, then it becomes imbalanced in terms of the home adapting exclusively to the child and relinquishing anything close to a normal home environment for the remainder of the family. In these instances, we may recommend that the parents consider custodial placement, or at least be very realistic of the limited goals they may anticipate for their child. Furthermore, it is emphasized that any decision the family makes may only have to be temporary; custodial care does not have to be a final and forever disposition.

Even with a child for whom custodial care is required, when that decision has been reached, we alter the treatment regimen to train the child to make an optimal adjustment to such an environment. We wish to train the child so as to diminish the possibility of his or her being retired at such an early age to an understimulating environment for whom treatment gains are considered to be exhausted. This means training the personnel at the facility where the child is placed on those programs which had the greatest value for the child.

Upon admission, the possibility of the child being retained in the home is actually planned for. In order for him or her to survive in a community, continuity of the treatment programs has to be planned for, which is begun by a contract with the home stipulating that staff will provide long-term follow-up there and in the school. Furthermore, referring mental health agencies are strongly encouraged to provide social worker time to learn the techniques successful with the child, so that they may be of assistance in maintaining the child's treatment programs following discharge. We do not assign the social worker the responsibility of reinstating all programs after discharge when there is retrieval of referral behaviors. Rather, we expect that professional to be able to recognize when there is decay in treatment effects with the child, and then alert us to intervene in the home. It has been predictable that difficulties will occur and that we will have to intervene in the home. This intervention is anticipated and scheduled at three months, and then at least at six-month intervals thereafter, particularly at the beginning of a new school year.

As will be explained in chapter 2, a child's treatment program will always require periodic intervention. When the child does experience difficulties after returning to the home, it is not economical to have the family resort to professionals who are unfamiliar with the child's programs. Rather, it is more effective to have the staff members who have worked directly with that family to be given the long-term responsibility for maintaining that child back in the community. This reduces the communication time necessary across professionals, and provides for a simpler learning situation for the child if the treatment programs are identical to those which he or she had previously adapted.

EIGHTH PREREQUISITE: COMMITMENT
TO THE PROGRAM

← Parental commitment to a treatment program involves an unknown amount of suggestion with the aura of placebo effects. The effect is often that the parents who are strongly committed to the kind of treatment program you provide will, through such rose-tinted glasses of suggestion, see their child as improved when that may not be entirely the case.

In addition, commitment to the program extends beyond the definition of agreement, in that it implies an active investment in the program. Commitment does not mean only the family agrees to continue the child's program beyond the six-month residential treatment interval, but rather, that this investment is reflected in the referring agency personnel, in your treatment staff, in the public school system and all its teachers, and perhaps even relatives and neighbors in the community. If these people are not all involved time-wise, theory-wise, and effort-wise, one may not expect the child's program to be performed consistently over the years.

Commitment to the program is most necessary amongst the staff composing the treatment group. This may be established most effectively by hiring the correct kinds of individuals and training them appropriately. I have no secrets to predict the personality characteristics likely to produce effective child-care staff. It has been my experience that the more educated and intelligent the individual, the more effective their work. Staff with less training, and particularly those with varying degrees of social difficulties, are likely to be argumentative, rather than constructively questioning and capable of adapting a scientific attitude about their duties. To maintain staff commitment to the program, it is recommended that a supervised work routine be created, yet one with a balance where the individual is expected to work autonomously and creatively within the confines of the theoretical orientation of behavior modification.

The goal of the clinical program is not to maintain an employment situation for a staff member who does not have the same goals as required of the job. Such a point may seem as a foregone conclusion and hardly worthy of this space. However, if one looks at the state hospital facilities where union contracts are more negotiable than clinical needs, and professionalism has been bargained away at the cottage staff level, this simplified discussion cannot be overlooked.

A precursor to treatment is to establish a firm contract with the family regarding their commitment to the program, which we try to accomplish over three appointments and one home visit. This prevents the family from making an impetuous decision regarding placement of their child in treatment with all the obligations demanded by the program. During these visits, testing is performed, but more importantly, the family is clearly informed of all expectancies. We also send one staff member to the home to be present during an evening meal to evaluate the child's behavior and also to assess if the family can withstand that much intrusion from our staff. When they are fully informed of the numbers of hours, the parent training contract, the requirements of working with other children, our unscheduled observations in the home, and our unsolicited follow-up studies, they are then asked to make a decision. This contract is one of mutual consent; it is not written or in any way legally binding. The family contract is essentially an understanding of what will be required by the treatment program, and what kind of services will be afforded the family.

When possible, we try to establish a similar kind of contract with the referring agency so that they will allocate the staff necessary to provide the follow-up of the children referred from their facility. Similarly, an arrangement is established with the school system prior to the child's admission, in the likelihood that the child may be returned back to that community and school after discharge. This is often difficult to perform because you cannot predict, even if the child does return to the school, the particular classroom for which he or she would be eligible. Furthermore, the teacher usually does not have the time to be trained in the programs you have found to be effective with the child.

This contract with the family, which stipulates their agreement with your goals, does not identify the family as being "sick." There have been variations in this attitude with the exceptionally disturbed child, but for the majority of cases, families are accepted as being "well." They are not recommended for family therapy, but rather are dealt with on a didactic basis as being teachers for their own children. This is considered justifiable on the accumulating evidence that these multiply handicapped children represent a group of organic, genetic, and yet to be discovered conditions which are responsible for their adaptive deficits. Also, we offer them our service, clearly stated, which they may decide to have or not, and it is acceptable if they reject the service. The rejection of the service is not taken as an implication to defensiveness. This allows the family to make the choice again at a later time if necessary. One family described in the case study section required a year of approaching and avoiding such a decision before they could commit themselves to such a program.

It is crucial that the family contract be very clear in its stipulation that parents have requested a service for their child, which does not imply that they themselves are disturbed. I suspect it is an error when a family requests clinical services for their child, and if they refuse being involved in family therapy, that they are unequivocally demonstrating resistance and thereby validating some pathological patterns in the family. Even if they reject your treatment, and even if family therapy is obviously indicated by their interactions, one should honor the goal for these families of making a responsible and rational decision for themselves regarding their child. Unless they are so irresponsible that they require judicial intervention because of varifiable harm to themselves, the children, or others, they should be allowed to live within a normal variance that we typically tolerate in our society, without imposing some suspicion of pathology upon them.

Are we allowing ourselves to be in the circumstances of promoting "throw-away families"? This remains a justifiable criticism of our approach with families. For those families who will not accept treatment, who refuse to change, who do not wish to have intervention, we allow that decision to be made by them, just as if they were purchasing any health or educational service. It is questionable if one can coerce or convince such families that they need help, and have them respond to that intervention when they have not been granted the privilege of seeking and accepting it on their own choice. When the professional resorts to psychological rhetoric to convince families to participate in treatment which they neither solicit nor understand, that professional is liable for the ethical debacle of the coerced patient, regardless if that coercion to treatment is by adjudicated commitment behind institutional brick or blind acceptance of an individualized educational plan.

2
Retrieval

Retrieval is when the child reacquires behaviors which initiated his or her referral that had been successfully decelerated, and ceases the preferred social behaviors which had been taught during treatment. This definition of retrieval is not synonymous with recidivism. Traditionally, recidivism implies that the appropriate manner to assess effectiveness of a treatment regimen is to monitor the patient for several years after termination of treatment. The time lapse between treatment completion and when the patient returns for inpatient service is used as a measure of the value of the treatment procedure. This evaluative procedure probably evolves from medical research, in which it is decided that after a certain number of years without treatment a new etiological condition is responsible for reacquiring pathology.

The implication of recidivism is that the treatment technique is comparable to giving one an "inoculation" of mental health, and the patient will thereafter be "mentally well." That which we know about social learning and abnormal behavior patterns would discount this approach to document the value of a treatment procedure. The environment, unless drastically altered, will most probably reinstate the stimulating and reinforcing conditions which maintained the child's behavior prior to treatment. Hence, as long as the child has a memory, his or her repertoire contains those responses which may again operate upon the environment. If that environment is slightly receptive to reinforcing those behaviors, there will indeed be retrieval of the deviant responses. The cogent point is that retrieval does not indicate the failure of a treatment procedure, but rather serves as a cue of when there should be reinstatement of those treatment conditions which have been experimentally documented to be effective for that child. The treatment techniques would be reinstated in the child's environment where the behavioral retrieval occurred. Behavioral retrieval, then, should be interpreted as a helpful signal to resume treatment. When you return the child to his or her natural environment, it is similar to exposing him or her to an extended ABAB experimental design, in which, despite your efforts, the child returns to baseline, which is retrieval.

FOLLOW-UP STUDIES

The concept of behavioral retrieval is not incorporated in the follow-up studies of psychotic children. Several examples will illustrate this point. In comparing these studies, it should be recognized that there is considerable diagnostic disagreement among investigators. A child diagnosed as autistic in California may well be labelled as brain-damaged in Wisconsin and schizophrenic in Great Britain. DeMeyer et al. (1971) compared five popular diagnostic systems for identifying psychotic children, and clearly demonstrated the variance among investigators on providing a similar diagnostic classification for a child. This confusion means that one is stymied in comparing group data across investigators on the relative effectiveness of the treatment procedures. Unfortunately, this is hardly relevant, since few investigators stipulate their treatment procedures.

Accepting that psychotic children represent a heterogeneous group, with unknown but supposedly varied etiological circumstances, exposed to a variety of treatment curricula which are undefined in follow-up studies, the extent to which they adapt to a normal environment is reportedly very limited. Lockyer and Rutter (1969) explained in their five- to fifteen-year follow-up of a heterogeneous group of psychotic children that intellectual and social test scores were surprisingly stable across time; in fact, comparable to that expected for normal children. The results obtained were not statistically attributable to age, sex, evidence of brain damage, onset of reported psychosis, or even the completeness of the original intelligence testing. The facts were that, *as a group*, these children's intellectual and social quotients as first assessed would most probably hold constant to a later age when they were again examined. This prediction does not take into account the individual variance of children within the group. This variance in children is what we are interested in with the experimental-clinical approach. The most general prognostic statement that could be derived from Lockyer and Rutter's report was that if youngsters do not have speech before age five, and were retained in an institution, they would likely show the greatest detriment in intelligence and social quotients at a later age. As mentioned previously, children placed in institutions are those who may have adapted most poorly regardless of where they were placed. Yet, most clinicians would agree that institutional environments are not conducive to growth in adults or children, regardless of how low they may be on the continuum of intelligence and social quotients (Goffman 1961; Ullmann 1967).

The follow-up studies of psychotic children are not encouraging. Even in Kanner's (1971) original eleven autistic children, only two showed a marginal social adjustment at adulthood. This was 18 percent of a small sample, the remaining children of which were either custodial regressed or always in need of control and direction from other persons. Kanner (1972) also followed nine of ninety-six children he had seen, all of whom were initially diagnosed as autistic. These nine children made the most optimal adjustment of the entire sample, and only represented nine percent of those youngsters who met his original criteria for childhood autism. All nine children had speech before age five, and were not retained in institutions. However, he did indicate that these children who made the most progress would not meet the criteria which would satisfy a clinician's definition of normalcy.

Loretta Bender (1969) tracked thirty children she had worked with, who, in her estimation, met Kanner's original criteria for childhood autism. At approximately age thirty, the individuals in this group were broadly categorized as one-third reported as being "fair," one-third chronically defective or regressed institutional cases, and the remaining third rotating in and out of institutions and constantly requiring care by other persons or organizations. These patients demonstrated a range of schizophrenic disorders in adulthood, with the exception of some who appeared purely retarded. She, like Kanner, emphasized that the one-third that had progressed optimally were by no means what she would describe as socially comparable to the normal adult.

Bender (1969) also cited the results of a study by Havelkova who performed a four- to twelve-year follow-up of seventy-one children diagnosed as autistic or schizophrenic. The children's ages ranged from eight to seventeen at the time of the follow-up study, with 37 percent residing in custodial institutions, 10 percent residing in residential programs which were treatment-oriented, and 53 percent remaining in their homes. Recognizing that it is not entirely legitimate to make predictions from different studies when such variance among diagnostic categories exist, there is the viable hypothesis that as these children increase in age, the probability increases that they will be residing in institutions outside of the home, and most likely in custodial care. In Havelkova's follow-up of these children who are high school age or less, 53 percent are able to reside in their homes. Yet, in Bender's follow-up (1969), it was learned that approximately one-third are able to reside in a home-like circumstance by the time they reach thirty years old. The suggested hypothesis is that with increasing age, it becomes less tolerable for the family to retain these children in their home. The lamentable fact is that with the variety of undocumented treatment approaches represented in these follow-up studies, one may not predict that these children will make a heuristic adjustment to the home as they approach adulthood. This overgeneralized hypothesis is reached when one has only available group data where individual variances are statistically washed out. Since these follow-up studies do not provide a detailed account of the treatment procedures used as related to the eventual disposition of each child, it is not legitimate to be pessimistic *in all cases* on the basis of these broad follow-up studies.

Adult Patients

The grim reality of the prognosis for psychotic children as determined when it is not related to specific treatment techniques is also applicable to adult populations. Anthony et al. (1972) summarizes a number of follow-up studies on recidivism in hospitalized adults. The two major assessment variables common to the studies reviewed were percent recidivism (return to the hospital) and percent full-time employment, both of which were related to time since discharge. Reviewing the summarized tabulations, it appears painfully obvious that hospitalization alone is ineffectual for an extended period of time with adult patients. Six months after discharge from hospitalization, one may expect that 30 to 40 percent of the patients will return to the hospital, and 30 to 50 percent will have full-time employment during that period of time. One year after discharge, 40 to 50 percent of the adults will return to the hospital for continued care, and only 20 to 30 percent will still have full-time employment outside of the hospital. By three to five years after discharge from hospitalization, these adult patients will demonstrate 65 to 75 percent recidivism as defined by their return to the hospital, and a mere 25 percent will be retaining some employment adjustment.

These percentages are improved with half-way house programs, but as Anthony explains, optimal adjustment for these patients is maintained only to the extent that they remain in the half-way house program and receive continued support from that agency. A half-way house is a continued extension of treatment with dependency upon professional supervision for the patient's employment adjustment. The data suggest that once adults are so disabled as to warrant hospitalization, the probability is greatest that they will require continued care, and least that they will demonstrate self-sufficient, full-time employment. High-rate recidivism is not exclusive to the conglomerate of psychotic children, but also pervades the varieties of diagnostic classifications in adult patients who may not have had a history of childhood psychoses.

Why are our treatment approaches so untenable after discharge, presuming that they were effective during hospitalization? Anthony reports that the reasons for discharge often include the patient's making an optimal hospital adjustment. Unfortunately, such discharge criteria are not based upon demonstrable adjustment to actual environmental conditions, but rather those which exist within the hospital environment which is admittedly quite different, if not socially bizarre (Goffman 1961).

These follow-up studies with adults, as with children, do not relate recidivism with particular treatment procedures used during hospitalization. Presumably, the majority of patients, both adult and child, demonstrate behaviors which would be of assistance to their adjustment to the natural environment while they are in the hospital. Why is it that those behaviors do not generalize or maintain after discharge? I hypothesize that retrieval of the pretreatment behaviors occurred because of lack of generalization of treatment effects and reinstatement of the maintenance reinforcement condition in the environment, which combine and supercede the treatment effects. This hypothesis does not negate the efficacy of the treatment techniques used, but rather is cognizant that patients have two major behavior patterns, one of which they acquire during treatment, and the more dominant one which initiated the original diagnosis and referral and is most likely to be maintained by their natural environment.

Behavior Retrieval

In our earlier studies (Browning and Stover 1971), we were chagrined by the rapidity of retrieval of referral behaviors and the failure to maintain treatment effects. However, when we simply compared the number of years in which deviant behaviors were rehearsed by a six-year-old psychotic child against the months of treatment in which he had acquired new, incompatible responses and deceleration of deviant ones, it was obvious that the greater habit strengths were in favor of the original abnormal responses. Furthermore, those deviant responses had the advantage of being on a multitude of reinforcement schedules, rehearsed thousands of times in the natural environment, which gives them the advantage of being very resilient. In the treatment approaches documented in this book in which the child is usually in residence for six months, only four and a half of which are actually effective treatment, the clinician must remember that this treatment interval may be pitted against up to six years of deviant habit strengths.

There is an analogy we use in explaining to parents the difficulty in training their child, and the likelihood that the child will retrieve the behaviors which prompted the referral for treatment. A six-year-old child learns to ride a bicycle, which he becomes very proficient at and enjoys immensely. At ten years of age it is decided that riding a bicycle is an "abnormal" behavior for him to indulge in, regardless of how reinforcing or enjoyable it is. This is analogous to a psychotic child's aggressive, self-destructive behaviors which are deemed abnormal. The treatment program for this "abnormal" behavior would be to train the child to no longer be able to ride the bicycle, yet after such training, bicycles would still be available for him to ride. The analogy is drawn to the child who communicates with aggression and tantrums, which have been effective as primitive, but operant, behaviors for years before treatment. A treatment program would be designed to teach the child to no longer display those behaviors, but to perform alternate responses. When the child is returned to his home, the original stimulus conditions are there to reinstate those behaviors, just as it would be for the child who is taught to no longer ride a bicycle, but to stay off it and walk as an alternate response. Obviously, the child would have only to climb on the bicycle once to be able to ride it as efficiently as before treatment; just as with a psychotic child, it would take only a few of the original reinforcement conditions to begin reinstatement of the abnormal behaviors of tantrums and aggressions which have contributed to the original diagnosis of childhood psychoses.

Psychotic children are disposed for retrieval of behaviors because of specific learning handicaps which further compounds their retardation. Lovaas has tentatively demonstrated the discrimination handicaps of psychotic children (Lovaas et al. 1971). The less proficient the discrimination ability an individual has in a learning task, the more likely it is that generalization of that response to similar stimuli will be correspondingly weak. Clinicians who have worked extensively with psychotic children do not require the facts of the laboratory to know that what is taught to these children in one location is exceedingly difficult to transfer to another. One may anticipate in treating psychotic children that what is taught in one place has to be taught in all places. Our recommended program is designed around this generalization deficit of these children; one never hopes for generalization, but must always train specifically for it. This is a primary reason why it is inappropriate to judge treatment effects of a particular program with a psychotic child by using the model of recidivism. Recognizing that generalization is a major handicap for these children and comparing previous habit strengths against duration of time in treatment, one's best prediction is that these children will retrieve their old behaviors and extinguish those they have acquired in the treatment program. This hypothesis indicates that the value of follow-up is not for assessment of treatment effects in residence, but rather as a monitoring device to indicate when one should intervene with the child and reinstate the treatment programs documented to be effective when he or she was in treatment. Acceptance of this hypothesis indicates that follow-up is a necessary and continuous part of treatment, which means that treatment is never terminated, only the intensity of its reinstatement may diminish.

Self-Control

Gollin & Moody's (1973) discussion of Browning and Stover's text (1971) regarding maintenance of treatment effects included the recommendation that greater emphasis should be placed on training self-control techniques with the children. This is an appropriate suggestion, and is an area which we should have researched more diligently. Our approach has been to train the child to adapt maximally to his or her environment, and also to correspondingly train the environment to maintain the child's behavior because of the aforementioned learning handicaps. We have relied almost exclusively upon environmental control to support treatment effects rather than a self-control approach. The techniques of self-control have just begun to be productive with intact adults, and have yet to be predictably effective in controlling behavior such as smoking, drinking, or psychotherapy effects. Self-control techniques presume that the child is capable of becoming operantly autonomous. In contrast, the data we have suggests that the majority of children might acquire operant autonomy for a few behaviors, but they are predominantly respondent youngsters dependent upon a sustaining environment trained to stimulate and reinforce the preferred habits.

Behavioral Void

Presuming that retrieval is a most probable pattern for these children, I would like to speculate further on the response characteristics which are most likely to be retrieved. When we have been called back to the home or school to reinstate treatment effects for a child, usually their retrieved behaviors are those which have an operant/avoidance value. Recognizing that psychotic children are intellectually and linguistically limited youngsters who have acquired at best a respondent form of language during treatment, they retrieve what has historically been very effective "body english." These are children with a history of repeated failures in their early operant training, with a restricted repertoire of communication, often composed of tantrums, aggressions, and self-destructive responses, and who are successful in avoiding or in stimulating others to appease them when they are unable to verbalize their needs. When these children are placed in a school setting where complex operant behaviors are required, and where they are confronted with academic and social failure, then the conditions are ideal for behavioral retrieval. Under these conditions, when the children do not have spontaneously available correct responses, the behaviors which were historically successful in similar circumstances are likely to be elicited. They are typically those primitive operant behaviors which have the effect of avoiding other persons' demands for a complex operant behavior. The aggressions, tantrums, and similar deviant responses characteristic of psychotic children are not only a form of communication for diffuse needs which the children cannot verbalize, but also serve to avoid training requirements which historically were neither rewarding, nor understood by the children. Many of these youngsters probably prefer a situation where they are alone and in an ostensibly behavioral void. When placed in a demanding operant environment, such as a classroom where they fail and receive minuscule reinforcement, they begin to operate with these avoidance behaviors.

We are not sure *why* these children appear to operate for a behavioral void, but it has been our observation that for many psychotic children this is a preferred state. Whether this is an organically driven condition, or simply acquired by finding it more reinforcing to be operant for isolation rather than exposed to repeated failure which never results in reward, is a theoretical question at this time. Because this is a dominant response mode for these children as observed prior to treatment, it is one most likely to be retrieved. When a psychotic child is placed in a special-education classroom, where respondent training is performed but appropriate operant responses are in greater demand, it will require constant stimulation to maintain their performance. The positive reinforcement, time-outs, and behavior shaping hierarchies necessary to sustain the treatment effect are seldom performed because the teachers are not accustomed to such arduous child-rearing demands. The results are that the treatment effects are subjected to extinction, and the child's original repertoire composed of avoiding with deviant responses will emerge. The only self-control technique we have used to counter this problem has been to train the child to say, "Please help me." Even this simple self-control technique is not infinitely autonomous; it has to be maintained and rehearsed with the child repeatedly.

Training Environment

These children are most likely to retrieve behaviors which will naturally reinstate their own maintenance conditions. For example, tantrums, aggressions, self-destructs, darting, and mutism will elicit various kinds of attention from others in their efforts to control these responses. These are the child's dominant behaviors prior to treatment—lingering infantile preverbal communicative responses which make known their needs that they were unable to explain, much less comprehend. With the rehearsal and persistence of such behaviors, be it in demanding attention, play, food, or simply avoiding the demands of other persons, these behaviors cause parents and teachers to cease their demands of the child. Instead, they attempt to settle, soothe, and appease the child, just as one would normally treat an infant.

One autistic child, Tim, retrieved his crying in the complex school setting in which he was returned after treatment. His crying was a predictable response whenever he was placed in a situation where he did not have a trained response. Historically, Tim's crying was a highly effective avoidance behavior and inadvertently reinforced by the family prior to treatment. His parents had recognized his confusion, just as one would respond with a normal, preverbal child who is crying because he could not make known his needs, and they would try to comfort their youngster. This had the unfortunate consequence of removing him from potential learning situations, and made crying and whimpering an avoidance behavior maintained by the parents' and teacher's attempts to cajole, please, and comfort him. When in the classroom after treatment, and confronted with the complexity of moving from one classroom to another, where his eye-contact training was not maintained, where the reinforcement schedules were approximations of extinction, where he was unable to communicate effectively with other children, he once again began to avoid that situation with his crying. By the time we intervened, he had the principal, teacher, school counselor, and speech therapist all taking their turns sitting with him in the hall when he would cry to avoid the classroom, and even offering chocolate milk to settle him. In a short time, he had regained the skill of crying in the classroom to avoid the instructional demands. We reinstated the techniques of timing-out crying, positively rehearsing the responses demanded of him in the classroom which he had been avoiding, and tried to establish higher rates of reinforcement for success. We had to train the environment to control his handicaps in order to perpetuate the earlier training effects.

← Negative Reinforcement

Perhaps another overgeneralized hypothesis may be made about the abnormal behaviors demonstrated by these children which make them stand in such contrast to normal youngsters, and increases the likelihood that they will train their social environment to provide the reinforcers which will favor behavioral retrieval. The hypothesis is that these children function predominantly on negative reinforcement paradigms, which sustains not only their avoidance behavior but the supporting reinforcement conditions. It is the child's termination of his or her tantrum, aggression, and self-destructive responses, which rewards the parent for having provided the kind of attention, food, play, or avoidance which "causes that behavior to stop." The definition of *negative reinforcement* is the termination of a stimulus which accelerates a response. The termination of a temper tantrum in an autistic child may reinforce the parents for having provided a variety of measures to comfort their child, such as carrying him or her, providing different kinds of food, or even leaving the child alone and not making further demands of him or her.

If the self-destructive child is left alone, presumably with no obvious reinforcement for that behavior, it will diminish. The erroneous conclusion derived from this observation is that social attention is maintaining the behavior. Rather, it may be that when you leave the child alone, avoid him or her, make no further demands, this is just the reinforcement condition for which the child terminated that response. This is likely to be the experience of parents with a self-destructive child, and the erroneous presumption of the professional that the parents' attention to that behavior was the sustaining condition. The termination of a noxious behavior may serve to reinforce the response the parents provided, which in turn reinforces that abnormal behavior in the child. In this respect, the psychotic child may be operating for a behavioral void, rather than one of learning new responses. It is a strange interaction; the child is least intelligent, but yet he or she is in control. With the best of intentions, the parents and teachers are trying desperately to teach the child, but they only succeed in teaching him to avoid learning by their natural tendency to diminish the child's screams and tantrums. They have taught him to continue the tantrums and aggressions, and the child has taught them to reinforce these behaviors by his or her ceasing them.

This is an unusual training interaction, but a logical and observable one. The psychotic child is most socially reinforcing for ceasing his or her abnormal behavior, which means the child is most enjoyable when in a behavioral void. When the child avoids such behaviors, the termination of those responses would only reinforce the parent or teacher for having quit trying to intervene with him or her. This is what is meant when it is said that the child operates for a social vacuum, which is reinforcing to other persons and they inadvertently perpetrate that kind of behavior. Since the child is least annoying when in that behavioral condition, the logic of this hypothesis follows that a program in which comforting, cajoling, rocking the child, and making no instructional demands with contingencies for responses demanded, would only serve to exacerbate the deviant responses. With continuation of such habit patterns, it would be very likely that such children would eventually be maintained in institutional environments, rather than in their homes. Families unknow-

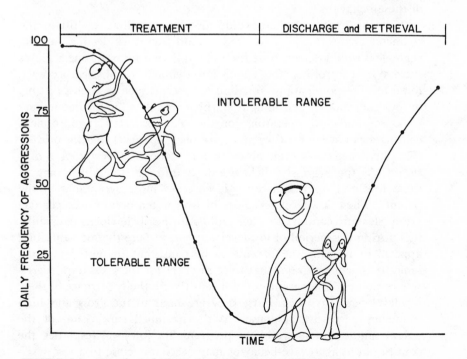

FIGURE 2-1 *Hypothetical Illustration of the Process of Retrieval*

ingly trapped by this reinforcement paradigm gradually accelerate the deviant responses, until their child eventually becomes so obnoxious that he or she has to be removed from the home.

Symptom Substitution

There are numerous conditions which foster retrieval of pretreatment behaviors of psychotic children; the one presented next is again hypothetical and remains unsubstantiated by our data. To clarify this hypothesis, figure 2–1 illustrates the child's behavioral status during and after treatment. As shown in the vertical axis of the figure, at the beginning of treatment the child is demonstrating fifty aggressive responses per day. These responses are on a gross level, defined as actually making physical contact directly with his or her body or with objects thrown at another person. This rate of aggressive behavior would be intolerable to the home and school, and would be one of the dominant behaviors which would necessitate the child's admission for treatment. During the course of treatment, aggressive behaviors would decelerate, perhaps due to a time-out program, until that behavior approaches what we would define as a tolerable range of aggressive responses for the family relative to the pretreatment level of these behaviors.

During treatment there would also be a qualitative shift in the character of the response. Not only would frequency decline, but the aggression would demonstrate itself in a different form. As one achieves success in controlling the aggression defined by physical contact, lower-level response approximations will occur, such as almost hitting, or touching another person lightly, which are related to the decelerated responses and still operating for the old, preferred reinforcement contingencies, whatever they may have been. I suspect that historically this phenomena has been observed and defined as *symptom substitution*. As the aggressive behavior falls into the tolerable range of these low-level approximations, it becomes more acceptable to the parents. These low-level responses of five or ten occurrences per day are a pleasant contrast to their child's former behavior. Predictably, it is during this period of low-level responses where the most difficulty appears in training the parents to be consistent in performing the same treatment programs that were in effect for the gross-level aggressive responses. The parents are not sensitive to the occurrence of these low-level aggressive behaviors; they are used to the gross and high frequency aggressive responses. With continued supervision of the parents and maintenance of the programs for low-level responses, the continuum of aggressive behavior may decelerate close to a zero level. Treatment effects are satisfactory and the child is discharged. Upon returning home, these low-level responses are the most recently rehearsed on the hierarchy of aggressive behaviors in the child's response repertoire. It becomes increasingly imminent that these behaviors are the first to be reinstated in the home, and least likely to be observed and treated by the parents since they are tolerable in comparison to the aggressive behaviors that characterized their child for so many years prior to treatment.

Unknowingly, the parents allow the child to rehearse these low-level behaviors, accidentally reinforce them, and gradually the child begins to operate more pervasively with this continuum of aggressive behaviors. The child then gradually progresses up the hierarchy of aggressive behaviors from slightly touching another person, to shoving, until he or she eventually begins to hit again. Frequency correspondingly accelerates with the qualitative shift of the behavior until the child has returned back to the intolerable range of aggressive behaviors. The parents, for reasons varying from embarrassment to disillusionment with behavior modification, do not ask for help. It is therefore necessary to not rely upon the family to call for assistance, but to anticipate the reality of retrieval, and to routinely visit the home to monitor for the gradual reinstatement of such behaviors.

Behavior Habits

There are habits in the home and school that will nurture retrieval of behavior. Just as the child may have had six years of deviant habits prior to treatment, and only four and one-half months of effective intervention, this same ratio applies to the parent's child-rearing practices which historically sustained those deviant behaviors. It is useful to remember that not only does the parent train the child, but conversely, the child is also training the parents. Regardless of the parent training performed, habit strength is greatest with those child-rearing techniques they demonstrated prior to treatment. It is by mutual reinforcement for subtle changes in behavior that the parents will gradually reacquire the original interaction they had with their child.

Furthermore, the parents, just as the child, will have difficulty in generalizing what they have been taught. Observations in the home frequently reveal that techniques like consistency, reinforcement, and extinction by ignoring annoying responses are seldom generalized to child-rearing practices with the other normal children. The parents also infrequently incorporate these techniques with new and different behaviors occurring with the child who was in treatment. It is not uncommon to learn that when the discharged psychotic child acquires unique but aberrant behaviors, even in homes which have been vigilant and successful in controlling retrieval of behaviors, parents will be unaware of the deviancy of the new behaviors and fail to employ techniques which would be effective and in which they have been trained. In retrospect, one wonders if it is reasonable to expect families to be this vigilant and objective about their own child.

Retrieval is usually rehearsed during the weekend visits throughout treatment. This effect is easily demonstrable during treatment if data are taken all days of the week. On Monday following the child's return from a weekend visit, there will be a higher incidence of the pretreatment levels of behavior. The child was probably successful in operating with his or her old behaviors at home during the weekend visit. This may cause some staff morale problems when it takes until Thursday to have the child under effective training again. Even well-trained families employ the treatment techniques currently used for their child, but only for those behaviors which occur in the intolerable range, and they remain oblivious to those which occur in the tolerable range as depicted in figure 2–1. The necessity of monitoring and interrupting this pretraining of behavioral retrieval is obvious; the administration of doing so is arduous and expensive by its requirement of having a staff in the home on weekends.

Schools are fertile grounds for fostering retrieval of behavior in children. When the child receives a new teacher at the beginning of the school year, communication with the previous teacher is limited, so one has to begin anew in training the latest teacher. A similar problem is apparent after summer vacation when the child is returned to the same teacher, during which time the child retrieved a level of intolerable behaviors which the teacher was not exposed to during the previous year. The teacher is unfamiliar with these behaviors, which may operate extensively for avoidance, and so may begin to inadvertently reinforce those retrieved behaviors.

Browning and Stover's (1971) text studies a child, Will, who has been able to reside at home and attend a special-education class. At the beginning and middle of each school year, and always whenever a new teacher was introduced, Will would retrieve aspects of his aggressive behaviors, which requires intervention in retraining the teacher on how to control these behaviors. Aggression will likely be problematic for the rest of Will's life. One ominous speculation is that each time a child does retrieve some pretreatment levels of behavior of an intolerable quality, that behavior is placed on a new reinforcement schedule and retrained again, which may render it more durable and more liable for retrieval at later times. It is the same problem as an ABAB same-subject design; it may only train the child to reacquire the behavior more rapidly.

This argument for consistency in programs after discharge shows why it is unwise to presume that one may treat a child for an interval of time and expect to retain those treatment effects as if they were indelible. The maximum one may perform in treatment is the training of new responses; one does not eradicate old habits. Once a habit, always a habit, regardless if it is learning $2 + 2 = 4$, how to ride a bicycle, or to aggress to make known your needs when language is unavailable.

WHAT CAN BE DONE TO RESTRICT BEHAVIORAL RETRIEVAL?

Before parents and professionals can begin to curtail retrieval, they should assume proper perspectives about it, namely, that it will occur, it is expected, and it is a natural phenomena. This perspective indicates that treatment never terminates, that the environment to which the child is returned is never static but always capable of reinforcing the pretreatment behaviors. Furthermore, parents and teachers should not feel guilty about behavioral retrieval, or ashamed to announce its occurrence, but rather consider it as a signal for a continuing prevention program for the child. Just as youngsters will always have to visit the dentist, that they will always have tooth decay, and will always need those services even though they may be diligently brushing their teeth every day, the same prophylactic services apply to the psychological needs of disturbed children.

It is recommended that the treatment team retain its relationship with the family, and remain in the ascendent treatment role when services are required. There is a definite place for local services, but it is questionable at this time if such services are capable of providing the consistent follow-up and treatment for these youngsters. The professional most qualified to reinstate treatment effects is that individual who has worked directly with the child in performing the training programs documented to be effective with him or her. With a diverse treatment approach composed of various professionals and/or with the follow-up service relinquished to another health agency, it is unlikely that the child will be retrained on those programs researched to be most effective with him or her during treatment, but rather exposed to entirely different approaches. With some of the traditional treatment procedures, it is likely that the professional will inadvertently reinforce retrieval of the behaviors. This would likely be the case in play therapy and psychotherapeutic relationships in which the child is permitted to behave as he or she wishes during the therapy hour. I am stating that these children do not require unqualified love and attention; but rather, that the love for the learning handicapped child is likely to be most effective when used in teaching and maintaining behavior, and may be destructive if it is contingent upon behaviors which involve avoidance or socially inappropriate responses. The outpatient program should be oriented to sensitize the parents and teachers to their habituation of the child's gradual retrieval of behaviors. This may be offset by their acquiring periodic samples of the pretreatment behaviors of the child. This would be more objectively performed by staff members originally affiliated with the treatment team of the child, since the teachers and parents habituation is liable to make them less reliable in observing the child, particularly for low-level responses. Professionals not acquainted with this kind of approach, much less the habit hierarchies specific to the child, are unlikely to recognize these behaviors.

One should not presume that teachers and parents will seek assistance. This is not only administratively problematic for the school teacher, but their gradual habituation, their work load, and the employment setting which requires them to work autonomously does not lend itself to their seeking assistance when difficulties arise. Special education teachers are expected to handle problems by themselves until they reach an intolerable level. When it does become intolerable, it often means there has been a massive retrieval of behavior in the child, which indicates they will have little likelihood of success in reinstating treatment effects. The role of the follow-up team is to prevent this kind of social disaster.

Many teachers have been trained in behavior modification, but it is likely that many have a popularized and oversimplified notion of the approach. Through no fault of the teachers, this approach has been unfortunately popularized as "praise, praise, praise," rather than the recognition that behavior modification, properly performed, is a complex series of synchronized shaping programs that require thousands of trials and demands constant monitoring for minimal results.

CHAPTER
3
Treatment Techniques

The treatment techniques presented here are intended to be a co-ordinated sequence. Additional programs will be illustrated in the case studies to correct unique disabilities which may be found in this divergent group of children. The majority of the programs are designed to be performed sequentially to prepare the child for participation in a small group, special education setting, and living in the home. A secondary goal is to ascertain if this is a reasonable disposition, or if it may be necessary to recommend placement outside of the home because of the child's massive learning handicaps. The children for whom these programs are designed are variously diagnosed as autistic, schizophrenic, retarded, brain damaged, and emotionally disturbed. There are some behavioral problems common to this diagnostic conglomerate of children to which this treatment regimen is addressed. Such problems include failure to respond to social control, inability to be retained and attend in a learning situation, primitive or no language, weak or absent social reinforcers, eating problems, and numerous bizarre and antisocial behaviors which exclude them from public school settings. To the extent that these kinds of handicaps are common, this treatment sequence is designed to assist in the compensation of those problems.

SEQUENCE OF TREATMENT

Figure 3–1 contains a rough outline of the sequence of treatment programs which will be presented. The initiation of the programs during the six months of treatment overlap, and when particular programs begin depends upon the data obtained on prerequisite steps. For example, eye contact training and attention to task will not be successful until foods are conditioned so that they have a reward value. Furthermore, strengthening the value of social reinforcers is a function of first training the child to enjoy eating a wide variety of foods. A prerequisite to academic and language training includes compliance training, as well as deceleration of avoidance behaviors which may occur in the classroom setting. The time intervals shown on figure 3–1 are not intended to be specific dates when a program is initiated, but serve only as a guideline. Item number 12 indicates special programs, which refers to unique behaviors that have to be trained and are not contained in the previous eleven treatment steps. These may be a number of different responses, for example, teaching playground skills, holding a pencil correctly, controlling stealing, or toilet training.

Curriculum

The format of the treatment sequence is a curriculum which progresses from primarily respondent behavior in the child to more

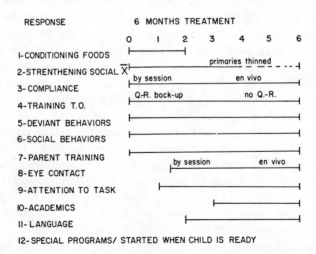

FIGURE 3–1 *Treatment Sequence for Psychotic and Neurologically Handicapped Children*

open, free operant behavior. The rationale is to teach the prerequisite behaviors necessary for the child to function operantly, however delimited, before exposing him or her to a demanding environment. Just as with a first grader, one does not begin on long division; with the psychotic child, one does not teach free play on the playground until he or she has the skills to play the games. This means the child has to have the language to interact with the other children; and before acquisition of that language skill, he or she has to acquire reinforcers, and compliance, and attention to task, and eye contact. The program, then, is a multiple shaping program for social behaviors. Within each program there will be a number of shaping steps provided as guidelines; they may have to be tailored to the ability level of the child.

Initiation of the special programs cited in this book will be a function of several variables. Is the child sufficiently compliant to follow the instructions of the program? Does the child have the prerequisite skills necessary to perform the responses expected in the program? And, perhaps equally important, are the staff ratio and time allotments available to implement the programs?

In reference to the treatment sequence in figure 3–1, all children will not necessarily begin on this treatment hierarchy at the same treatment level; this will have to be individually programmed. The treatment sequence is offered as a curriculum guideline, but at all stages progression through the treatment hierarchy would be determined by an experimental-clinical approach. Rather than explain the entirety of the experimental-clinical approach, refer to Browning and Stover's text (1971). Simply stated, it is a same-subject experimental approach taken to document the effectiveness of each program with a child. The behavior of each child is monitored by behavioral charting throughout the treatment curriculum. When the data indicate the program is effective, it is only on the basis of that information that one progresses to the next and more complex shaping step. If the data show that the treatment effects are negligible or ineffectual, then one must cancel that program and devise a new one to fit the special needs of the child. The steps offered in this treatment hierarchy are graduated so that prerequisite ones are trained before the latter, more complex behaviors are taught to the child. During the course of this treatment sequence, the parents are trained to perform each of the programs. Their implementation of the programs is managed through biweekly visits and under direct supervision of staff, with this supervision being diminished to the extent that the parents are successful in following the programs. Home observation is necessary to verify if parents are able to perform the program as they were under our supervision. When this approach is not effective, one may resort to video taping, and request parents to review the video tapes to indicate their correct and incorrect implementation of the programs.

It is recognized in this treatment sequence that the singular effects of the individual programs are confounded with each other. This is admitting no more than that it is a multiple shaping curriculum progressing from very primitive responses to more complex social ones. Thus, one cannot separate out the unique effectiveness of any singular program as it contributes to the total treatment effect. However, if the treatment programs begin with a child who is 30 percent compliant to simple commands, assaultive, self-destructive, sustained on few kinds of food, undernourished, and noncommunicative, and at the end of six months the child is speaking in a special education classroom, although still very retarded, but compliant 80 to 90 percent for all commands directed at his or her comprehension level, that confounding can be tolerated; it is satisfactory evidence of the effectiveness of the total shaping curriculum.

Reinforcement

Social reinforcers are conditioned during all phases of the treatment curriculum whenever primary reinforcers are used to reward responses. This is presumably accomplished by preceding presentation of the primary rewards with social reinforcers. The rationale is to associate the primary reinforcer with a praise statement so that the latter will acquire a reinforcing valence. In the treatment curriculum for the case studies offered in this book, we have not verified that the social reinforcers were indeed counterconditioned or strengthened by this approach. We have used this approach as a standard one, based upon earlier research which is detailed in Browning and Stover's text (1971). This is admittedly an unwarranted assumption since it is based upon so few cases, and is subject to that criticism. Furthermore, those earlier studies were individual cases; they were not group studies to demonstrate that this program is necessarily effective with all children. As a further note of caution in performing the treatment sequence with very retarded and learning handicapped children, it may be found that social reinforcers may never acquire an effective value with a child; their social reinforcers are as poorly acquired as are the majority of their other responses.

Compliance training is begun immediately in the treatment sequence, using both primary and social reinforcers initially, with this being coordinated with a time-out shaping program for noncompliant behaviors. Compliance is a necessary response for these children, to render them responsive to parental and teacher instructions so that they are behaviorally available to learn, whether it be at home or in school. Compliance is a primary handicap for these children, and is one of the most primary responses to exclude them from community living. The emphasis upon compliance, being performed so strictly, is often subjected to the criticism that the children appear very mechanical in following the commands made of them. That accusation may be questionable on the grounds that psychotic children, whose repetitive flapping, aggressing, and restricted repertoire of behavior expel them from any school setting, are destructive to the home, and constitute the behaviors which make them look more like a mad mechanical soldier bent upon social destruction. Children who are compliant, who like to do that which is expected of them because it has been historically rewarding, are children who begin to smile and laugh, who can learn and be operant, who first begin to show joy in their world, in fact, no longer appear so mechanical in their behavior as they did prior to treatment.

Time-Out

Training the psychotic child to take a time-out also begins at the initiation of the training program. These children have a variety of behaviors which have to be controlled by some extinction/punishment procedure. A training sequence is described here which initially requires use of a quiet-room for training the child to take a time-out while concurrently decelerating deviant responses. This is gradually shaped so that the child is able to take a time-out seated on the floor in a place where the deviant behavior occurred. The time-out training sequence described here requires the child to be on a time-out for only two minutes; in some instances five minutes have been used, but preferably by the conclusion of the program this may be diminished as low as thirty seconds.

The deviant behaviors which are controlled in the treatment sequence are subjected to the time-out program from the beginning of treatment. This is performed sequentially for the most disruptive and highly frequent responses to the least disruptive, and in some instances, less frequent behaviors. This is performed in a coordinated fashion in the program so that it is not overloaded on the negative side with the child receiving too many time-outs. The deviant behaviors include such responses as aggressions, darting, tantrums, self-destructiveness, and noncompliance. The social behaviors indicated by number 6 in figure 3–1 will vary with the skill level demonstrated by the child. These social behaviors include dressing, self-care in the bathroom, eating appropriately, making the bed and cleaning his or her room, going to school unescorted, playing with other children, learning recreational skills, and playing independently. Obviously, in the six-month interval we are only beginning to train social skills; this task is primarily relegated to the home and school. The treatment curriculum is geared to train the child to become available and susceptible to acquiring these more complex behaviors after treatment.

Eye Contact

Eye-contact training is another basic response taught since it is a prerequisite for delivering instructions in language acquisition and academic training. Eye-contact training typically commences after food has acquired a reinforcing value, as evidenced by amounts eaten in a time-delimited period of thirty minutes per meal. These children have a handicap of discrimination learning evidenced by their failure to attend to the appropriate stimuli incorporated in the learning task. They demonstrate a tendency to drift and focus on irrelevant stimuli, which impedes their performance. Attention-to-task training, listed as number 9 in the treatment sequence, is an academic prerequisite, also necessary for individual play. This is training children to be seated at a desk with their head down and working, regardless of whether they are making errors or correct responses. The time interval in this program is expanded until the child is able to work from time intervals which began at fifteen seconds and progressed to at least twenty minutes of task-oriented work without redirection, and progressing from primary to social rewards for maintenance of that behavior. This is necessary if the child will be immersed in a group setting in a school where the teacher will not have the time to be monitoring and redirecting the child constantly to a task.

The academic curriculum cannot really commence effectively until eye contact begins, and the child is able to attend to a task long enough to be directed by the teacher, and compliance has progressed to the point where he or she will follow commands or instructions without relying excessively upon time-outs, and the deviant behaviors have decelerated sufficiently so that they will not interrupt the classroom. The academic curriculum will vary with the extent of retardation discovered in the child, with that level being determined during the course of the entire program. If it appears that academic pursuits really will not contribute to employment for the child after high school, then it is recommended that the training be directed toward prevocational behaviors. The multitude of academic programs which have stemmed from these research studies are too numerous to include in this text, and are currently in separate manuscript preparation (E. Browning 1979).

Language

Language is the critical turning point in the entire treatment curriculum. Without the previously mentioned behaviors being trained or controlled, language is less likely to be acquired. When the child has sufficient eye contact, then one may begin in one's efforts to train language. The behavior prerequisites necessary for initiation of language training include conditioning foods and social reinforcers, compliance, training the child to take an appropriate time-out, control of deviant behaviors, eye-contact training, and attention to task. This does not mean that the final goals of each of these programs have been achieved, but that they have been successfully started. With many of these children, language is never really attained. For some youngsters, by the conclusion of the language training program, they are actually demonstrating large blocks of echoed responses, which is the maximum they have been able to acquire. In such circumstances, the child often remains as a retarded but respondent, compliant youngster who requires constant monitoring and supervision by other persons, and will remain linguistically dependent upon them. Such a youngster should not be allowed to retrieve his or her old communicative operant behaviors, such as tantrums and aggressions, but may be mute much of the time. The child can follow the commands he or she comprehends, and is continually reinforced for the few speech responses he or she acquired which allow him or her to be more socially acceptable.

Children who acquire operant language are the most rewarding to work with; they "blossom" or become operant in their behavior with the acquisition of speech. It should be noted that we will occasionally be using the words *speech* and *language* interchangeably in the case studies. It is recognized that different definitions are usually given to these terms. However, with many of these severely handicapped children, their language persists as a limited form of speech, which, as mentioned, consists of large blocks of echoed words in which they have been trained. Some of the youngsters acquire what we may define as language in terms of their demonstrating unique combinations of words to make known their needs, to explain, and to learn. But they, too, often have a repertoire of pretrained speech responses which were trained specifically for certain situations, which they are able to use operantly at times, but predominantly remain on a respondent level. So, even with the most fruitful child in this research, speech and language are never comparable to what one would find with a normal youngster. Often, after a successful program these children sound very much like a prerecorded tape in their language. When this is the case, quite often they are demonstrating pretrained sequences of language which are emitted under certain stimulus conditions when you are speaking with them. But even with that shy repertoire, it may be that the child will progress to be more operant in language.

DATA ACCUMULATION

This treatment sequence requires that behavioral charting be performed to assess the effectiveness of the shaping steps contained within each program, and across the entire sequence. For the purpose of efficiency, it is useful to obtain a one-week baseline before beginning each child's treatment sequence. After accumulation of the baseline, we sample the behavior in question for each child, all responses under training at that time being counted simultaneously, one day per week, a different day each successive week, so that we are able to sample across all days during the course of the entire six-month treatment curriculum. This is designed to remove some of the order effects one would obtain if they always sampled on the same day. Obviously, order effects should vary with months in residence. If one always sampled the child on the same day each week, one would obtain a very biased view of the efficiency of the programs. For example, under a very highly structured program, on Thursday the child is likely to appear very good throughout the course of the treatment. This would not reflect the normal variance one would expect to observe on Mondays. It is important that all days be sampled cyclically during the treatment sequence so that you may assess how effective the child is in generalizing back to his or her home, which is usually demonstrable by the data obtained on Mondays.

In Browning and Stover's text (1971), it is recommended that all behaviors for all children be counted continuously all days of the week. This is subjected to the criticism of the staff time involved in obtaining that massive number of counts, with the inevitable occurrence of their habituating to the behaviors which were being observed continuously, with the end result that reliability deteriorated. When staff have only to count on one or two children per day, a different child each day, they are more likely to be sensitized to that child's behavior since it breaks up the routine of always observing the same behaviors, and it also counters the danger of their habituating to the child's behavior. Furthermore, since it takes weeks to train a response with these children, weekly samples are usually sufficient to assess the effectiveness of the program when those counts are maintained over a six-month interval. Bank counters (Lafayette Instrument Corporation) are used to count the behaviors during each shift, and the data are entered on a daily data sheet for each child and filed in a data book. One staff member is assigned each day to be responsible to assure that during his or her shift all data are logged appropriately. At the conclusion of the evening shift, that one staff member checks all data books. The special staff for each child are allocated research time each week to check their data, and update all graphs so that they may use this information to counsel the parents on Friday evenings.

There are always a number of programs which are nondata based for each child. These programs are usually performed with a general management order in which the data may not be accumulated continuously, but rather sampled at the beginning and termination of the program. Examples of some nondata programs are contained in the case studies. They are usually in the form of training sessions for specific problems the child may have, in which the effects will be comparatively obvious.

CONCLUDING STEPS OF THE TREATMENT CURRICULUM

By termination of the treatment curriculum, positive practice should be a dominant technique in training the children, and reliance upon time-outs should diminish considerably. Positive practice is simply having the child rehearse error responses to success with diminishing supervision. By discharge, time-outs should be delivered for lower-level approximations of the original decelerated behaviors. At this stage of the program, the child is being dealt with more on a verbal level, his or her environment is much freer, and he or she is allowed and encouraged to be more operant to the extent of the acquired language and prerequisite skills. The commands given to the child will be expanded, this again being dependent upon the extent of language acquisition. At conclusion of treatment, the child should have advanced to the point of performing longer sequences of commands, such as putting on all clothing and making his or her bed before coming down to the nursing station for his or her tooth brush. At the beginning of the program, this single command may have been broken up for each article of clothing, and each step of making the bed, as well as going to the nursing station.

At the conclusion of the program, staff time will be increasingly directed toward training the social environment to sustain the behaviors which the child has acquired. This requires training the teacher in the community classroom and more frequent visits in the home to ascertain if they are maintaining the child's programs. The child's time at home will increase from weekends to three- and four-day intervals for the remainder of the time in the treatment setting. The routines demanded of the child in residence should not be inconsistent with those likely to be available in the home. At this terminal stage of the program, one should have frequent consultations with the parents about the prognosis based upon the learning rates of the child. If the parent training has been successful, and they have been amply involved, the concluding recommendations will be no surprise. Also, regardless of one's counsel to the parents at this time, those recommendations are always left open. If it is decided at this time that the child will return to the home, this is with recognition that it is on a trial basis, as the next phase in the child's life. Even if residential care is recommended, this is explained to the parents as not necessarily a permanent status for the child, but a decision which can always be rescinded.

ADMINISTRATIVE OUTLINE

The administrative structure used with the groups from which these data have been derived is designed to serve two goals: consistency and continuity. It is necessary that everyone perform the same programs in the same manner, not only consistently, but long enough to assure that there is optimal generalization of treatment effects.

The curriculum presented in this book is designed for outpatient use, specifically the public school, and inpatient circumstances, namely residential or institutional programs. Considering the state and federal mandates for special education privileges being provided for developmentally disabled children, it appears reasonable that the public school shall assume primary responsibility for the behavior management of the child, even when the child is residing in a residential program and attending a public school during the day. The program authority has to reside with one agency; in fact, there should be one person primarily responsible for the program of each child. The treatment programs presented have been used in both facilities: in public or day school settings, as well as residential programming, with parent involvement in both conditions.

The recommended administrative structure is that of an autonomous team in which roles are delegated and trained for, and responsibilities are not subjected to bureaucratic chains of command. The preferred educational group is small, usually only six children being served by one team under inpatient conditions, but the program has been used successfully with outpatient groups of eight and ten varied youngsters in one classroom with two teachers or a teacher and one aide. Decisions regarding clinical or educational choices are derived within the group, and not constantly subject to approval by persons not clinically affiliated with the treatment team. This eliminates the cumbersome and unnecessary communication pitfalls so characteristic of larger institutions or school environments using departmentalized administrative structures.

Communication time within the group is scheduled to be as goal directed as possible. Time is scheduled each day, either at the end of the school day in that setting, or at shift change time in the residential programs. We determined that 16 percent of total staff time was involved in communication or ongoing training to implement this program. That figure may seem high, but it was child-directed, and it allowed us to assure that everyone was doing the same thing, the same way, in managing the children. If this goal of consistency is not achieved, the programs will be administered variably, treatment effects will be marginal, and it is a greater possibility that the child will retrieve the original referral behaviors. The value of the administrative autonomy of a small group allows the communication time to be relevant to problems to which the group is addressed. The roles of business office, food service, housekeeping, transportation, and similar items are support operations designed to perform their services on request, thereby allowing the group to function independently. In particular, if food is required from the kitchen it may be ordered without progressing through memorandums, different departments, and permissions from persons not sensitive to the needs of the group. Items to be purchased are requested, but in emergent situations, it is possible to obtain purchase orders within an hour for most items. The majority of expenses are ordered on a monthly-estimate basis without the necessity of lengthy justification.

This administrative model excludes the departmental structure where professionals are parceled out to various treatment or educational units within the institution or school. Those professionals would not have responsible authority nor understand the needs of the treatment unit. The departmental model is not liable for continuity of programs: it perpetrates role confusion, and is pondersome in its attempts to coordinate communication among departments. The departmental model is excluded because the individual is really responsible to that department and its maintenance, rather than to the child directly. Delineation of roles and responsibilities within departments becomes primary, and the child's education assumes a secondary role; in fact, he or she obviously serves the needs of the department. The departmental model also ignores the fact that many different kinds of people can perform similar tasks if they are trained and supervised correctly. The departmental model does not recognize that social workers can give children baths, and sufficiently trained class-room aides can design behavioral management programs for the children, and psychologists are not the only persons who can analyze data.

In a small autonomous treatment and educational group, promotions develop within that unit as a function of the value of the staff's performance, rather than longevity of service which is characteristic of many state mental health operations. Large institutions and schools with departmental administration are confronted with the problem of union demands superceding child needs. With such a situation, the position of a child care worker, or classroom aide, as a professional mental health and educational person, becomes an impossibility. It is our impression that in the departmental structure, the professionals work for their own individual identities, each one receiving a separate piece of the child, and the puzzle never really becomes integrated, much less the child. Perhaps the greatest error committed in the departmental model is that there is no one person who knows entirely what was done in the treatment and education with each child because no one person is primarily responsible. It is our impression, with our justification of a cost analysis, that the small, task oriented, and autonomous treatment unit as described here is actually less expensive in its treatment costs, and more effective.

In both the inpatient and outpatient projects, the nurses, child care workers, teachers, classroom aides, social workers, and psychologists are responsible for performing all treatment programs for all children in all places. It soon becomes apparent that everyone is able to perform the classroom programs because of their greater detail, and availability for people to be in the classroom. Each child has a special staff person assigned to him or her, and that special staff's duty is to be the child's advocate between the family and the treatment or educational group. The special staff coordinates visits, parent training schedules, and follow-up studies in the home after discharge. They are responsible for maintaining the data books on their child, and are allocated two hours per week to perform this task. They are also required to explain the weekly data to the parents when they take their child home for the weekends, or in the day school setting, to still provide that service at least weekly. The special staff, with the director of the program, reviews each child's program weekly, and then on a weekly staffing shares the child's progress and problems with all staff involved in the group. One afternoon a week is allocated for the rounds. In the residential program, a "subgroup" rounds is performed each week so that there is enough time to closely scrutinize the data of each child. The special staff's job also includes making sure that other staff performs the child's programs correctly.

Hours of staff for the group on the inpatient program are autonomously determined and usually posted one week in advance. Personal requests are honored on a sharing basis among staff for days off and vacations. This is necessary for staff morale. The staff in the group are not subjected to "rotations" for which they may be pulled from the research group and placed in another project simply because the other project is short staffed, or someone else had seniority.

EATING

Behavior Taught: Eating an Appropriate Variety of Foods

Severe eating problems are characteristic of many severely disturbed and retarded children. In order to teach attention and then language, it is necessary to have a predictable reward, and we often rely upon food for that effect. However, it is not beneficial to the total program of the child to use a few highly preferred foods, such as cereals or candies, since they are detrimental to the child's mealtime eating, and may serve to perpetuate the eating problems which may already exist. It is more clinically advisable to teach the children to eat an appropriate amount and variety of foods, which then in turn can be used in teaching other more complex skills requiring a very strong reward system. The physical health of the child is as crucial as his or her psychological health, and being able to eat appropriately would render the child more adaptable to home and school meals, or in any residential facility where the child may eventually reside. Furthermore, the food is paired with social reinforcers when the child is being trained to eat a variety of foods, as well as when food is used as a reward for attention and language training. Thus, we extract considerable service from food: the health of the child, adaptation to the child's natural environment, strengthening social reinforcers, and teaching attention and language.

Data to Monitor Program

The data necessary to monitor the effectiveness of this training program are expensive because it requires a 1:1 staff supervision to implement the program, and considerable preplanning to order the hierarchies of food to be trained during the course of the program. There will be a qualitative shift in the kinds of responses being monitored. Initially, it may be one or two foods which are being strengthened with one preferred food, and later this will progress to more varied kinds of foods. One has to monitor the effectiveness of the reinforcement effect of preferred foods on learning to eat the new and different foods. This requires staff time spent in reviewing menues, placing orders with the kitchen, and monitoring percent success in eating different kinds of foods for successive meals. For each kind of food being trained, one records the number of trials in which that food was offered and the number of trials in which it was successfully eaten and reinforced with a preferred food. This will be clarified in more detail in the general management order to follow.

Typical Status of Child

Frequently, these children have had a long-standing history of eating problems, often traceable back to infancy. Also, these are children who are retarded by any examination, if it is possible to administer. They demonstrate abnormal behavior patterns, minimal compliance, confusion in following verbal commands, and have limited skill in verbal expression. These are children who, again, have worn the labels at various times of autistic, psychotic, retarded, disturbed, and brain damaged. They are typically young children, signifying that the extent of their disability was so obviously severe that the parents sought help at an early age with their child, which again restricts the prognosis.

Often these children eat a very limited variety of foods. Sometimes the variety is rigid—they will only eat a certain few kinds of foods, and always the same ones on successive days. With some youngsters, there will be variability in the few kinds of foods preferred, which will not hold constant across days. For example, the child may prefer potatoes and bread on one day, and the next day will reject either food. These youngsters often, but not necessarily, are below age expectancy heights and weights, which one may suspect is interactive with their eating patterns and developmental lags. However, it is our impression that these children are not very active and do not require as much food as other children. They may appear as more active because much of their behavior is obnoxious, but as far as engaging in different kinds of activities during the day which would involve running and playing vigorously, there is very little of this more normal activity. It seems that they have adapted to a schedule where little food intake is necessary to maintain them.

Where Implemented

The training program is performed during all mealtimes, all days of the week. During the first weeks of treatment, when the child is home for weekends, the program is not performed by the parents until we have had success in teaching the child to eat most foods. After the child begins to adapt to the program, the parents are trained to perform the program and to provide a diet which the child is known to be able to succeed on, which is the generalization training of the program. This program requires the parents to be well versed in the training curriculum, capable of consistently following a management order, and having supervised experience in performing it successfully at the treatment facility.

Staff Required

During the majority of the shaping steps required by this program, it is necessary that initially a 1:1 staff ratio be available for the child during the mealtimes. Shortly after the program begins, it is feasible for one staff to train two children, by alternating trials between them. In addition, staff time in the kitchen cannot be overlooked. A cooperative arrangement must be established with kitchen personnel so that they will prepare the kinds of foods to be used as reinforcers, as well as the foods arranged in the hierarchy from least to most preferred. It does not require much experience with food service costs to recognize that individually prepared meals substantially increase labor costs. However, it is our impression that this is a necessary cost in the clinical service for such children, which is counterbalanced by successful cases who do not require protracted residential placement.

Reinforcers Required

Food is the reinforcement used in training the child to eat a variety of age-appropriate amounts of food. It is necessary to arrange a hierarchy of least to most preferred foods, with the latter being used to reinforce eating increasingly less preferred foods. In fact, the reinforcers will shift if the program is effective, and as the child learns to eat a greater variety of foods, they in turn will be used successively, in a sequenced fashion, to reinforce eating still other unpreferred foods. We recommend the use of social reinforcement preceding the presentation of preferred reward foods. It may not be the case that the social reinforcement will have an accelerative effect on the eating, but rather, the reinforcement valance of the social reinforcers will increase by association with the preferred foods.

General Management Order

The child is seated at the table, unlikely to be distracted excessively by other children or events taking place in the room. One staff sits at the table with the child. Later in the sequence it is advantageous to have the child eat with the other children, but it is often necessary at the beginning stages of the program to be seated at a separate table with the child. Two plates are used. One is set in front of the child and contains the nonpreferred food or foods; the other plate has the foods used as the reinforcement and is placed before the instructor. The proper utensils are placed on the plate in front of the child (presuming the child can use a spoon or fork appropriately at this time) with a very small amount of nonpreferred food on it. In front of the child on the other plate is a larger amount of the preferred, or reward food, which the child is told he or she will receive after eating and swallowing the nonpreferred food on his or her plate. When the child takes the utensil and eats the nonpreferred food, he or she is then given a large amount of preferred food, preceded by social reinforcement. The remaining trials of the meal proceed in the same fashion. We usually interrupt trials by at least 10-second intervals. The length of the meal is typically limited to thirty minutes, which is the average amount of time a youngster has when eating at home or school. When the child reaches at least 85 percent success of all trials with the nonpreferred food, a new nonpreferred feed is added. Now the previously rewarded food may also be used alternately as a reinforcer in conjunction with the other rewards already available.

Specific Shaping Steps

There are a variety of concurrent shaping steps in this eating program. Different children will begin at different levels of these sequences, so the program has to be customized for the child. The concurrent shaping steps are as follows:

1. Before the inception of this program, one must determine which foods are preferred by the child and which are nonpreferred. This may be accomplished by interviewing the parents, but further demonstrated and validated by having them available at meals during the week of baseline and recording those which the child eats in a free setting. In this baseline, the staff does not require the child to eat any particular kind of food, but allows the child to select at his or her own rate, with the staff simply recording what the child eats and the estimated amount. According to the tallies obtained from these observations, a hierarchical order may be arranged showing which foods the child prefers from most to least. Those that are at the top of the list and are most consistently preferred will be used as the rewards for eating increasingly more of the remaining nonpreferred foods on the list. One would work

down the list, progressing from the most to the last preferred foods. It may be necessary to begin with foods which are reinforcing at breakfast to be used only at breakfast time, with the same decision being made for foods to be used at other meals. Or, it may be the case that ice cream and toast are highly stable preferred foods, and could be used as reinforcers for all meals. This would have to be ascertained from the observations and tests with the individual child. When one begins this program, it is advisable for the child to be on vitamins in the event that his or her food intake is initially low. Furthermore, if there is difficulty in taking fluids, it may be necessary to offer water and other liquids at various times during the day to maintain proper hydration.

In this food hierarchy, one has the preferred and nonpreferred foods available at each of the three meals during the day. One then uses the most preferred foods to reinforce eating progressively large amounts of the *least* nonpreferred, then the next, more nonpreferred food, and so on. For example, perhaps chocolate ice cream is used at breakfast, first in large amounts, and then decreasing amounts, for eating increasing amounts of scrambled eggs. After the child has succeeded in eating offered bites of scrambled eggs 85 percent of the time at the criterion of one spoonful amount each time, then ice cream *and* scrambled eggs may be used in a round-robin fashion for reinforcing the child to eat toast, which would also progress from small bites to larger bites.

2. The next shaping hierarchy within this program is the amounts of foods. At first, a large amount of food reward will be used to reinforce eating an extremely small amount of nonpreferred foods. As the child achieves 85 percent success, then the amount of non-preferred foods is increased, and the reward amount is correspondingly diminished. As one progresses, for example, the shaping steps should move so that the child is eating the entire amount of the eggs for a couple of spoonfuls of ice cream.

3. The third shaping hierarchy is the location of the training. As mentioned earlier, it is first conducted on a 1:1 relationship at a table aside from the other children so as to minimize distraction. As the program progresses, the child is integrated gradually closer to the main dining table until eventually he or she is eating with the other children.

4. The fourth shaping hierarchy is the amount of supervision as performed by what persons. The beginning steps of the program are on a 1:1 ratio at each meal. Different staff will be instructing different meals. This is intended to assist generalization across staff. As one progresses with the program, the family is expected to per-

form the program during some of their visits, this being conducted with diminishing staff supervision. By termination of the program, the child will be eating food in a round-robin fashion, after which he or she begins to eat those foods he or she wishes, with dessert at the end of the meal. At this final stage of the program, a staff member does not have to be directly involved with the child, but only casually observing the child while working with other children to be sure that he or she is eating some of all foods provided.

Learning Theory Explanations

There are two ways to discuss learning theory relative to this program. One is simply to use a known reinforcer contingent upon the response of eating the nonpreferred foods. By such repeated pairings, the nonpreferred foods by their association with the preferred may acquire a reinforcing valance themselves, or at least be acquired as a more probable habit. The other explanation would be in accordance with the views of Premack (1959). In this interpretation, a high probability behavior, namely, eating preferred foods, is used contingently upon the low probability behavior of eating nonpreferred foods. It is a combination of both of these views as concurrently operational in this training program. The preferred foods are of a high probability occurrence, because that is what has been available for the child habitually in the home prior to treatment. If they were deleted from the diet entirely, the probability of the other foods on the hierarchy of acquiring a reward valance would correspondingly increase because of increased higher drive. This is actually what occurs in this program; the preferred foods are deleted until the nonpreferred food is eaten. This may mean that a child may go for several meals without eating, but it is likely that he or she will succeed since a large preferred reward is so obvious to the child and readily visible, and the nonpreferred food is so small that there is little avoidance. The treatment paradigm seems to fall between both of these views, although some investigators may argue vehemently for either position.

EYE CONTACT

Behavior Taught: Eye Contact

Eye contact training is a prerequisite to social, language, and academic programs for the severely handicapped child. This program is recommended for children who are unable to learn in a structured setting; part of this deficit may be attributed to their failure to attend to the relevant stimuli being presented. This behavioral deficit seems characteristic of psychotic children, and various techniques have been reported in the literature to train eye contact (Lovaas 1977; McConnell 1967; Marr, Miller, and Straub 1966; Ricks and Wing 1975; Simmons and Lovaas 1969). This is compensatory training, derived from the premise that to capitalize optimally upon the native intellectual skills of the child, one should train the child sufficiently so that he or she will attend to the necessary stimuli in the learning task.

Normal children have the capacity to learn difficult conceptual tasks while daydreaming, throwing spit balls, and only periodically attending to the teacher. They seem able to fill in the instructional voids themselves with a minimum of information. The children we are training lack that capacity of generalization and alertness. They must make a more definite response to all stimuli for habit acquisition, and they are dependent upon external conditions to guarantee that response. Furthermore, these youngsters do not learn well by observation; they are characteristically deficient in imitation and modeling skills. In addition, organic deficits such as aphasia (Churchill 1972) may further impede their language acquisition, which accentuates their learning problems. Eye-contact training will not assure that a child will acquire language, nor does it guarantee academic improvement. It is only a psychological crutch to facilitate the child's learning to its maximum, however delimited that may be.

Data to Monitor Program

Sample counts during training sessions will provide the data to measure the progression of eye-contact training for the successive steps outlined next. In these training sessions, one will count the number of trials in which the cue for eye contact is delivered, and the number of times in which eye contact is held for the time interval being reinforced at that particular shaping step of the program. In each shaping step, when two or more days of 85 percent success for all trials administered per day are achieved, then advancement to the next shaping step is recommended. This is an arbitrary delineation for movement to the next shaping step; with some children one may wish to strengthen the response by requiring a greater number of days at the criterion level of success. With other children, one may never be able to achieve 85 percent success; less predictable behavior in the child may need to be tolerated.

Typical Status of Child

Diagnostically, children who lack eye contact usually fall in the mysterious categories of brain damage, psychosis, autism, schizophrenia, and retardation. This program is recommended for youngsters with a minimum of operant language, whose comprehension is correspondingly low, and for whom samples of eye contact reveal that when their name is presented, with a glance being accepted as sufficient eye contact, they are successful less than 50 percent of the time. These children usually have had an abortive attempt at language training, but during the course of instruction the child does not attend to the teacher and the speech gains are minimal. These are children who seem oblivious to other persons, are unable to stay with a task, and demonstrate a minimum of structured play both by themselves and with others. Attending responses, whether directed at other persons or in play, are restricted.

Where Implemented

Eye-contact training is first performed in training sessions, usually administered during meals and additional sessions during the day. We have used mealtime with the food available as reinforcers for training eye contact. The remaining two or three sessions provided during the day are typically twenty minutes in duration, using other preferred foods, of small quantities, as a reward system during those sessions. Eventually, social reinforcement may be used exclusively during these scheduled sessions, which allows food to be reserved for mealtimes.

During the eye-contact sessions, the child is seated at a table across from the instructor. The instructor holds his or her face approximately one foot away from the child's during the first shaping step, with this distance being increased with successive steps. Correspondingly, there is an increase in the time intervals of eye contact which is reinforced on the successive shaping steps. In the beginning of the child's program, eye-contact sessions should be performed at the same time and place each day, but with varying staff. The reason for this requirement is because these children have difficulty generalizing, so we first teach the response in specific locations for all persons, and after it acquires an 85 percent criterion level, then begin training in other surroundings. Again, we do not hope for generalization; we train specifically for it.

Staff Required

During the early shaping steps of the eye-contact training sessions, it is necessary to have a 1:1 staff ratio. Later, when the child is more compliant to the task, and when sessions are conducted in the school setting, two to three students may be taught together with sequential trials. The final steps of eye-contact training are performed in vivo, at all places, during which the staff may be working with a group of children while introjecting eye-contact training trials periodically with the child.

Reinforcers Required

The reinforcers we have used in this program have been food at mealtimes, and half pieces of preferred cereal during the remaining training sessions. Presentation of these rewards is always preceded by praise with the hopes that these verbal statements will acquire a greater social reinforcement value. During the latter steps of the treatment regimen, one relies exclusively upon social reinforcement, having faded out the use of primary reinforcers. When eye contact is demanded conjointly during speech and academic training, the child should be rewarded socially for that response, regardless of whether the language or academic response was incorrect. Furthermore, during the final steps of the eye-contact training, the schedule of social reinforcement should be thinned. This is usually accomplished naturally, but if response delay is observed one would then increase the reinforcement for eye contact to reinstate that response.

General Management Order

With some children, prior to beginning the program we obtain samples of eye contact at the various steps which are performed during the course of treatment. This information may be useful in predicting how long one may anticipate having to conduct the program, as well as the level at which the shaping steps should be initiated. Typically, we find with these samples that eye contact drops precipitiously with increasing distance.

The next step is to identify which foods will be used during the training sessions. It is recommended that one successfully complete teaching the child to eat a variety of foods, so that most foods available at mealtimes may be used as reinforcers for eye-contact training. It is imperative that if food during meals is to be used as rewards in teaching a response, that in so doing the child will also be provided a well-balanced diet. It is suggested that one be rather parsimonious in the use of cereals during the other training sessions since they are filling and do not contribute to a balanced diet. Cereals are preferred over candies, however, since the latter are likely to be more deleterious to the child's appetite at meals.

Furthermore, it is crucial that before eye-contact training begins, the child is sufficiently compliant to remain seated and attempts to follow the requests being made of him or her. During the course of all shaping steps, the staff member should give the command for eye contact; the cue should be held constant throughout the program so that it may readily be transferred to the school teacher. The cue is usually the child's name, but with some children at the beginning of the program, one may add, "Look at me." Eventually, this latter phrase is deleted with just the child's name being used. Eye-contact training should begin at a level where the child is most likely to succeed, such as requiring only a glance in which momentary eye contact is reinforced. When the correct response or criterion response is achieved, the staff member makes a positive evaluative statement, such as "Good looking!" and then offers the primary reinforcer if that is still in use at that step of the shaping program.

Specific Shaping Steps

1. The child should be seated approximately one foot from the in-structor at a table. The instructor holds the reinforcer being used close between his or her own eyes and states the child's name. The child is allowed approximately 10 seconds in which to glance at the instructor's eyes, or more likely the case, the rein-forcer, which would be the criterion response for which the child receives the reinforcement of praise and the food. If the child does not give that glance, the instructor may gently turn the child's head while giving the command, and if the child then glances momentarily at the instructor's eyes, the child re-ceives the reinforcer and praise. On trials when the child does not glance with this much prompting, then the instructor would place the reinforcer out of sight, and turn his or her head away for approximately five seconds. This physical prompting gradually fades on successive trials by moving the child's head less distance, with less pressure, until the child is able to perform it in response to just a cue. The duration of time in which the instructor looks away between trials should vary so that the youngster does not become interval trained rather than responding to the cue. This is an arbitrary time interval given in which the child has to initiate the response after the cue of his or her name has been delivered. We have cited ten seconds as an example of the time most often used; this may be decreased depending on the status of the child as ascertained from baseline studies. Assisting the child by turning his or her head manually at this first step also is

an arbitrary decision; some clinicians may prefer to wait for the child to initiate that response.

2. In this step, the instructions are the same as for step 1, with the exclusion that you no longer assist the child by turning his or her head to "prime" the response. If the child does not respond within ten seconds of the cue, you are to look away for a few seconds, and then repeat the trial. At this step, one may begin shaping for a quicker response, and allow only eight seconds for the child to initiate the response, with still only a glance being required. And as in all steps, the trial interval should vary. The clinician may find that as some children begin to acquire the response, they may even say the cue of, "Look at me," and then focus their eyes on the instructor. This is good, and it means the child is beginning to comprehend the task. However, we do not deliver the cue for a trial until the child has stopped looking directly at the instructor. You want to elicit a clean response to your stimulus of the child's name, with you being the one in control of the behavior.

3. The instructions are the same as in step 2, but now the reinforcer is no longer held between the instructor's eyes, but approximately at shoulder level. At this step, one allows a maximum of six seconds to elapse between when the child's name is given and the response has begun for it to be reinforced. As in all steps, 85 percent success is the criterion before moving onto the next step.

4. The instructions in this step are the same as in step 2, but now the reinforcer is held closer to the instructor's lap. The child is allowed four seconds in which to initiate the response after the cue of his or her name has been delivered.

5. The instructions are again the same as in step 2, but now the reinforcer is held out of sight, such as beneath the table, and four seconds delay is tolerated for a reinforceable response.

6. With all remaining steps, food reinforcers are always held out of sight when the cue for eye contact is presented. And as usual, social reinforcement precedes delivery of the primary reinforcer whenever it is used. For the remaining steps, the child is allowed two seconds in which to initiate the eye-contact response after his or her name has been stated. At this sixth step, the child is required to hold eye contact for one second, at a one-foot distance between the instructor and child's face.

7. This step is identical to the requirements of step 6, with the exception that the child is now required to maintain two seconds

eye contact, at a one-foot distance, as the criterion response to be reinforced. As usual, 85 percent success is necessary before moving to the next step.

8. Requirements are the same as in step 6, but now three seconds eye contact at a one-foot distance is required for reinforcement.

9. Same requirements as in step 6, but now four seconds are required of eye contact, at a one-foot distance.

10. Same requirements as in step 6, but now five seconds are required at a one-foot distance for a reinforced response. Also, one may begin at this step to fade the primary reinforcers, but still maintain 100 percent social reinforcement for correct responses. The manner in which the primary reinforcers are reduced is arbitrary, and depends on the progress the child is demonstrating. It is recommended that the primary reinforcement be faded first, with maintenance of the eye-contact response being retained by social reinforcement, with that contingency gradually being reduced in the latter steps of the shaping curriculum.

11. For all remaining steps, eye contact is demanded for five seconds, but now the distance between instructor and child will increase for successive steps. Correspondingly, the reinforcement ratio will also diminish. With some slow learning children, it may be more successful to progress through all steps of the program before the reinforcers are faded. At this step, eye contact is maintained for five seconds, and the instructor's face is two feet from the child's.

12. The instructor is seated three feet from the child's face, and eye contact duration remains at five seconds.

13. Distance between instructor and child is now five feet.

14. Distance between instructor and child is now ten feet.

15. Fifteen feet now separates the instructor and child.

When eye-contact training has been established at five seconds and fifteen feet, this response is now trained in vivo in both the cottage and classroom. We have found it helpful to have twenty-minute training sessions in the classroom, just as in the cottage, to assist generalization. With some children, these training sessions are performed for all steps of the eye-contact training in the cottage. The five-second time interval is accepted as a minimum time in which academic and language training instructions may be delivered to the child. The fifteen-foot distance is reasonable considering the distance the child is likely to be from the teacher in a special education classroom.

This is actually the second phase to the eye-contact training, in which the response is rehearsed in all conditions in the cottage, the school, and the home on weekends. This is generalization training. The purpose is to prepare the child so that he or she may attend sufficiently for positive practice on speech error responses, for attending to peers, parents, and teachers, and to be psychologically available in the classroom. During this in vivo training, staff may be using primary reinforcers, if that is necessary, but this should diminish as the response becomes available in all these natural surroundings. To assure that this training is performed, we may schedule a minimum number of trials which have to be delivered to the child for eye contact at various distances throughout the day. These trials are scattered during the day, performed at different places, with all staff, so that the child is trained to stop and attend for instructions and rewards which will be used in later training programs.

INTRODUCTION TO TIME-OUT SHAPING:
THE PREREQUISITE OF
BALANCED PROGRAMMING

The program recommendations exemplified in the case studies which follow show a clear reliance upon a short time-out to control inappropriate behaviors. This orientation has to be clarified, since time-out has become one of the more abused procedures. The treatment recommendations given here reflect twelve years' experience and research, which have not only taught us that one can easily misuse this approach, but also the conditions under which one can almost guarantee failure of time-out.

Time-out is not locking up children for interminal periods of time as punishment. The "lock up" procedures used with delinquent children, even with emotionally disturbed and developmentally handicapped youngsters, are fruitless; they assure counteraggressive behavior, they are likely to countercondition the positive aspects of the adult world, and there is a noticeable absence of data to support it as a viable approach.

The treatment goal of the behaviorally disturbed child is to learn in a neutrative environment, to have external, and preferably, self-control of problem behaviors, and to be behaviorally available for instruction. It is necessary that the youngster is trained to be enjoyable to teach. This is more likely to assure that the child shall have the advantage of an affectionate and caring environment, providing he or she is easy to work with, and *not* obnoxious. The noncompliant, aggressive, bizarre, out of control, and developmentally disabled child will receive little spontaneous and noncontingent reinforcement from the supporting environment as an adolescent, much less as an adult. It may be possible with the very young child to provide a highly contrived neutrative environment, while concurrently decelerating problem behaviors. But one should not be deluded. If that child is not successfully trained to be compliant, behaviorally controlled, and able to follow the home living routines, the child will receive increasingly less nurture and training from his or her social environment. The contention of this book is that one specifically arrange to have a neutrative, loving environment for the young and severely behaviorally disturbed child, while concurrently using a time-out to decelerate asocial behaviors. The alternatives are obvious: asocial behaviors will not spontaneously extinguish and, if allowed to flourish unchecked, they will catalog this person from being a participant in the normal community environment.

There are certain advantages of the time-out approach. One is that you are definitely "doing something" about the problem behaviors, rather than allowing the child to "burn staff out" by requiring them to perform the impossible task of ignoring the child's antisocial behaviors. Remember, ignoring behavior is useless if there is any self-reinforcing component to the behavior. The time-out prevents one from implementing an aggressive model, such as scolding, spanking, or physically restraining children who are out of control. The properly trained time-out precludes reliance upon physical handling, such as overcorrection which has a tendency for the difficult child to train the staff to counteraggress against the youngster. A rule of thumb which we have used whenever possible is to "keep your hands off the child, unless you are hugging him or her." Certainly, there are times when facilitation is useful in guiding a child's initial learning of some fine or gross motor response, but this would be performed in a very positive training atmosphere. Whenever punishment or extinction procedures allow the staff physical contact with the child, one should be extremely vigilant for the emergence of counteraggressive reactions.

In the early stages of time-out shaping, some children may have to be guided to the time-out place. The eventual goal of time-out shaping is to train the child to take his or her time-out without supervision. This is a delicate initial stage of time-out shaping. The teacher and parents should be monitored closely, and they should perform their physical guidance swiftly, silently, and without counteraggressive behavior. Time-out is basically an extinction approach, and while punishment certainly is involved, it is not the basic ingredient of an effective time-out. Furthermore, the time-out shaping curriculum allows one to move into self-control approaches, such as relaxation training.

Correct instruction of a time-out is difficult. There are some very fine details, which, if overlooked, will literally guarantee that a time-out shall be an ineffectual approach. Some guidelines follow:

1. The environment has to be dominantly positive for the youngster, or else the extinction approach embodied in time-out will be a "removal from nothing." Time-out theoretically presumes the child is being removed from a reinforcing environment for having engaged in an inappropriate behavior. The child has to be literally bathed in a neutrative and positive environment, the removal from which, even for thirty seconds, is a significant experience for the child. Just how significant will be evident in your data. If the environment is not dominantly positive, the child will experience no contrast effect between the time-out and the home or classroom environment. This is often the case when the child demonstrates a plethora of negative behaviors, severe retardation, noncompliance, and is unresponsive to the usual forms of social reinforcement. Under such conditions, the staff may be trying to train a response that is too difficult for the child to comprehend; avoidance behaviors occur, and time-outs are found to be ineffectual for noncompliance, aggression, etc. In this instance, the child has no appropriate behaviors to command affectionate attention from his or her environment. So, the first condition is: do not embark upon a time-out program unless you first establish that you have a very nurturing and enjoyable environment for each particular child. A neutrative environment is not simply saying, "good boy," or "good girl," but is a very complex environment which has to be constantly monitored, and to sustain this will require as much effort as performing and monitoring the time-out itself.

2. The child may be unaware of why he or she is being timed-out. It is often an erroneous assumption that the child understands what you are talking about, even when the teachers verbally tell the child what he or she has done wrong. Give visual gestures, point to the response the child made, use very short explanations if any at all, and be certain that the child understands why he or she is being timed-out. Remember, a child's verbal comprehension is best when the language used is comparable to his or her level of verbal expression.

3. Keep a close vigilance on the frequency and the duration of time-outs. If the child is receiving too many time-outs during the day, which accumulate to several hours in a time-out or quiet room condition, this effect will countercondition the positive environment that you are trying to establish. The data will tell you if you are using too many time-outs by simply adding the time in time-out per day.

4. Do not time-out error responses. Quite often a child may receive a time-out for noncompliance, when in fact the child simply does not have the response available. It is similar to punishing a child for saying, "two plus two equals five." This is not noncompliance, but simply reflects that you failed to teach the child the correct behavior to begin with. It is preferred to train the correct responses in sessions before making a compliance issue of the behavior with the child.

5. Do not fail to persist in the time-out shaping program. For example, there is a normal phase in time-out shaping in which the time-out continues to have a decelerating effect on the behavior in question, but suddenly the child deliberately engages in that behavior, and may even give himself or herself a time-out. This leads one to think the child enjoys time-outs, or that it is a meaningless experience for him or her, and surely it is time to cancel the program. Do not be deceived. The child is beginning to comprehend the consequences for his or her behavior, and is rehearsing it like any new learning experience. Developmentally, it is no different than the two-year-old child who retorts with "no" to every inquiry, apparently enjoying being oppositional. That two-year-old is only enjoying his or her discovery of the meaning of "no." The higher-functioning child may simply "test out" the program by resisting your control.

6. The time-out shaping programs may not advance rapidly enough. One may find the child "habituates" at some level of the program, and you never seem able to achieve the criterion necessary to move to the next level of time-out shaping. This usually indicates that (a) the child does not understand what behavior is being timed-out, (b) the behavior is self-reinforcing and independent of your neutrative environment, (c) the environment is not dominantly positive, or (d) you need to reduce the percentage of correct time-outs used to advance to the next shaping step (for example, reducing your criteria from 85 percent success to 65 percent).

7. The staff should be monitored by an outside person to determine if they are overdependent upon the use of time-out. They may be

performing time-out in a perfunctory manner which will teach the child to become habituated to the approach.

We have noticed that when we demand responses too difficult for the severely handicapped autistic children they operate with aggressive behaviors to receive a time-out, or quiet room, simply to avoid the instructional setting.

8. The data must be reviewed weekly, which is not to be construed as making impetuous changes. Rather, the weekly checks are to determine if everyone is performing the time-out shaping correctly. Hold steady, have months of patience; the greatest error is to presume that your data will tell you in just a few days or weeks if the program is working. Just as teaching any new behavior will take hundreds of trials for the severely handicapped child, the same experience applies to time-out training.

The two alternatives to time-out are different kinds of punishment or teaching alternate behaviors to replace the asocial behaviors. Punishment procedures outside of a time-out are not recommended because of the iatrogenic effects, that is, they will train the staff to be negative with the child. Outside of time-out, the other form of punishment recommended is "response cost," where the child is losing some reinforcement for having engaged in an asocial behavior, which is simply a variation on the theme of extinction. Punishment procedures involving the intrusion of some stimulus are not recommended because of the legal questions involved, and corporal punishment runs the risk of teaching the child to also use that same kind of behavior to control other persons. Simply through modeling effects one may be training the child aggressive behavior.

Teaching substitute behaviors is to be routinely performed whenever time-out is used. In the case studies that follow, the children were trained, by the use of time-out, to not engage in aggressive or other asocial forms of behavior. But remember, each child is simultaneously trained in the use of language, or alternate forms of communication, as substitute responses for aggressive behaviors. Bizarre mannerisms may be countertrained by teaching children to keep their hands down at their side, and reinforcing increasing time intervals for displaying that self-control behavior. It is required that whenever time-out is being used, one concurrently teach behaviors to replace those being decelerated.

If one is to train substitute behaviors, and not rely on time-out in the curriculum, it will require that the child be sufficiently compliant and available for learning so that these other intrusive behaviors will not interfere with the instructional setting. The acquisition of these substitute behaviors may be performed during the day in the child's environment, such as using positive practice when the child makes an error response. Positive practice is not a form of overcorrection. Positive practice is having the child rehearse the response under highly reinforcing conditions, and there is no difficulty with his or her complying with the rehearsal of that response. One may "foreshadow" a situation where the child is likely to engage in inappropriate behaviors; for example, taking an aggressive child to a playground and rehearsing prior to recess how the child should act instead of using aggression. Another approach is to have very specific training sessions during the day in which the child is taught not to engage in the behavior which you wish to decelerate for increasing time intervals. Such may be the case when teaching a child to keep hands down at his or her side, rather than to engage in bizarre mannerisms.

Teaching substitute behaviors without concurrently using time-out presumes that "ignoring" will effectively decelerate the behaviors. Ignoring presumes that you have control of all the reinforcers in the child's environment, and that your social reinforcers are sustaining *all* of the child's asocial behaviors. Be cautious. It is likely that you are responsible for only some of the attentional reinforcers the child receives for the inappropriate behaviors, but not all of them. When this is the case, and you ignore the behaviors, it means you have "thinned the reinforcement schedule" for the behavior the child was engaging in. Specifically, when you ignore the behavior which may also be self-reinforcing, you may remove much of the attentional reinforcement the child receives for the behavior, but not all forms of reinforcement. For example, instead of being reinforced 20 percent of the time for engaging in self-destructive behaviors, the child now receives some other form of vicarious or self-reinforcement only 5 percent of the time. You have then only succeeded in thinning the reinforcement schedule, thereby making the habit more durable and impervious to extinction or punishment effects. The message is not to be ignored—do not engage in ignoring as an approach unless you have known and complete control of the sustaining reinforcers. The advantage of time-out is that you have greater likelihood of restricting all forms of reinforcement the behavior may be extracting from the environment.

Our research in the last three years has led to a natural replacement of time-out as the child reaches preadolescence. The child is specifically trained in the self-control technique of relaxation, in some instances using biofeedback equipment, as a highly rewarded self-control behavior (E. Browning, 1979). This approach is a counter-behavior to replace aggressive and asocial behaviors. It requires that the child has advanced through time-out shaping, and that there is marginal reliance on time-out.

In conclusion, the important point to keep in mind is that if one can successfully teach the child alternate behaviors without relying on time-out, then do so. But, if one cannot achieve that goal, it is suggested that time-out shaping be used. Time-out is the last alternative. It is for the severely disruptive child; it has to be performed precisely (by all persons, all places, all times) for optimal generalization effects; and it is for the child, not the adolescent or adult.

TIME-OUT SHAPING PROGRAMS—I AND II

Behavior Taught

The behavioral goal is to teach the child to take a two-minute time-out in circumstances that would be available in the public school classroom and home. This means not having to rely upon use of a quiet room or similar facilities that would not be available in the natural environment. The goal would be to teach the child to take a time-out—such as turning around in his or her chair, or being seated on the floor beside his or her chair, or perhaps seated in a corner— with a very short interval of time as being an effective extinction/ punishment condition.

Data to Monitor Program

Periodic sample counts throughout the day will be sufficient to monitor the effectiveness of this graded shaping program. The data will be a comparison between the total number of time-outs given to the child, and the number of which were successful. There is a qualitative shift in the kind of time-out conditions the child is provided during each shaping step, which should be indicated on the graph. (Examples of the shaping steps are shown in the case studies contained in this book.) The percent success of appropriate time-outs are charted for successive sample days. An arbitrary figure such as 85 percent success for two consecutive days may be a sufficient criterion to progress to the next step of the shaping program. It is suggested that one stay with the same criterion level of success on each step of the program to assure that the response was acquired at that level. This way, if there is degradation of the appropriate time-out later in the shaping progression, there is an earlier acquired response level to which you may back up to reinstate the treatment regimen and progress over again.

Typical Status of Child

This treatment regimen is for children for whom ignoring aberrant responses is ineffectual, for whom various punishment procedures have been used unsuccessfully in the home prior to admission, whose deviant behaviors have a long-standing history, who are neither sufficiently compliant to follow a verbal command to take a time-out by being seated on the floor quietly for a two-minute interval of time, nor able to follow a rehearse to success program without a time-out. If these children were told to be seated and quiet until directed to get up and re-engage in the activity from which they were just expelled, they would not follow such a command. Instead, they would get up and run off, chattering, or commanding attention with deviant behaviors and receiving possible reinforcement from other observing peers or adults in the vicinity. These deviant behaviors may vary from aggression, self-stimulatory responses, self-destructive responses, and other behaviors which have a history of either being self-reinforced and/or reinforced by other persons. The occurrence of such behaviors during a time-out negates the effectiveness of the time-out condition since the child is continually reinforced for some other response and will not experience an extinction time interval following the response for which he or she received the time-out. These children are typically negativistic, noncompliant, and may not even comprehend the meaning of the time-out. Some profoundly psychotic children may not experience an extinction effect at the inception of the program if they are given a time-out by being placed on the floor and ignored for two minutes. In some instances, they may have just been timed-out from a learning situation that was difficult for them. Receiving a time-out under those circumstances would be reinforcing since it would serve as an avoidance or escape from the work situation. With such children, one should not anticipate very successful time-out effects until they acquired a variety of appropriate behaviors for which they receive considerable reinforcement. Being removed from such a potentially reinforcing event augments the effect of the time-out. For this reason, there must be concurrent positive programs.

Where Implemented

This program is initially conducted in a very circumscribed environment. As seen in the early shaping steps, one must be in close proximity to a quiet room. This means that probably in the first steps of the program the youngster will be contained in the cottage setting almost exclusively until he or she has progressed sufficiently to no longer require the quiet room to perform a successful time-out. As the shaping program progresses, the time-out is performed in a variety of places, and reliance upon the quiet room diminishes. One should be certain that as the children move through this treatment progression, leaving the environment where the quiet room is available, they are trained to take an appropriate time-out without requiring the quiet room as a "back-up." Otherwise, as may be seen in the following management orders, one is in the position of having to give the children a time-out in the quiet room for having failed to take an appropriate time-out. And if you are at some distance from the quiet room, you will have to transport the children, during the interim of which a variety of other responses are likely to be vicariously reinforced. Furthermore, children may not be able to associate the belated time-out in the quiet room with their failure of taking a correct time-out.

Staff Required

At the inception of either of the two time-out shaping programs offered here, it will be necessary that every time-out given requires *actual*, or in the second alternate shaping program, *possible* utilization of the quiet room. This necessitates delegating a staff member to have the time available to administer the time-outs. During the later steps of the program when the child is capable of taking time-outs wtih less supervision, such as would be available in a special education classroom or at home, a 1:1 staff allocation is no longer required. By the conclusion of the program, a simple verbal command will be sufficient and a 1:1 staff ratio for each time-out is no longer necessary.

Equipment Required

The quiet room should be small and without furniture or other possibly reinforcing items. A large room is not likely to be advantageous since the child may then indulge in running about and other possibly reinforcing behaviors. Small dark closets are not recommended because they are likely to produce fear effects, thereby overloading the punishment aspect of the time-out, and diminishing utilization of the extinction effects which one wishes to capitalize on the greatest in the use of a time-out. We have often constructed time-out cubicles for small children, $4 \times 4 \times 5$ feet in dimension, with a large door and a screened top to admit light. A cubicle as small as this may be useful for young preschool children. In the cottage setting, an 8×8 room has been utilized for this purpose, having a window with safety screens so the child does not break glass and get hurt. The window should be high enough so the child cannot readily see what staff and other children are doing. The psychotic child will be predictably angry when placed in such an extinction condition, so it is recommended that some rather strong doors be constructed. This emotional response diminishes as the child learns that he or she is placed in the room for only a short interval.

General Management Order: Shaping Program I

The general outline of this treatment curriculum begins with the child taking each time-out in the quiet room, then gradually working the child into the natural environment where he or she takes the time-out seated on the floor. As the child progresses out of the quiet room, whenever he or she does not take an appropriate time-out, the child then receives a "back-up" time-out in the quiet room. The verbal command holds constant throughout all steps of the treatment program. One simply states, "You take a time-out. You did. . . ." What the child did may be some inappropriate behavior that currently is being dealt with by a deceleration program, or the child may have been moving during the time-out when he or she was expected to be seated, quiet, and still. The following outlines the shaping steps through which one progresses in this program to teach the child to take an appropriate time-out.

Recommended Shaping Steps: Time-Out Program I

1. The first step is to determine the duration of the time-out the child will be given. In most of the case studies that follow, we prescribed a two-minute time-out and a five-minute back-up time-out in the quiet room for occasions when the child does not take an appropriate time-out. However, at the time of this publication, Ellen Browning and I have been studying the effectiveness of a one-minute, and even thirty-second, time-out, with a one-minute back-up time-out in the quiet room. The results are comparable to the two-minute time-out and five-minute back-up. Throughout all steps of the shaping program, the child should be praised for successful time-outs. In fact, tangible reinforcers may be used for correct time-outs, without any deleterious effects such as the child trying to receive more time-outs so as to receive those reinforcers. The manner in which to deliver a time-out is very matter-of-fact. There is no discussion about it; once you have indicated what the child did to deserve the time-out, it is implemented. No further

possible reinforcing statement should be delivered to the child at that time. Afterwards, with the verbal child, you may discuss why he or she received the time-out. Such understanding may facilitate the effect.

The first step requires that when the child receives a time-out he or she will take it in the quiet room for one minute, with the door locked if necessary. After one minute, the child is taken out of the room and very matter-of-factly returned to the activity from which he or she was removed, and if feasible, the child positively practices the correct behavior. One will continue this first step until there is evidence that the time-out is having a decelerative effect on those behaviors under that treatment. This is the only empirical way one is to ascertain if the quiet room is acquiring an extinction/punishment effect. It is illogical to progress to the next shaping step in this program if one is unsure that the quiet room had a decelerative effect on behavior. An arbitrary decision is involved here; it may be that even a 15 percent reduction in the rate of the aberrant behaviors being timed-out will be a satisfactory criterion to progress to the next step.

2. The next step of this program provides that when the child takes the time-out in the quiet room for the one-minute period of time, the door is shut, but now unlocked. If the child comes out of the door during the one-minute time interval in the quiet room, he or she is told, "You take a time-out. You came out of the quiet room." The door is then shut and locked for a one-minute "back-up" time-out for having taken an inappropriate time-out, namely, leaving the room. At this and subsequent steps, all successful time-outs are reinforced socially, and the quiet room is used as a "back-up," extinction/punishment condition for incorrect time-outs. When the child achieves the arbitrary criterion for two consecutive days of 85 percent success of taking time-outs in the quiet room by staying there for the prescribed time interval, we advance to the third shaping step.

3. In the third step, the time-out is still one minute, but the door is now left open. If the child walks out of the quiet room, he or she is told, "you take a time-out. You came out of the door." Again, when 85 percent success has been obtained for at least two consecutive days, in which the child on his or her first trial in the quiet room stays without leaving, you progress to the next step.

4. The fourth step in the treatment hierarchy is for the child to receive time-out in the quiet room, but remain seated in the same place while there, with the door open, so that one may observe him or her. If the child moves from the time-out place in the quiet

room, he is told, "Take a time-out. You moved." The door is shut for a one-minute back-up time-out in the quiet room. During those trials in which the child receives the five-minute back-up time-out in the quiet room, he or she may move around or do whatever he or she wishes while there, just as the child had been permitted to do at the first step of the shaping program. When the child is successful, again at 85 percent criterion, in sitting still in the quiet room with the door open, the following steps commence.

5. The remaining steps of this treatment sequence use the following progression: the child takes the time-out three feet from the open door of the quiet room, then progresses to five feet, to ten feet, and so on. The criterion for increasing the distance from the quiet room is based upon the child reaching 85 percent success of time-outs received under that condition. When the child is taking time-outs at a distance from the quiet room where it is not directly visible to him or her, then one may begin to expand the child's environment since control of deviant behaviors is maintained by appropriate one-minute time-outs. At this stage, you must be confident that the child will take a correct time-out, otherwise you will have to take him or her back to the quiet room for the one-minute back-up time-out, with all the possible vicarious reinforcement which can occur in the interim. In these later steps of the shaping progressions, there are likely to be many occasions in which the child is some distance from the quiet room and did not take an appropriate time-out, so he or she has to be walked or even carried back to the quiet room for the one-minute back-up time-out. At this time, however, the child should be sufficiently compliant so that when this problem arises he or she will walk back to the classroom or cottage and take a time-out in the quiet room with minimal supervision. We inform the classroom or cottage that the child is returning. He or she usually dutifully walks into the quiet room, is seated, and takes the one-minute time-out, after which he or she then returns to the activity. With some severely disturbed children, we place a small portable quiet room in the classroom to use for the back-up time-out in the shaping program so that it can be maintained in the classroom.

By the conclusion of this shaping hierarchy, the child may be given a time-out wherever there is an activity. If the child is in the classroom, he or she may be told to take a time-out being seated on the floor, in a corner, or behind a desk. When outside playing and he or she aggresses toward another child, and is told to take a time-out, the child may do so "on the spot," being seated and quiet for the one-minute interval. Shaping program II, discussed next, adds other behavioral requirements during the time-out, such as sitting still, head slightly down, and not talking, so the child has little probability of receiving reinforcement during the time-out condition. This is an important ingredient to the behavioral training program. It teaches the child not only to take a time-out under a variety of circumstances, but so that he or she is not demonstrating behaviors that may be accidently reinforced, which would negate effects of the time-out.

General Management Order: Shaping Program II

This shaping program is the converse of Program I. Instead of beginning at the quiet room and working the child out, we begin at the other end of the continuum, taking an appropriate time-out by gradually demanding the necessary behaviors. For errors incurred during those time-outs, the child receives a one-minute back-up time-out in the quiet room.

Recommended Shaping Steps: Time-Out Program II

Before beginning the program, one must decide upon the duration of the time-out. We recommend a one-minute time-out, with a one-minute back-up time-out in the quiet room through all phases of the program. Successful time-outs are socially praised. In earlier studies, we did not use primary reinforcements for fear that they may be sufficiently strong to generate a chain in which the child works for a time-out to receive the primary reinforcement. Subsequent studies convinced us that some pupils who become "stuck" in the program, not learning to take a time-out, do respond positively to the use of tangible reinforcers for taking a correct time-out.

The verbal commands are the same throughout the program, namely, that you tell the child very matter-of-factly to take a time-out, what he or she did to deserve it, and how he or she is to take the time-out, with no further interchange until after the time-out has been successfully completed. An 85 percent criteria success for some determined number of days is recommended before progressing to the next shaping step. If during the shaping program a child is not moving at a rate similar to what he or she achieved previously, it may be necessary to "back-up" and reinstate the behavior at the earlier shaping step. Periodically in this program, as with the first program described, verbally explain to the child what is meant by a time-out, and for what behaviors he or she would receive that treatment. This may facilitate the learning, but profoundly handicapped children may not understand the meaning of time-out until they have repetitively experienced it.

1. In the first step, the child is told to take a time-out in some designated place, typically where the aberrant behavior occurred. The child is led to that place and told to sit down on the floor. At this stage, the child is allowed to scoot about, as long as his or her feet are in contact with the floor. If he or she gets up, the child is then told to take a time-out for having risen, and escorted to the quiet room where the door would be shut and locked for the one-minute back-up time-out for having failed to take a time-out at criterion level established at this shaping step. Successful time-outs should be moderately praised.

2. The next step in the sequence is for the child to take the time-out as designated above, but now he or she would have to remain still and not move about. Failure to follow this expectation would result in the one-minute time-out in the quiet room. After 85 percent success at this level is achieved, the next step begins.

3. The behavioral criteria selected for the subsequent steps are arbitrary. Quite often at this stage the child is required to take the time-out where told, without needing to be led. We also add at this step that the child sit still, with his or her head slightly down, verbally quiet, and not engage in any kind of self-stimulatory or other behaviors which may have been self-reinforced or historically elicited reinforcement from others. These behavioral requirements may have to be broken down into smaller steps. Each time the child takes an appropriate time-out, he or she will be praised. But to the extent that any of these other behaviors occurred which interrupted a correct time-out, the child receives a one-minute back-up in the quiet room. When one has achieved this latter stage, the child may work farther and farther from the quiet room, since there will be less need for it as a back-up condition.

Parent Training

Parents of the children who are trained to use these treatment regimens always had the children home on weekends during their child's residential stay. Parents of children in day treatment performed the programs at all times at home. We require the parents to follow us in using each shaping step by at least one week so as to assure that the child is capable of demonstrating the response which he or she is being trained to perform at home. There is no evidence documenting that such a time lag is preferred; it was a clinical decision based on the assumption that if the child had achieved the response criterion at our facility, it would be easier for the parents to train that level of performance at home on the weekend and evenings. This required that the families alter a small room in their home for a quiet room, or construct one of plywood of the earlier mentioned dimensions. Before performing the program at home, parents are instructed in its use, acquainted with the data we accumulated with their child, and supervised in administering time-outs according to the shaping step in effect at that time. This supervised training is conducted by the special staff of the child.

There are two reasons for the importance of parents learning all the shaping steps for training their child to take a time-out. One is that after discharge when the child begins retrieving old behavior patterns, they have a repertoire of techniques with which they are experienced to reinstate the treatment effects obtained prior to discharge. Second, this assists generalization in that all components of the behavior taught the child have also been trained at home. One possible criticism of this parent training approach is that it may be confusing to the child if the management order for training him or her to take a time-out is at a different shaping step at home than at the treatment center. This criticism is a legitimate one. Toward the end of the shaping program, however, the programs being used at home become identical to those in effect at the treatment center.

Learning Theory Explanations

A few procedural points which are often violated in a time-out procedure should be emphasized. One is that a short time-out is recommended, since this leaves the child available for learning, rather than being isolated. Second, long time-outs make the entire environment in which the child is being trained a noxious one, simply because much of the time may be spent in that punishment condition. I think it is incorrect to say that a time-out is not in part a punishment procedure, for it is definitely a stimulus condition which has a decelerative effect on behavior. It is more than just preventing the occurrences of some presumed reinforcement, and you are definitely "doing something" to the child. I hypothesize that the longer the time-out, the more generalized that punishment effect becomes, and although it may decelerate the behavior, I suspect it has other deleterious side effects on both staff and parents as being more effective social reinforcers. In other words, you would be associated with that much time as a punishment agent, in addition to leaving you less time for being a possible reinforcer. Also, short time-outs allow one to make high rate out of low rate behavior, thereby facilitating learning by providing more trials of the same response. This occurs with low rate behaviors such as tantrums or aggression, which may not cease by the end of the two-minute time-out. One then has the opportunity to take the child out of the time-out condition and back into the learning situation. And, if the behavior persists at that point, the child then has another trial of time-outs for that same behavior. With slow learning children, it seems more beneficial to increase the number of trials per response, just as learning language, reading, toilet training, or appropriate eating takes more trials for these children.

A time-out shaping program such as those described here is indicated for the severely disturbed child who is incapable of taking an appropriate two-minute time-out from the onset. Depending upon the severity of the child's limitations of following through with such commands, one may begin at different levels on the shaping hierarchies. Whereas simply ignoring an inappropriate response may be satisfactory with a normal child, with moderately disturbed youngsters it may be necessary to use a time-out to interrupt the history of reinforcement they have been receiving for the deviant behavior. It is with the psychotic child and the profoundly handicapped child that one must resort to training them to take an appropriate time-out.

It is cautioned that these kinds of techniques are not recommended for normal children, but rather ones which are more useful for the severely handicapped. Keep in mind that the child's environment should be dominantly a reinforcing and enjoyable one. Time-outs are not enjoyable, and if used excessively, they will be destructive to the child's relationship with others and may contaminate a learning situation. For that reason, one should not try to time-out a massive number of behaviors at the same time. It may be necessary to decelerate different responses consecutively rather than concurrently, because otherwise, even with short time-outs, the child's daily life would be almost exclusively an extinction process. Excessive extinction procedures are likely to destroy your positive relationship with the child, and your expectancies on how to relate with the child will be primarily punitive. You have to regulate yourself to a regimen in which you require yourself to be primarily reinforcing and not to be overloaded on time-out type procedures.

Unfortunately, we have no systematic data to indicate which of the two time-out shaping procedures is most effective for certain children. It did appear that we were relying more exclusively upon time-out procedure II, but our preference was based on nothing more substantial than clinical judgment.

Alternatives to Time-Out Shaping

There are reasons to consider the alternatives to time-out. The most obvious is that the school or home may be adverse to such a program. Second, the teacher should be wary that there is not excessive reliance on time-out in the programming. This occurs quite frequently when the effectiveness of the program becomes realized. Such overuse has the unfortunate effect of making the classroom a very negative place for the children involved. Its use has to be judicious, not only in terms of behaviors timed-out for each child, but for the whole class-room setting. If there is too much time-out occurring, the classroom simply becomes a nasty place for everybody. It may be that the child is too old to be on a time-out program. We do not recommend this procedure being initiated past preadolescence, and during adolescence it must be replaced by some other procedure. It would be inappropriate to discharge a child from a school setting to the work environment with his or her behavior still dependent upon time-out.

It is often necessary to consider alternatives to time-out as a child becomes older, and the effectiveness of time-out "plateaus." There comes a time with some youngsters when they habituate to time-out, and almost perfunctorily go through it; hence, it becomes ineffectual. Perhaps this is not unusual—any punishment or extinction procedure is eventually going to negate itself. This is no different than a child acquiring deaf ears to his parents' admonishment. But at that time, it is certainly necessary to move on to other more self-control approaches. The following are examples of alternatives to time-out. It is not the intention of this section to cover in detail each of these procedures, but rather to present a few of the many alternatives.

Alternative Treatment Approaches

1. Transition from time-out to self control. A recommended alternative to discontinue use of time-out begins by reinforcing correct time-outs being taken, without relying on a quiet room. When a successful percentage is achieved, such as 80 percent or greater, then the youngsters will be reinforced for going to their room on their own, and returning at some signal from the teacher or parent. Later in the program, they return when *they* feel in control. The teacher or parent then reinforces the children for time intervals of not engaging in that behavior which prompted their removal. This approach requires reinforcing children to go to their room unescorted, return on their own, and also for increasing time intervals of not displaying the behavior which required them to leave the room.

2. Relaxation training. In this program, relaxation training is performed in sessions each day, with emphasis placed on deep breathing. With a low functioning child, it is questionable if deep muscle relaxation ever occurs. In fact, our experience with this approach has been that the behavior has been reinforcing to rehearse in

session training, and when commanded to perform during crisis, serves to interrupt the behavior which was problematic. Thus, when the child aggresses, he or she is commanded to go into relaxation, which is a highly reinforcing event for the youngster. This would be coupled with reinforcing time intervals after each incident of not re-engaging in that behavior. Hence, it is primarily a reinforcement approach, of rewarding the child for going into relaxation and interrupting the behavior which was causing problems, and also reinforcing time intervals of not engaging in that behavior after relaxation is completed.

3. Reinforcing time interval of no inappropriate behavior.   Some professionals argue vehemently that you cannot reinforce someone for not doing something. That question is academic trivia. One can effectively reinforce a child for increasing time intervals, on a shaping progression, for not engaging in aggressive behavior, tantrums, throwing objects, and so on. This does take a fairly verbal child to comprehend, and often when this program fails it signifies that either the reinforcers were weak or ineffectual, or the youngster simply did not comprehend the program. This approach requires verbal mediation by the child. One might begin this program by reinforcing the child for thirty seconds, or any time interval much less than the time range between the behaviors which normally occur. Thus, if a child is being reinforced for nonaggressive behavior, and the lowest time interval between aggressive behaviors is one minute, one may begin reinforcing thirty-second intervals of not being aggressive. The program then follows the usual shaping progression, perhaps using 85 percent for several days as a criterion for advancing to greater time intervals for reinforcement of that behavior not occurring.

4. Response cost.   This is a simple punishment approach in which there is loss of preferred reinforcement, such as tokens or points, with the child engaging in some inappropriate behaviors which you wish to decelerate. The effectiveness of this program can only be realized by first building an effectual reward program, for which its loss means a great deal. We have used this kind of approach with adolescents who have been on time-out for several years, and who have progressed to the point of token systems being meaningful. The time-out program is then replaced with loss of tokens for the remaining inappropriate behaviors.

5. Reinforcing alternate behaviors.   This approach is recommended to be performed in any time-out program. If a child is communicating his or her needs by temper tantrums, those behaviors may be ignored, and emphasis placed upon reinforcing communication

skills instead. Reinforcing alternative behavior requires some kind of consistent approach toward the inappropriate behavior; if it is not time-out, it is likely to be ignoring the behavior, or pointedly making some reaction toward it. That reaction could even be verbal admonishment or any of the alternatives already mentioned.

6. Positive practice.   This approach has the child rehearse appropriate behavior in a situation where he or she just demonstrated the inappropriate response. This is repeated for trials until the child performs correctly, which is positively reinforced. Thus, to decelerate the aggressive child from walking into a classroom and hitting another youngster, you have the child practice walking in the room in the same situation for repeated trials, until a series of correct ones occurs. Each correct response is reinforced. Furthermore, on successive days when that situation again occurs without any evidence of aggression, you again reinforce the child for having done that correctly. This is a good alternative to time-out, and in fact should be performed with time-out. That is, if time-out is used, the child should go back to the same situation where the behavior occurred after time-out, and rehearse the correct response, and be reinforced accordingly.

7. Ignoring/extinction.   If a child is highly reinforced for inappropriate behavior by attention from others, and you have good evidence for that conclusion, pointedly ignoring that child when he or she engages in that behavior may be successful as a form of extinction. If you know that you are the primary source of reinforcement for the behavior, your ignoring that behavior will be successful; in fact, you are performing a form of time-out. However, if the child is periodically being reinforced by other persons in the environment for that behavior, or is self-reinforcing for that behavior, ignoring as a form of extinction will not work. In fact, it may work against you. If you and others are reinforcing the behavior by your attention, and you stop reinforcing it, but the other persons persist, it is likely to place the behavior under a thinner reinforcement schedule and make it more impervious to extinction. This form of ignoring can be accentuated. You may even time yourself out with the child's interaction, such as walking away, focusing on other youngsters, or providing any form of cues that he or she has not gained attention from you for that behavior.

These are just a few examples of procedures which may be used to supplement or replace time-out. It readily becomes clear that this is only a small list, but of all the procedures they are either different forms of reinforcing incompatible and appropriate behaviors or forms of extinction for the behaviors which you wish to decelerate. Remember, it is also feasible to have some behaviors under time-out, and some behaviors on these alternate treatment procedures. In fact, such is likely to be a preferred approach, since you may find that one of the alternative procedures is more effective than time-out, which is sufficient information for one to delete reliance on time-out and move to one of the less restrictive approaches. This last point is very crucial to this discussion: one must be always attending to what is the least constrictive approach to use with the child. If time-out is the choice, it is a restrictive approach, and the rationale for its use is to prevent the child from degrading in his or her social behavior to such an extent that as an adolescent or adult his or her behavior in general will be intolerable, resulting in the child being placed in a generally restrictive and nonrewarding environment. Time-out should only be construed as an approach to render the child available for instruction.

Legal Issues of Time-Out

Time-out is probably the most abused procedure in the business. In 1978, there were even congressional investigations of child welfare facilities, specifically in regard to the interminal periods of time which adolescents were locked up in secluded rooms for rule infractions. Adult and youthful offender programs still use "the hole," which is isolation for noncompliant and/or aggressive behavior, without reliance on any data to discern if such extended isolation is effective in the first place. In fact, even suspension of school for inappropriate behavior has been called time-out.

Using the terminology of time-out, or behavior modification, does not whitewash the traditional, in fact, medieval approaches. But locking little kids up in small rooms looks very abusive. That is why we recommend using short time-outs, having time-out shaping so the child will self-control away from such seclusive places, and replacing this approach with alternate forms of self-control such as relaxation training. However, one is not going to sweep the issue of control under the rug by outlawing time-out or behavior modification. This will only lead to the return of chemical or physical restraint, extended seclusion, or trying to delude people into believing that the kids will grow out of these behaviors.

To be legal in prescribing time-out, or in fact any punishment extinction procedure, there should be *informed consent*. That means that parents, and if possible, the child, should understand all aspects of time-out. Essentially, they should be educated on time-out, they should observe it with other youngsters, they should understand the literature about it, they should be cognizant of the detriments that may occur from time-out, they must sign for it, they must periodically review the data with staff or teachers, and they must have the continuous option of a noncoerced decision to continue with time-out for their child, or to delete that program in the school or home. To be legal, by courtroom standards, means that time-out should be performed in conformance to the requirements of the professional literature. That means that baseline data should be taken, that the data should be constantly logged and reviewed, and that alternate behaviors should be trained with data taken of those responses also. Thus, if one is decelerating temper tantrums in the nonverbal child, not only data should be taken for time-out effects on that response, but also data accumulated for training some alternate language program, such as using cards to communicate with family or teachers. It is legally reasonable to stipulate in a child's program when the time-out program is discontinued, in terms of percent success, or frequency reduction of the behavior in a time-out. A time-out program should have options of replacement programs, such as training self-control by way of relaxation, response cost, conversation, etc.

DECELERATING DEVIANT BEHAVIORS

Behavior Taught

This is a general management order, variations of which are used for decelerating a variety of deviant behaviors such as those illustrated in the case studies. The purpose of the program, on one theoretical level, may seem as extinction of abnormal behaviors. The concept of extinction, however, implies that the response is completely eradicated from the child's repertoire. Permanent suppression of a response is mythical; perhaps the more recent use of the concept of "control" as used in the behavioral analysis literature is more relevant. At best, we attempt to control and decelerate deviant behaviors, and to maintain the extent of that control. We may use the term *extinction* at times, but in full recognition that extinction applies no more than deceleration and control, with these terms being synonymous in our definition. The extinction program recommended here is based on the use of time-outs, typically performed concurrently with a time-out shaping curriculum so that behavioral control will not always be dependent upon a quiet room.

At this stage in our research, we do not recommend physical punishment techniques, including the use of painful shock which has been tested with autistic children in previous studies (Browning and Stover 1971; Lichstein and Schreibman 1976). The reason for this rejection of shock or similar kinds of strong punishment techniques is that when one has to resort to such an extreme stimulus condition to engender control over behavior, this in itself is evidence of a very limited prognostic statement about the child. When such a massive punishment condition is necessary to produce a response change, the prognosis is limited to institutional care, and the homes are unable to maintain the minimal and tenuous treatment gains we achieved. If it is apparent early in the program that only a massive punishment condition such as shock would be effective in controlling the behavior, it may be rather futile to continue with parent training, or pursuing the goal of returning the child home since the child's profound intellectual limitations are likely to preclude that disposition. The use of strong punishment procedures should be relegated to the institutions providing custodial care of profoundly retarded children whose aggressive and self-destructive behaviors are not responsive to the more subtle stimulus conditions such as those available in time-outs, ignoring, or reinforcing alternate patterns of behavior. No recommendation is being made here for the use of physical punishment conditions; even in custodial care, this still remains a questionable recourse. Implementation and maintenance of physical punishment programs do have a destructive effect on the staff and family. One simply cannot expect individuals to perform punishment programs for children for an extended period of time and retain the necessary positive relationship with that child and the sensitivity necessary for continuing to work with all children.

Depending on the child, there may be a variety of deviant behaviors that will need to be decelerated and controlled. The kind of behaviors chosen are those which impair his or her being able to participate in a learning circumstance, beginning from one in a highly structured environment, to that which will eventually be available in the home and school setting.

The behaviors placed on decelerative programs should be arranged and treated in a stepwise fashion, progressing from those most deleterious to compliance training, eye contact training, eating, and those prerequisite positive behaviors that must be taught to the child before he or she can progress to more complex responses such as group play, academics, and language. The program should begin with only a few responses under deceleration so that there will not be a preponderance of behaviors being timed-out, which would contribute to a negative program for the child. Many of the behaviors placed on deceleration may all have the same reinforcers, such as with children whose aggressions and tantrums are forms of avoidance behaviors which in the past were reinforced by their being left alone. Sometimes a group of aggressive responses will function as a form of "body english" communication. These may be controlled sequentially, progressing from the most irate and disruptive behaviors to those which are low level and least disturbing to the entire program. As the behaviors are sequentially controlled, new ones may be added until all those which are interruptive to the child's learning in an admittedly controlled condition are sufficiently decelerative so that he or she may participate in a school setting.

It is useful to include the parents in the decisions of choosing the behaviors to be controlled. This is intended not only to give them objectivity about their child's handicaps, but also so that from the beginning they are assuming some of the responsibilities in the programming for their child. It is not usually recommended in the very beginning of the program for parents to be responsible for selecting all behaviors to be placed on deceleration since their lack of experience and information may lead them to choose behaviors which are not the most crucial ones. Toward the end of the program, this decision making would be gradually changed so that parents are choosing the majority of the programs or behaviors under deceleration, and you are performing those programs in collaboration with them. Ideally, by termination of the program the parents assume primary responsibility for all of the child's treatment programs. However, this is more often anticipated rather than actually achieved.

Data to Monitor Program

Accumulate a one-week baseline for all days, from 7:00 A.M. until bedtime, and thereafter sample daily frequency one different day each successive week, to ascertain the treatment effects of the program. Often three to four behaviors may be under simultaneous deceleration programs, and as each behavior reaches control, a new one should be added, with its baseline also being taken at that time. For a more precise test of the overall effect of the program, a multiple baseline study can be made, in which all behaviors anticipated to be controlled would be sampled together at the beginning of baseline, and sampled continuously throughout the program. This information may be useful, but it is an expensive approach since one would have to count a greater than average number of behaviors simultaneously, which is likely to require a 1:1 staff ratio on each sample day just to accumulate this evidence.

Typical Status of Child

Youngsters who are candidates for this type of program have had a long history of deviant behaviors, which often has a complementary value to their noncompliance, and there is usually an aura of communicative value to the responses. These are nonverbal children, or with a paucity of language skills, who may prefer seclusion. They may demonstrate a variety of related physical behaviors to make known their needs, which they are incapable of communicating other than with diffuse aggression, tantrums, or self-destructive responses. In recognition of this relationship between deviant behaviors and communication handicaps in psychotic children, if these deviant responses are extinguished, you would have the obligation of teaching language or alternate communication skills, such as the children taking you by the hand and showing you what they want if they are unable to acquire language. Prognosis drops precipitously when the children are unable to acquire such alternate communication skills.

Unfortunately, we professionals have been trapped quite frequently into accusing the parents of reinforcing these deviant behaviors as if there was some degree of calculated responsibility for having done so. Perhaps it is more realistic to point out that this is an inadvertent reinforcement, and likely to occur in most homes having such a learning handicapped child. Many of these deviant behaviors may have been acquired as a result of the child's attempting to adapt with his or her limited skills. Some of these behaviors also appear to be organically driven and self-reinforcing. As previously mentioned, many of these deviant behaviors are often a form of "body english" with which the child has learned to express needs that he or she is unable to verbalize or specify appropriately. These are youngsters who persist in displaying behaviors not uncommon for a young infant, but they stand in stark contrast relative to children of comparable age. It would be inappropriate to blame the parents; in fact, it has been our counsel with such families to point out that we would wager that their "psychotic" child would look very similar if he or she had been placed in any other home at birth.

Given this assumed status of the child, deviant behaviors have a purpose. The intention is to control these behaviors so as to make the child more amenable for learning alternate social responses. This may mean that the child is incapable of acquiring language, and that the eventual goal will be to have a child who is very complacent, obviously retarded, but minimally disruptive and more acceptable to other persons. This approach is to the child's advantage, regardless of whether his or her placement is in a home or an institution since it is more likely, if the child is less deviant and more compliant, he or she will receive greater attention and reinforcement of a more positive nature than if those deviant behaviors are retained.

These psychotic youngsters seldom have alternate responses that may be reinforced to the exclusion of the deviant behaviors. This is

fortunately not the case for children who are verbal and also demonstrate aggression and tantrums and similar kinds of behaviors. In
those cases, one is more likely to have alternate behaviors to reinforce.
It is a much more difficult task with a child who is devoid of language
skills and demonstrates deviant behaviors as his or her only form of
communication. Your goal, again, is first to control these behaviors
which make the child asocial, and then to devise a series of shaping
programs to train the child to be more socially operant. If the child
does acquire language, or some rudimentary forms of communicative
skills, he or she is likely to be more operant in behavior. *Operant*
means the child generalizes in his or her training, and spontaneously
"operates" on his or her environment to attain desired rewards. If he
or she remains at a respondent level, always subject to your directions, and trained not to use the normal forms of communication, that
child's adjustment may not be complementary to normal family living.
Respondent means there is a minimum of generalization, there is
little variety or spontaneity in the child's behavior, and very circumscribed stimulating and reinforcing conditions have to be maintained
to keep the habits in his or her repertoire.

At initiation of their treatment, all of these children are being
trained on a respondent program where they respond to the stimuli
you present and are reinforced for following your command, with a
minimum of avoidance behaviors to prevent their responding. After
they have been taught a variety of other prosocial behaviors, particularly language, then one may progress to a more operant environment where they select the stimuli to which they wish to respond and
in which they operate for the kinds of preferred reinforcers available
for having done so. When they are capable of making that much
growth, of moving from a respondent to an operant existence, then
the treatment documented disposition is in favor of placement in the
home. When control of deviant behaviors is not reliably achieved,
and language does not improve appreciably, the children are most
likely to be retained on a respondent level. Continued training is
then designed to maintain that status, so that they may adapt, however limited, to a custodial existence which may actually be in the
home or in an institution.

Where Implemented

The program will first be conducted in a highly structured environment, such as a residential setting or classroom. As the more grossly
deviant responses are brought under control, and lower-level responses
are being subjected to treatment, then the program may be expanded to
an in vivo situation. And, at the latter stages, positive practice may

be indicated to replace time-outs for the weaker, deviant responses. When the child is returned home for weekends, which is usually indicated, the parents should begin their treatment of the deviant behaviors that have already shown a definite response to treatment. Parents should begin treatment with only a few behaviors so that they are not overloaded, which would only diminish their chances of success and impair generalization effects. As the program progresses, all behaviors are treated under all conditions, that is, everywhere by everyone. This requirement has to be coordinated with the availability of a quiet room if the child is still dependent upon that condition for a back-up for taking inappropriate time-outs. A useful approach to determining the number of programs the parents perform is to add only one at a time, but only when you have determined that they can perform them correctly, and they have returned weekend data demonstrating that they can satisfactorily conduct the other programs which have already been assigned to the weekend.

Staff Required

A 1:1 staff arrangement will be necessary to begin the program. As the behavior decelerates and the child learns to take appropriate time-outs without requiring a back-up in a quiet room, then the child may be gradually introduced to a group setting. This is providing the child is responsive to verbal direction for taking a time-out or to initiate a positive practice trial without undue interruption of the group.

Contingencies Required

The quiet room for training the child to take an appropriate time-out will be the necessary contingency for the extinction/punishment condition. This is performed on a 1:1 basis—every defined deviant response under a management order receives a time-out. This approach has to be coordinated with teaching the child to take a correct time-out. Social and primary reinforcement may be used to strengthen behaviors that are incompatible with the deviant responses and known to occur in similar circumstances, which helps provide the child with an alternate response. For example, if a child has been assaultive on the playground during peer play, and you control that behavior with a time-out, you may wish to use primary and later social reinforcement for increasing time intervals in which he or she does not demonstrate the deviant behavior. This, of course, will be a function of the child's verbal comprehension. It has been our subjective impression that nonverbal children learn better in ratio reinforcement schedules that have many obvious visual cues, than they do in interval reinforcement schedules. Some interval schedules cannot be divided, such as teaching the child to be "in-seat," "on-task" for increasing time intervals.

General Management Order

This will vary depending on the level of the time-out training the child is receiving for those behaviors under deceleration training. There are some prerequisites which will have to be satisfied when the program is put into effect. If the child is not responsive to social rewards, oblivious of their absence, and obviously operating for isolation, the time-out program is doomed to be ineffectual. The reason for such failure is that the child is receiving a preferred consequence for his or her deviant behavior by nature of the time-out condition, and he or she experiences no loss of other reinforcers. In simplified terms, the child has to have known reinforcers if the time-out condition is to be effective.

It is necessary for optimal control of those behaviors under deceleration that alternate responses be trained, which will require their prompting and providing massive reinforcement. If the child is highly compliant, demonstrates a minimum of deviant behaviors, and is readily responsive to social rewards, it may be sufficient to use a positive practice regimen for the deviant behaviors and to socially reinforce the appropriate responses. There is a point of caution with a positive practice program. The child may learn a response chain composed of demonstrating the deviant behavior, rehearsing it to success, and then receiving the anticipated reward. This problem may be avoided by having primary rewards reserved for the child's demonstrating fewer trials when he or she rehearses the response to correction, and social reinforcement for just its eventual correction, regardless of numbers of trials. This technique may be performed in parallel with a program of reinforcing the child when he or she does not demonstrate the deviant behavior in circumstances where the behavior usually occurred. If you are unable to localize the circumstances which typically elicit the deviant behaviors, or if the responses are mysteriously variable, one may perform this program on an expanding time schedule. That is, the child would be reinforced for not demonstrating the deviant behavior for five-minute intervals, then for ten-minute intervals, with a predetermined criterion level to be achieved before progressing to the next step in the time period. Ideally, this type of program should be implemented at the later stages of treatment so that the child is rewarded for not demonstrating the deviant behavior as well as for correcting it when it does occur, thereby acquiring control over that behavior with a minimum of cueing from other persons.

This interval reinforcement program also assists in removing the child from total dependence upon your control with time-out contingencies. To teach the child control over the response, in order to please others and to receive reinforcement for having done so, is the ideal goal of any program.

Recommended Shaping Steps

The first step is to prepare a hierarchy of responses that are to be decelerated. It is preferred to identify the conditions under which these behaviors occur. These conditions may be experimentally contrived to demonstrate that with their presence or absence, the behavior will vary in its frequency accordingly. This behavioral analysis will provide some hypothesis of those reinforcement conditions which should no longer be available to the child for those responses. The behaviors that are to be decelerated should be placed on a hierarchy in accordance with their frequency and the extent of their disruption to the child's learning in the treatment setting. For example, physical aggression should be controlled before bizarre mannerisms. You also have to consider the value of the deviant responses as a form of language, as well as their escape or avoidance value. The program will progress through a hierarchy composed of the most frequent and disruptive to the least frequent and low-level behaviors.

The management order may now be prepared, which must have a clear and concise definition of the behaviors that are to be decelerated. The management order should stipulate that once the baseline behavior has been accumulated, the administered time-out condition should be coordinated with the step the child is currently on in his or her time-out shaping program. This requires that all staff administer the decelerative treatment programs in the same manner, which provides an easier discrimination for the child. When the staff administers a time-out for one of these behaviors, they should explain in the same two or three words what the child did and then tell the child to take a time-out. The explanation should be clear, simple, and not confused with the usual kinds of adult compound sentences which such a child will never comprehend.

A schedule should be established to train the parents to implement the deceleration programs. It is suggested that the parents initiate these programs on a weekend visit following a definite deceleration trend at the treatment facility, and they should already have been trained to perform the programs correctly with minimal supervision. It is necessary to record the frequency of the behavior at home to ascertain if there is generalization of the deceleration on the week-

ends, as well as to indicate when parents are ready to add new behaviors to their home-treatment regimen.

Before any program begins, at least a one-week baseline should be
obtained and a schedule established to determine the sample days
to be used on successive weeks to assess the effectiveness of the program. It is recommended that one specify only a two-minute time-out
for reasons which have been discussed earlier in this text. It should be
recognized that one is relying on evidence of almost complete control
of the behavior before one can ascribe a definite treatment effect.
Furthermore, the behavior will be retrieved at various times, so the
management order should be retained in general effect during the
course of treatment and after discharge.

Specific Shaping Steps

1. Behavior definition.   Example: Aggression. Child makes physical
   contact by hitting, spitting, kicking, pushing, throwing objects that
   actually, or almost, hit you.

2. Baseline management order.   Count the total daily frequency of
   these responses between 7:00 A.M. and 8:30 P.M. for five consecutive
   days. An aggression response is counted for each physical contact
   or near miss of objects thrown at you. There are two alternatives to
   how the baseline is accumulated. In the *uncontrolled* baseline, you
   respond to the child however you please, but without counter-
   aggressing. This is seldom possible with well-trained staff as they
   will probably treat by ignoring the response, without their being
   aware that they are responding in this way. In the *controlled* baseline, you ignore each aggressive response, but if these become un-
   bearable, walk away from the child. This can only be construed
   as a definite form of treatment.

3. Treatment management order.   Each time one of the above responses occurs, you are to say, "You don't hit (or spit . . . , etc.). You
   take a time-out." Then administer the time-out according to where
   the child currently has progressed on the time-out shaping program.
   Time-out duration is two minutes, with the exception of a five-
   minute back-up time-out when the child does not take an appropriate time-out or if that is the first step of the time-out shaping
   program in effect. After the time-out, take the child back to the
   same situation where the aggressive response occurred and continue
   with whatever you were doing with him or her, preferably repeating
   the same conditions that prevailed when he or she last aggressed.

4. As a gross aggressive response is controlled, you may find emergence of low-level aggressive behaviors, such as spitting at the

ground, swinging at you but missing, etc. These should be then placed under a deceleration program according to the above steps since they are response approximations operating for the preferred consequences obtained by the gross aggressive responses.

5. If the child can comprehend your reinforcing for a time interval during which he or she does not demonstrate the aggressive behaviors, that order may be put into effect when there has been definite control by use of the time-out. The management order would require a series of time intervals, perhaps beginning as low as ten minutes and being stepped up at five-minute increments, for each time period in which the child does not demonstrate the behavior, he or she would be reinforced. The reinforcers may progress from primary plus social to partial primary plus social to exclusively social. This should be stepped to at least one-hour intervals. When one reaches that time interval, you are likely to have habituated to the child and will forget to reinforce. Ideally, this should be stepped to match time intervals found in school so that the teacher or parent can reinforce at the end of the day. For some children, this may be too great a delay, but this will have to be judged empirically.

6. If the circumstances that trigger the aggression are well documented, you may add to the original management order, as well as to the above time interval schedule, that the child be taken back to that situation and positively practice appropriate behaviors. He or she would be reinforced for not aggressing during the behavioral rehearsal.

Learning Theory Explanations

There are several concurrent steps involved in a deceleration-type program that are derived from learning theory. First, you are attempting to decelerate, to control, the frequency of asocial behaviors by a punishment/extinction procedure. You are assisting generalization of the treatment effect by having a program performed at first under very circumscribed conditions, and then extending this to cover the child's general environment. You are preparing for generalization by training the parents to implement the program on weekends, so that as the programs advance, parents assume total responsibility and have had the monitored experience of being able to perform these techniques. Furthermore, the program employs verbal cues to assist in the discrimination of the correct and incorrect behaviors. This is fulfilled by indicating the inappropriate behaviors prior to the time-out, by verbally directing the positive practice of correct behaviors after the time-out, and by socially reinforcing the child for increasingly longer intervals of not demonstrating inappropriate behaviors. The technique enters the hazy ground of self-control by diminishing the cues being used to indicate the appropriate and inappropriate behaviors during the course of the program. It also is reinforcing the child to correcting himself or herself spontaneously, as well as not demonstrating the behavior for increasing intervals of time.

The management order requires that you reinforce incompatible responses as these are identified. For example, consider those children using aggressive and self-destructive behaviors as a form of "body english." Not only would these behaviors be decelerated through time-outs, but children would be concurrently taught language skills or comparable behaviors to replace these primitive forms of communication. The child is taught two things: not to display the old behaviors, and to use another socially appropriate form of communication. If the child cannot learn to speak, then he or she may be taught to be a compliant child who points and takes you by the hand to indicate what his or her needs are, which is less disruptive to a home and a classroom.

The program recognizes low-level approximations of the original disruptive behaviors will operate for the same reinforcement contingencies. It is recommended that when these behaviors emerge, they be subjected to the same treatment procedures. This is reflected in aggressive behaviors, which at first may be identified as making actual physical contact by striking another person. Later, however, this may just be an almost tic-like movement of the child's hand directed at another person when he or she wishes to be alone. It is indicated that such low-level approximations be decelerated and controlled, since their being allowed to remain in the repertoire will only increase the probability of retrieval of the original behaviors.

COMPLIANCE TO VERBAL COMMANDS

Data to Monitor Program

All-day, weekly sample counts are sufficient to monitor the effectiveness of the program. It is necessary to count the number of trials in which commands by staff are directed to the child and the number of times that the child complies to those commands as expected at that stage in the training program. This yields a ratio between compliance and commands, which, if the compliance count is divided by the number of commands given, will yield a percent success/compliance. This is simply graphed out across time with a vertical axis of the graph showing the percent success and the horizontal axis showing days of training. Slope of the graph will show if acceleration occurs and when one may progress to the next shaping step of the program, which involves increasing the variety and complexity of commands. It is cautioned that one perform the counts as inconspicuously as possible to avoid inadvertently reinforcing an inappropriate behavior by the mechanics of the counting itself. With continued training, one may progress to more requests than commands on the assumption that the child will like to do what he or she is asked because of the previous reinforcement.

Typical Status of Child

It has been our experience that all varieties of disturbed children will demonstrate difficulties in complying to commands made of them by adults. Children ranging from simple behavioral disorders in the school and at home to the autistic child all have their own deficits in complying. Quite often this behavior is dominant in preventing the child from interacting appropriately with adults, and impedes their play with peers. Needless to say, compliance is a prerequisite behavior for successful adjustment to the group-classroom setting. The intent of the program is not simply for the child to comply to avoid being timed-out, but eventually that the child complies because he or she likes to, because of the reinforcement history, which makes for a much more relaxed and enjoyable relationship with the child.

Where Implemented

The places where this program is performed varies with the level of complex behavior the child is demonstrating. With a profoundly disturbed child in a residential treatment program, it may be necessary to begin the program exclusively in a structured cottage setting where he or she is most of the time. With a more intact child, the program may be implemented from the very beginning in the cottage, school, and home. A critical variable to the success of the compliance training program is consistency. Everyone should perform the program the same, and it is in effect at all times, at all places.

Staff Required

Since it is necessary that every command directed to the child be consequential, it is likely at the inception of the program that a 1:1 staff ratio will be required to satisfy this requirement. Programming should be graduated so that as a child demonstrates more compliance, he or she will be more autonomous, require less staff supervision, and be more conducive to group placement and training. The requirement of positively practicing compliance to commands when the child does not comply, will mean that several minutes, or perhaps an hour or more, may be necessary to elicit the compliant behavior which is demanded of the child. The administrative requirement, then, is to make available a trained person who will have the time to implement the program at each of the shaping steps. With successful progress, less staff time will be required by the program.

Reinforcers Required

The goal reinforcer that will eventually maintain compliance is social reinforcement, on a very thin schedule as may be anticipated in the normal environment. However, at the beginning of the program, in order to realize an effective reinforcement for compliant behavior when it does occur, one may have to rely heavily on primary reinforcers. This will immediately precede social reinforcement. Gradually this schedule will be thinned to using social reinforcement with occasional primaries, and eventually deleting the primary reinforcement entirely from the program. Token systems may be suggested at intermediate stages of this shaping program, but it is cautioned that reliance on artificial reinforcement systems which are not typically delivered in the child's natural environment may hamper generalization effects back to the home and community. Therefore, it is recommended, as in all programs, that thin social reinforcement be the goal reward system by the conclusion of the program.

General Management Order

The most simple outline of the management order is that the staff will make commands of the child, at a language and response expectancy level that they know the child can succeed on by evidence of past history or observation. Each time a command is delivered, the child has a set interval of time in which he or she may comply or not comply. It is recommended to use a time interval such as five seconds, after which the child is either reinforced for compliance, or given a short time-out for failure to comply.

The manner in which the time-out is administered is crucial to the program. If the child is capable of responding to such training, it is recommended that the time-out be given "on the spot," where the command occurred that the child failed to follow. If the time-out occurs in the classroom setting, it is recommended the child leave the chair and sit at another place away from where he or she is working. He or she should not be allowed to talk, fidget, or do anything in any way which may be potentially reinforcing or attention-getting from other peers. In some circumstances, simply the child's looking at other peers and receiving some vicarious reinforcement by their glances and expressions either directly or by past experience may be detrimental to the time-out effect. In such instances, it may be necessary to turn the child to face a corner, or to remove the child to an adjacent room or behind some furniture. After the two-minute time-out has transpired, the child is then given the command over again, to which the child again has the choice of complying or not and receiving reinforcement or, again, another time-out. It is necessary that the command be repeated following each time-out until compliance is achieved, regardless of how long this may require. If the child does not take the two-minute time-out correctly, he or she may then be taken to the quiet room and placed there for five minutes as a back-up time-out for failure to take the two-minute time-out. The rationale for the back-up time-out is that the child will then decelerate in the behaviors which were occurring during the two-minute time-out by the effect of the five-minute back-up time-out. Again, it is a choice situation in which the child may be in the quiet room or take the time-out "on the spot."

When a child does comply, he or she should be reinforced with a reward system currently in use, at its ratio. A combined positive reinforcement, certain praise statements, a smile, a pat on the shoulder, etc., may be conjointly sufficient. For lower-level children, this may have to be paired with primary reinforcements, such as a preferred cereal or other items. This reinforcement is given even if it takes hours to reach that one compliant response to the same command. This point cannot be stressed enough. It should be remembered that the objective of the program is to teach the child compliance, not simply to teach compliance as a behavior to avoid a time-out, which may initially be the case. The reward should be emphasized, and one that is from the start strong and frequent in its scheduling, but this being thinned so that you approximate what is more typically available in the environment to which the child is discharged. With the seriously disturbed child it is unlikely that the reinforcement available for compliance in the school environment will be heavy enough to reliably sustain the behavior. It would therefore be necessary that the teachers be trained to administer the reinforcers at the schedule demonstrated to be successful at the treatment facility.

Recommended Shaping Steps

There are a series of shaping steps that may be run consecutively, and some concurrently, to train the child for increasingly complex compliant behavior. This treatment progression from simple to complex behavior is a qualitative shift which is seldom illustrated in the final data of a child. Monitoring the data is recommended for determining when one may shift to more complex behavioral expectancies. Again, we use 85 percent success as a criterion for moving to the next level in a training sequence. The number of consecutive days in which a child accumulates at least 85 percent success may range from one day to perhaps several, this being at the discretion of the clinician. One should then maintain 85 percent success until that behavior has stabilized. This training will have the value of rendering the child more capable of achieving the next shaping step successfully. The suggested shaping steps that may be incorporated in compliance training are given below. These proposed programs are recommendations only, and their sequential ordering will depend entirely upon the uniqueness of each child. One child may have to begin in sessions using food at the meals as a reinforcer for training very simple compliance, such as handing the staff a block; whereas another child may begin at a level using social reinforcement in cottage, school, and home from the very beginning of treatment.

1. Sessions.   With the profoundly handicapped child who is seriously disturbed with very little, and mostly primitive, compliant responses, it may be necessary to begin training for compliance in special training sessions. This is usually performed by scheduling several twenty- to thirty-minute training sessions each day. Frequency and duration of sessions are expanded corresponding to the increasing success of the child in following the commands made during the training sessions. This begins by working in one room with a child for several half-hour sessions during the day giving very simple commands. These commands may be requests to hand you a block, to sit down, or to stand, all contrived to be at a level where it is anticipated that the child will succeed, or have potentially an available response for success. These sessions may then be conducted under more complex circumstances, such as in different rooms, in the hallway, eventually outside, and then gradually in the school, and finally with parents present. It is recommended that all staff use the same commands for responses they are training at the beginning of the training session, and monitor their success on different commands, so they may program commands in the sessions which will maintain a high success ratio. This is consistent with the program goal that the child complies because it has historically been rewarding. This is achieved by simply preparing a list of the commands you are training, and keeping a continual diary of the child's success on each command. As you achieve cri-

terion success, such as 85 percent on a command, that one may be deleted from the list and a new one added. This monitoring assures that you are moving in some orderly progression for complexity and variability of commands.

The session training may then move to all-day training on compliance. Again, at the beginning of this phase, the training should progress from prescribed commands that you teach the child, adding new commands as earlier ones are acquired. This approach teaches the child an expanded repertoire of commands to which he or she may respond appropriately.

2. Simple to complex commands. The key to this training progression is that you want the child to experience success throughout the course of the compliance training as much as possible. You want to be assured that the expectations given the child are ones which he or she can comprehend, and very probably can perform correctly. There are two ways we have used to monitor the shaping steps from simple to difficult commands:

A. The number of words in the commands may be graduated in steps, from one-word commands to two-word commands to three-word commands, etc., until full and spontaneous sentences are satisfactory. Some children may never advance beyond comprehension of four- or five-word commands. The more simple the command made of the child, the greater the probability of success. This again indicates that the management orders for the staff conducting the program should specify the number of words they may use, and at the beginning of the program the exact words may be indicated so they can monitor which words the child has learned to follow. Examples of this would be "Sit," and a two-word command might be, "Come here," a three-word command may be, "Give me block," etc.

B. The comprehension expected of the child in the number of words used in the command should match the complexity of the movements required by the command. For example, if the child is directed to do something, he or she also has to be able to remember the sequence of steps asked of him or her. By nature of experiential deficits of many profoundly handicapped children, they may comprehend a certain command, but have a paucity of experience in recalling and performing the sequence of responses commanded of them. It may be necessary to train each response step separately, to assure the child has them available in his or her repertoire, and then gradually combine these responses so that he or she may perform them consecutively. This training may be accomplished by a series of management orders, progressing in the number of movements the child has to make to the command under training. For

example, the first management orders may demand only one movement, such as "Sit down," "Stand up," etc. This series of training
steps would progress to more complex commands such as, "Come
here," which may be across the room, to "Come here," which may
be down the hall, to "Come here and sit down," which involves
progressively more movements.

3. Staff ratio.   In the early training steps, it will be necessary to provide a 1:1 relationship when each command is delivered. This ratio
is necessary because if the child does not comply, you must have
the time available to follow through with administering the time-
out or sequence of time-outs and positive practice of the command
until he or she has reached success. The progression should then
move from the 1:1 ratio to a two- to three-child group, to a large
group, such as will be available in most classroom settings. It would
be detrimental to begin training at a complexity level where the
child is least likely to succeed. It would be predominantly a punishment program if one began training a primitive psychotic child
compliance to commands for performing academic material for
which he or she did not comprehend the instructions, amidst a
small group, and without the benefit of structured sessions. Everybody, particularly the child, would be doomed to failure under those
circumstances, and it is fairly obvious how negative the relationship
with the child would become.

4. Parent training.   The progression of this program should include
training the parents to perform each successive shaping step for
compliance. You not only train the child to a sequence in learning
to follow commands, but you also train the parents to parallel the
child's growth. Essentially, you are encapsulating several years' experience into a few months of what would be normal development
in following complex commands. Furthermore, when the parents
have the child at home on a full-time basis, the child may be expected to retrieve old behaviors, so parents may need to "back-up"
on the training hierarchy used for training compliance. If they
have had the experience in conducting the training sequence with
you, they are more capable of reinstating those programs and re-
gaining control. It should never be forgotten that the child belongs
to the parents, and that orientation has to be sanctioned for ethical
and the obvious treatment reasons. The parents are the ones who
will assume the total responsibility for the child. It is more likely
to sustain their success if from the very beginning they know the
entirety of their child's development to the extent that you are
instrumental in facilitating it. The goal, then, is eventually for the

parents to be the "therapists," and you only retain the role of a temporary "pseudo-parent" for the child.

5. Reinforcement systems. The reinforcement systems recommended for compliance training also shift concurrently with the changes from sessions to open cottage training, from simple to complex commands, from 1:1 training to small-group to large-group training, and with a corresponding increased reliance on the parents to perform the training. These reinforcement systems will progress from primary reinforcers, which would be various kinds of preferred foods, to social and primary reinforcers being paired so that the former may be associated with the reinforcement effects of the latter. After primary and social reinforcers are conjointly successful in maintaining at least 85 percent compliance, the primary reinforcers may be deleted from the program. At this stage, it may be useful for some children to establish a reinforcement program shifting from simple to more complex token economies which are also paired with social reinforcement. Following this program, token systems are deleted and replaced exclusively by heavy social reinforcement, which is then gradually thinned so that the child is being reinforced only occasionally for compliant behavior.

Within each of these programs of primary, social plus primary, social plus token, social, and then diminishing social reinforcement, the reinforcement ratio may be correspondingly thinned when the criteria level of success is achieved. To illustrate, one may begin by reinforcing every simple compliant response elicited in sessions with a bite of food. This is then gradually changed to having food plus social reinforcement paired together, and this then is altered so that every other compliant response receives food, to every fourth response, to every sixth response, etc. The same progression of the reinforcement schedule likewise applies to the token system. At first, the tokens should be ones which are obvious and quickly redeemable for some preferred reinforcer the child has demonstrated he or she likes. The token ratio is then gradually changed to require a greater number of compliant responses to receive the same reinforcement, and then perhaps altered so that the tokens are replaced by a monetary system, which is comparable to an allowance the child may receive at home, which would also be contingently performed during the week, such as washing dishes, making the bed, etc. The complexity of such a changing reinforcement system depends upon the intellectual capabilities of the child. The primitive psychotic child is unlikely to understand a complex token economy, so that system may be deleted entirely from the progression suggested. It may be necessary to move from primaries to primaries plus social to social reinforcement exclusively for the more retarded child.

Learning Theory Explanations

There are several explanations that justify the use of the time-out and reinforcement in training compliance. The purpose of the time-out itself is not intended to be a punishment contingency, although, to a certain degree, it may indeed be just that. The earlier literature on time-out defined it as an extinction condition. That is, it was presumed that for many children their deviant behavior, and in this instance, noncompliance, was being reinforced, however vicariously, and that preventing the occurrence of that reinforcement by the time-out would place that noncompliance on an extinction schedule. It is questionable if an extinction procedure is all that is operational in a time-out. A time-out is a definite stimulus condition that has a decelerative effect on behavior, which, by definition, would make it a punishment condition. And yet, there are occasions when it appears that the time-out is neither extinction, nor punishment, but a combination of these with "new learning."

In our work with autistic children it has been frequently observed that the time-out condition is effective. In fact, it is difficult to describe it simply as a punishment condition, since the child may even "work" for the time-out. To illustrate, one youngster would noncomply and then say, "Take a time-out," and shut himself in the quiet room. If you tried to interrupt that sequence of behavior, he would be very distraught. It was not that the child was necessarily receiving some vicarious reinforcement when he was noncomplying, but rather that, due to his lack of comprehension and lack of structured training trials, he never learned to make the appropriate response to begin with. The reinforcement used for compliance seemed useful, but it may have been that the learning was not so much an effect of reinforcers and extinction, in the usual operant sense, but rather by contiguous association the correct and incorrect responses became separated out.

Perhaps a Gutherian learning theory model is more suitable in explaining the learning that takes place in that circumstance. With some children, the time-out is quite obviously a punishment condition as evidenced by their tearful reaction to it, yet it is recognized that extinction programs will also stimulate emotional reactions when there is a loss of historically preferred reinforcers. It is often the case with primitive children that they have neither learned many behaviors, nor have they "learned how to learn." These are not primarily "operant" children, but more "respondent," and with an inconsistent environment, appear very aimless and uncontrollable. With a structured environment, they then become more predictably "respondent" to your commands—but they still remain dependent upon someone else directing their behavior. Spontaneous and creative behavior at a normal age expectancy seldom emerges with the psychotic children we have worked with, regardless of how impressive their gains may seem to be.

The aspect of the program that requires that the alternate response of compliance be reinforced should be quite obvious in terms of learning theory. The goals are to teach the child compliance, while concurrently teaching him or her to diminish noncompliance. Positive practice is built into the program by the requirement that the child succeed by taking the child back to the situation where he or she failed to comply and having him or her rehearse it again to success. This approach provides mass trials of practice on an error response, noncompliance. It is imperative that one not allow the error response to remain uncorrected, since that may simply thin the reinforcement schedule the child had been receiving for noncompliance, which will only make the response more durable and resistant to extinction. Thus, what the child may be learning by your occasionally failing to follow through with positive practice after he or she receives a time-out, is that he or she can indeed maintain the old behavior of not complying.

The back-up time-out of five minutes administered when the child does not take the two-minute time-out correctly, or perhaps the one-minute time-out program, is another training condition crucial to the compliance program. The intent is to teach the child to take a time-out in circumstances likely to be most available at home and in the public school. It is more feasible that the school teacher may administer a time-out in the back of the room or a similar place rather than to rely on a quiet room, which would hardly be available in the public school room. We have had psychotic children for whom the school provided a small, portable quiet room for temporary use when there was retrieval of behavior, but this is understandably difficult for most school systems to provide.

The compliance training program is intended to produce some generalization from commands to requests. Commands, it must be remembered, are when the child does not have an alternative to the expectancy given him or her. The child is simply told to do something; the child's choice is either to do it, or to have a time-out, after which he or she has to do it anyway. With the request, the child is given a choice, and that should be honored by the parent or staff providing such a cue. In the request, the child is asked if he or she would like to do something, to which the child may respond either yes or an adamant refusal to do so. This response to a request should be acknowledged, namely, that you allow the child some individuality to choose, this being part of normal development which should be cultured. That distinction should be kept in mind, but it is hoped that with successful compliance training, in which there is a preponderance of positive reinforcement available and a minimum of the time-out by nature of a graduated program, the child will generalize from commands to requests, and when requests are made of the child, he or she would be more likely to respond appropriately.

POSITIVE PRACTICE

Behavior Taught

Positive practice is probably the most useful teaching technique in this program, and it is a primary learning approach to which the child must adapt. The definition of positive practice is simply teaching the child to rehearse an error response to correction, for the successful completion of which he or she is awarded. Physical assistance, such as in overcorrection, is not used. This treatment curriculum is performed in collaboration with timing-out deviant responses and begins when the rate and intensity of those responses are sufficiently low that neither a quiet room nor a time-out is frequently necessary. Positive practice presumes a compliant child who will collaborate with your efforts to stay on task, without being unduly reactive to being incorrect. If the child refuses to attempt to rehearse to correction, this would be a noncompliance, for which the child would receive a time-out. However, if this is resulting in numerous time-outs per day, then the child is not ready for positive practice. Spontaneous rehearsals should be reinforced whenever they occur.

Positive practice may be used at the inception of a program with low-level intensity behaviors for children whose language skills are higher than the majority of children referred to in this text. An example of positive practice would be as follows: A child, who has been in training for aggression, takes the toy truck she has been playing with and throws it at another child. She would receive a time-out for that aggression, after which she would be taken back to that play situation, given the truck, instructed how to push it around in parallel with the other child, and rewarded for doing this correctly. This routine may be rehearsed and reinforced repetitively with several toys at that time. Another example may be when a child enters the dining room and emits a bizarre screech. You would take him out of the room, instruct him to walk in quietly, reinforce his doing so correctly, then repeat this sequence several times.

Positive practice requires that the children have sufficient language skills to comprehend the command indicating what behavior should be repeated for success. Often one encounters youngsters who may not be able to express themselves at a level comparable to that which they can comprehend, which still indicates that positive practice may be useful. This treatment technique relies heavily on reinforcement, and hopefully these reinforcers will have long passed the stage of tokens and primaries, since it is a treatment regimen that should be utilized naturally in the home and school. Quite often this treatment technique is used later in the child's program rather than at its inception. It is a program that is verbally directed at varying distances, so that the prerequisite behaviors of compliance, eye contact, and attention to task have been successfully trained.

There are usually two forms of data required to measure the success of positive practice in either controlling a deviant response or acquiring a new behavior. If the behavior is under deceleration, the frequency should be tallied, and second, one records the trials and success in which positive practice was used in rehearsing the correct responses. To illustrate, perhaps aggression was initially under a two-minute time-out regimen and successfully diminished, but low-level approximations of that behavior were retrieved at the termination of treatment upon the child's returning home. These low-level approximations may not require a time-out, rather, positively practicing the correct alternative response would be sufficient. One would then be notating the frequency of the deviant behavior, and also the numbers of times that positive practice was used. One may find that a great number of trials in positive practice are continuously necessary for a very minimal effect on the behavior. This kind of information may then indicate a back-up time-out to control the behavior, after which the positive practice would then be reinstated.

In teaching an entirely new response, such as in language, where positive practice is used most frequently, one counts the number of trials in which a response was rehearsed as well as the frequency of the behavior. If positive practice was used in articulation errors, or in expanding spontaneous speech, one counts these responses and compares them to the daily frequency of positive practice trials. The reason for this is the same as in controlling deviant responses, namely, to determine if the positive practice trials are diminishing across time. If there is diminution in the behavior, it may suggest that some alternative treatment program will have to be devised. Positive practice is an arduous task for a child, and if the child has difficulty performing the response so that he or she is rehearsing a preponderance of error responses, this may negate the total effect of the program. The value of positive practice is evident if fewer trials are being required for the child to correct an error response, and if there is actual diminution in the occurrence of that error response.

Typical Status of Child

The child must be willing to rehearse the response, and have a history of reinforcement with the instructor so that he or she may anticipate that such compliance will receive reinforcement. Furthermore, one must be assured that the child is able to perform the response which is being rehearsed. If this criterion is not satisfied, then positive practice is not indicated but rather a shaping program to build in the correct response, which may later be subjected to positive practice to assist this generalization across the child's environment. It is presumed that the majority of bizarre and socially deviant behaviors of the child are under control, so that these are not used as escape responses during positive practice trials. The program is obviously favorable for the higher-level child who has already made considerable gain in his or her treatment program. The goal is to develop a technique that can be used in the normal environment by the teachers and the parents, which also avoids "power struggles" with the child in practicing correct responses.

At the beginning of the program when the child is learning how to positively rehearse a response, a 1:1 staff ratio will most likely be required. As the program progresses, and the child acquires the skill to rehearse with a minimum of supervision and trials, it may be performed in a group setting with few instructions. Initially, the program will have to be performed in a highly structured setting where you have control. As the child acquires the ability to positively practice, this program may be performed anywhere in the child's environment. In fact, the intent of the program is to gradually shift it from heavy supervision and structure, to minimum structure and staff direction.

Reinforcers Required

When the positive practice program begins, preferably the child is no longer being maintained in programs requiring primary reinforcers, but rather social reinforcers. However, there may be variations in the reward systems depending upon the youngster, and if primaries are employed, they should be gradually replaced with social reinforcement. Primary reinforcers may be used occasionally simply to make the entire training technique a more pleasant and preferred one for the child. In the utilization of social reinforcement, it is often useful to have the entire group in which the child is involved to participate. Everyone clapping when the child successfully practices articulation errors may be very helpful to all the children. In colloquial terms, the child's pride in achievement is a subsidiary goal of positive practice. You should make it very clear to the child how proud you are of his or her achievement so that he or she may likewise adopt that attitude. As the program progresses, you may wish to add the management order that the child indicate to you when he or she has successfully rehearsed the response correctly. This helps train the child to monitor his or her own behavior, and be less dependent upon others for discriminating correct from incorrect responses. This is accomplished by giving the child fewer cues to indicate the error response to be corrected, as well as fewer cues to direct him or her to rehearse the correct response.

General Management Order

One should begin with responses which the child is capable of rehearsing easily and successfully. This is to assure that the program itself will become rewarding, and that the child will more readily acquire the technique of positive practice. It would not be recommended to initiate a massive number of behaviors under positive practice at the same time. The reason for this is that the child will be practicing with very few rewards being received. This program should be built up in a step-wise fashion as you add more behaviors for positive practice. The guideline for positive practice is that it is a technique designed to facilitate generalization. It is a program that one uses for available responses, which have not generalized sufficiently to be reliably elicited in a variety of places. Again, it is a compensatory technique that can be readily utilized by persons outside of the treatment center, and one that is easily trained to those persons.

When error responses occur during positive practice, one has to persist in eliciting another response until the correct one occurs. Nothing else happens with the child until success is achieved, so that it is a rewarding experience which concludes with the correct behavior, and does not finish with rehearsal of an error response. The question may have to be repeated time and again, and on some language training steps it may be necessary to go back through some of the original shaping steps and gradually lead up to the criterion response. For example, if one is practicing the word *cat* and the child is unable to produce this in a few trials, one may then possibly practice the *ca* sound and then the *t* sound and then practice these together for the formation of *cat,* which would then be rehearsed for five correct positive practice trials to facilitate the response. This latter point should be stressed. In positive practice, one may take ten or twelve trials to achieve the correct response. It may be most useful then to repeat the positive practice on that sound so that you conclude not only a success for several training rehearsals, but that you have diminished the number of trials necessary for the child to achieve that response by the last positive practice series. One may take twenty trials to eventually achieve the word *cat,* but then go through the positive practice again for another five times so that on the last series of positive practice on that word, it only takes three trials to achieve the correct response. After the child has correctly produced the response, then you move on in the activity in which he or she was engaged prior to the positive practice, particularly if this was being conducted in the natural environment.

It is arbitrary how many responses will be subjected to a positive practice regimen at any one time. Perhaps three to four would be a guideline, but this would depend upon the success rate of the child, how amenable he or she is to positive practice without becoming discouraged, and the effectiveness of your reinforcers. It is also based on what you can reasonably expect the staff, parents, and school teachers to possibly rehearse with the child. If there is a preponderance of behaviors that have to be rehearsed, one may expect that there will be a delay in everybody's performance in following through with such training schedules. If you overload the child with positive practice, staff will not reliably practice all the behaviors, which means that error responses will be rehearsed rather than correct ones. This may have the unfortunate consequence of placing them on a thinner schedule, and contribute to their resistance to eventual extinction.

Training Guidelines

1. The first step is to choose a response that will not be too discouraging to positively practice, which requires generalization training. The response should be readily available to the child with a minimum of error responses occurring, so that the child begins on a dominantly positive program.

2. Second, one must select the reinforcement system. If primary reinforcers are used concurrently with social, the former should be faded during the program. Reliance on social reinforcers should be correspondingly diminished so that it has some semblance to what is likely to be available in the public school classroom.

3. One may now establish a schedule of where the positive practice will be performed, by whom, when, and the steps by which one will move to an in vivo structure of the program. This should be

specified clearly on management order sheets, new orders being prepared for successive steps.

4. The data which will be logged to test the program should now be ascertained. One will have to decide what criteria will be used to add new responses to the program. This is a rather arbitrary distinction, and will have to be determined by what the child may achieve, without demanding response expectancies which will lead to unreasonable frustration for the child.

5. It should be indicated in the management orders the procedure by which one will diminish the corrective cues necessary for successful positive practice of the response in question. For example, if the child is initially saying *gat* for *cat*, it may be necessary to prompt with a cue for the child to be sensitive to the error that he or she has committed and to correct it. In other words, you want the child to acquire less dependence upon you for correction of his or her error responses, and to become more self-monitoring. It would also be indicated to have a rather strong reinforcement system available for when the child corrects his or her own responses spontaneously without further cueing from you.

6. One will also have to observe the staff to assure that they are not habituating to a low-level performance in the child, tolerating error performance, and failing to have the child rehearse the response to criterion. Staff's tolerance or habituation of the child's errors will only serve to place the error responses on a thinner schedule and render them more resistant to extinction.

7. And finally, in the shaping steps you have established, you should anticipate the hierarchy of the responses that will be trained so there is goal direction to the program. This is not intended to be an invariant hierarchy, but rather one which may be modified with experience as you progress through the behaviors selected. Selection of such behavioral goals is an important ingredient in parental training, for it presumes that training their child can be a planned endeavor.

Learning Theory Explanations

The intent of this program is to teach the child how to rehearse error responses to correction, how to be more alert to his or her own error responses by your fading the cueing you have given to prompt the child's recognition of those responses, which all contribute to that cloudy area of learning theory called *self-control*. Self-control is obviously no more than retention of your cueing, which the child performs to spot his or her error responses. The program is designed to be of assistance to generalization because if a child is trained to be responsive to positive practice for a variety of behaviors, then the technique may be implemented anywhere and readily generalized to use by the parents and school personnel. The prerequisite behaviors of eye contact, attention to task, and compliance must be taught before this program can be successfully employed. This places positive practice in a training sequence of the compensatory behaviors which are necessary for teaching the seriously handicapped child.

INDEPENDENT WORK AND PLAY

Behavior Taught

The objective of this program is to teach the child to function with diminished supervision in some constructive activity, be it in the form of play or independent work such as that anticipated in a special education classroom. The goal also includes that the child eventually learns to enjoy these tasks and that they would eventually acquire sufficient reinforcement value to maintain the child's performance as you fade the direction and reinforcers later in the program. One reason for this training is that the child may be unsupervised for intervals of time at home, which is an important respite for the parents. This training is also critical for the child's acceptance in a group setting such as that found in a special education classroom. If the child's behavior is dependent upon a 1:1 staff ratio, obviously the community will be unable to maintain him or her, much less teach the child new responses.

A useful goal is to achieve fifteen minutes of unsupervised participation on task within a group of six more children in a classroom setting. This is still considerably less than what is expected for normal children, but with a group of youngsters in a special education classroom, that time interval is probably satisfactory for the teacher to use as a limit. After this time limit, the teacher may need to redirect the child back to task and reinforce him or her for having performed satisfactorily for that time interval. One strives to have tasks or play that the child may take some satisfaction in, but with many of these children their performance is at best perfunctory. As the program progresses and new material is added, the teacher will gradually identify the child's maximal level of task complexity or play, and this information contributes to the treatment documented prognosis of the child. With the parents' continued participation in this program, they too will comprehend the reality of their child's abilities.

Data to Monitor Program

Throughout the course of this curriculum, trials and successes are recorded to monitor the child's progress in working independently for increasing time intervals. Trials are determined by the frequency of directions given to the child to work or play. Success trials are the number of occasions in which he or she performs at the criterion time level. Constant monitoring of these trials and successes is necessary to ascertain if you may have progressed too rapidly in the steps, which would indicate the necessity of backing up to a previous or intermediate step. This assures that the child progresses at a pace which is predominantly successful, rewarding, and with a minimum of failure.

Typical Status of Child

The children for whom this program is indicated are characteristically hyperactive, who are out of their seat and bounding about the room a few moments after being directed to a task. While in a play or work task, their behavior is typically nonconstructive relative to that task. These youngsters have difficulty following verbal commands directed to their remaining in their seats and performing sequences of behavior. They usually have a history of rejection from classroom settings, during which they accumulate the nebulous diagnostic labels of brain damaged and emotionally disturbed. Nonconstructive behavior for some of these children is characterized by aimless wandering, annoying or bizarre responses, and often an absence of behavior. The latter described children may indeed sit at their desk and approach the play or academic material sporadically and lethargically, but most typically do absolutely nothing with the materials. It has been our experience that the compliance level of these children is low and that eye contact is correspondingly very restricted toward persons and activities. Before this program is initiated, there should be an upsurge of compliance already in effect, as well as acceleration of eye contact so that these two prerequisite behaviors may facilitate the child's following the directions of each step.

Where Implemented

This training program begins in five- or ten-minute training sessions spaced during the day and performed both in the cottage and the school. As the child acquires success, these sessions are gradually introduced to the home on weekends and performed by the parents, but only after they have been trained in its implementation. As the program advances, the sessions become more spontaneous in their employment, and not always conducted in the same room with the same desk and the same materials. This latter requirement is to support generalization of the training effect.

Staff Required

A 1:1 ratio is necessary to begin this program. As the shaping steps progress to group integration, the staff ratio will be gradually faded to the 1:2 ratio, 1:3, 1:4 until six children are successfully on task with one staff. This staff requirement is also expanded correspondingly with increased time on task. This can only be accomplished if it is supported by a corresponding improvement in the child's compliance as well as his or her acquiring a variety of tasks which are in themselves intrinsically reinforcing due to their past training history.

General Management Order

The goal of this program is to arrange a planned shift in the duration of time on task, this being coordinated with diminishing supervision while on task, with the reinforcers changing from reliance upon primary and heavy social reinforcement to occasional social reinforcement. Furthermore, the number of other children present while the child is on task progresses from none being present to eventually six other youngsters, or a number reasonable to expect in a classroom setting. The complexity and variety of tasks and play materials correspondingly increase during the course of the treatment program. The administrative difficulty of this program is to coordinate all of these variables concurrently. Prerequisite behaviors must be identified before the program can begin, and rectified if necessary. To illustrate, with the hyperactive child there may be a considerable amount of *darting* responses, defined as the child bolting away from the table and running with the presumed gleeful hopes that someone is going to chase him or her, which is more rewarding than staying on task as evidenced by the history of the behavior. Other bizarre mannerisms, self-destructive behavior, etc., all preclude successful implementation of this program. It is necessary that such program behaviors show satisfactory deceleration before this program is begun. If these behaviors, which are the antithesis of the child's success in this training sequence, are not controlled, you will be in the unfortunate position of having excessive time-outs for those behaviors during the teaching sessions. This is likely to produce the unfortunate effect of contaminating the potential reinforcing aspects of successful on task work or play.

The shaping steps of this program are obviously simple. They progress in a sequence of expanding time on the task or play materials for which the child is reinforced. When the child achieves the time interval satisfying the criterion necessary for reinforcement, he or she will receive that reinforcement, as well as a simple verbal explanation of why he or she was successful. If the child fails to make the time criterion in effect at that time, his or her failure would also be indicated in a very matter-of-fact way.

Specific Management

The child is seated at the table facing the materials during the training sessions. The materials selected should be enjoyable to the child, or at least ones that he or she moderately tolerates. One may even select items that were used previously in training compliance so that it is more likely the child will be successful. The staff may be required to stand beside the child at first, but as the shaping steps progress, staff should gradually move out of the child's field of vision. The program should begin with a time interval which you have found from previous baseline observations that will not require redirection to the task or play materials. This may require a time interval as low as five seconds, preferably determined from baseline studies. After five seconds have transpired, in which the child has worked consistently with *head down* and *attending to the task*, the child is interrupted momentarily, socially praised, provided a primary reinforcer and a short verbal explanation of why he or she was reinforced, and then redirected back to task. If the child fails to meet that five second time interval, or raises his or her head, the staff may say something to the effect, "You looked up, no candy, put puzzle together." With higher-level children, one may not need to verbally explain the erroneous response, but simply restate the command and wait until the successful time interval has transpired for which the child is reinforced.

When the child achieves 85 percent success for some arbitrary number of training sessions, the time interval necessary for receiving the reinforcer is increased. For example, the child may begin at a five-second time interval at which he works at the task or play materials before receiving the reinforcer. After succeeding at that level for five sessions averaging 85 percent success, the child then progresses to ten seconds as the necessary time to receive reinforcement. The same behavioral expectancies are maintained; namely, looking at and working directly with the task, not merely sitting or staring off into space, but manually at work with the materials. When you progress to the next shaping time interval, the child's performance will temporarily decay. This is to be expected since the child has been trained on an interval schedule and is trained to look up at the termination of five seconds in anticipation of the reward. This previously correct response now becomes an error response since the child has to remain on task now for ten seconds. This five-second on task response must be extinguished as he or she works for the new criterion of ten seconds. One may expect with each new shaping step that the performance will drop off momentarily before it begins to accelerate to more successful trials again. If the drop in performance is precipitous, and if the child shows a much greater delay in achieving the ten-second criterion in comparison to the previous step, it may be indicated to back-up and retrain at a level between the first and second step. This decision is ascertained empirically from the data, and of course the usual clinical judgment is involved in selecting the time increments to be used in the shaping steps.

As this program advances in time on task, other behavioral expectancies are gradually introduced, which are admittedly arbitrary but selected from the estimated capabilities of each child. These new variables include having different staff perform the program, conducting sessions at varying times during the day, arranging the sessions in different settings, and employing numerous activities and play materials introduced at graduated levels at which the child is likely to succeed. It may be necessary to provide special training sessions to train the child how to play or work appropriately with the materials. This coordinates quite neatly with academic training programs, but perhaps is more difficult to determine with play materials. When the program advances to at least a five-minute success on task behavior, the child is integrated into the school setting for the remaining shaping steps. The teacher applying this program will gradually introduce more children to the time on task program, directing and reinforcing them alternately.

Learning Theory Explanations

This program follows a very simple format of shaping behavior as well as fading techniques. The graduated steps of increased time and performance on task are arranged at levels to assure success. It is hoped that with enough trials and successes, these tasks will become more intrinsically reinforcing, and thereby capable of sustaining performance with less reliance upon social reinforcers. Achievement of this goal is particularly important if you wish to approximate the normal classroom environment. As the concurrent programs achieve greater success there will be a diminution in bizarre behaviors, darting, noncompliance, etc., which will contribute to fewer error responses occurring during the training sessions.

In all steps of the program, reinforcement should far exceed the frequency of time-outs, even if it means backing-up to an earlier level of time on task. Generalization is facilitated by performing the identical programs at home. Typically, parents should begin a few steps behind the time interval currently in training at the treatment facility so that they are assured of success with the child at home. This helps avoid the inevitable retrieval of nonattending behaviors which will occur on the weekends and hamper the child's performance on the program.

TABLE MANNERS

This program is designed to teach the youngster the appropriate use of utensils and foods, to remain seated during the meal, ask for foods, take appropriate bites of foods, request to be excused, and interact verbally with the other persons at the table.

Data to Monitor Program

Because of the large number of other data-based programs typically in use with a child in our treatment regimen, one seldom places these behaviors under a continuous behavior count. At best, one accumulates a periodic sample of specific table manners that are exceptionally inappropriate. Often this count will be low rate, so one takes a count of errors occurring per meal for each behavior taught in succession. One usually monitors the error responses, but continues to reinforce the correct responses to retain their stability during the course of training.

Typical Status of Child

Before a program for table manners is initiated, one should be far beyond the earlier programs of conditioning food to be a reinforcer and using food to reinforce eye contact and language. Hopefully, the child has obtained enough autonomy and diminished dependency upon such strong rewards that he or she eats meals without assistance. This program usually begins near the termination of the treatment program with a severely handicapped child, and is intended to train the child to eat as expected in the home. The table manners trained should be consistent with those expected at home; some homes do not require one to say, "Please pass . . ." or "Excuse me."

At this time in the program, the child should be sufficiently compliant that he or she will *rehearse to success* new responses being taught, such as how to hold utensils appropriately. Time-outs should be effective and may be applied without resorting to a quiet room so as to be least disruptive when certain bizarre behaviors emerge at the table. The child is most primed for success when food is reinforcing, he or she is under optimal social control, responsive to more reinforcers, capable of positively rehearsing errors, and time-outs decelerate inappropriate responses. It is at this stage when the child may sit without constant supervision, and attends to the task of eating his or her food.

Where Implemented

This program is conducted at all meals at the treatment facility, as well as on home visits during the weekends with the child.

Staff Required

Since the child is advanced sufficiently so that close supervision is no longer necessary, this program may be performed with groups of children. Of course, if the child has not progressed this far, one could establish a shaping program of working directly with the child aside from the others at a separate table, and gradually reintegrating the child to the regular table as he or she gains control and success. Staff supervision is then correspondingly faded as the child joins the regular table. This 1:1 shaping program is indicated for the exceptionally low-level youngster who requires constant assistance and heavy reinforcement, as may be the case with some anorexic or severely retarded youngsters who cannot follow directions. These would be youngsters for whom language programs are beyond reach, and they are being trained for the most simplistic behaviors necessary to function in the home or perhaps in a custodial facility. But for the majority of cases, the child is seated with a group with one staff present, preferably on a 1:3 ratio, so that one person is able to monitor all children and praise, practice, and if necessary, time-out individual youngsters.

Reinforcers Required

Social reinforcement used for appropriate responses, and the food present as attained while eating appropriately should suffice as reinforcement. Positive practice may be necessary to stabilize the sequencing of these reinforcers for correct responses. For exceptionally deviant responses, a time-out may be necessary to which the child simply pushes the chair back from the table and remains seated quietly for one or two minutes and returns to the meal.

General Management Order

The first step is to break down the responses that you wish to teach the child from simple to most complex. If the child is in deficit in a wide number of responses, it is necessary to work on these in a step-wise fashion. If the child is more intelligent and has fewer deviant behaviors, these may be trained concurrently. Your clinical judgment will be involved in this decision, but the best choice would be based on samples taken of the child's progress in the training curriculum. If the progress is minimal and different from what the child was typically capable of acquiring as judged from other behaviors in the program, it may be necessary to delete some of the required responses and train these in succession rather than concurrently.

With some responses, you may need to assist the child, such as manually showing him or her how to hold the fork, beginning by reinforcing very specific behaviors as they occur appropriately under such supervision and planfully diminishing your supervision. It is hoped that the child will require less verbal direction, and eventually one can shift from a ratio to an interval reinforcement schedule. This means that you would progress from reinforcing a child for every correct response, to a less frequent reinforcement schedule, and eventually progressing to increasing time intervals of eating appropriately, with the final step being considerable praise for finishing the entire meal without error. It should be noted that when the child is returned home, he or she will probably be reinforced infrequently for correct table manners, and perhaps never in the school cafeteria setting. Therefore, it is necessary that the reinforcement schedule be thinned to be compatible to the contingencies that are available for that behavior in his or her natural environment.

Recommended Shaping Guidelines

1. If the program is to be monitored with data, it is necessary to assess the frequency of inappropriate manners. This requires first defining specifically which responses the child will be taught as well as those inappropriate ones which will be monitored for deceleration. Several options are available with these data. On a sample day one may wish to tally the frequency of the responses which will be taught and those to be deleted. The responses to be trained should be listed from easiest to most difficult as rated by their apparent frequency and anticipated difficulty in teaching those behaviors. For example, you may wish to teach the child how to eat with a spoon rather than his or her hands. The next level would be teaching the child to hold the spoon correctly, then to

eat with a fork afterwards, and finally, using a knife. With this kind of program, a weekly sample is likely to be sufficient data to monitor the child's progress.

2. A thirty-minute meal is usually compatible with the time allotted in school or at home. The child has that thirty-minute time interval to eat, with time-outs obtained during the meal being deleted from that time, as well as time spent in positive practice. One may argue that it seems more positive to extend the time period until the child has been satiated at the meal rather than limiting it to just thirty minutes. The rationale for the time interval is that it is a goal time; time deleted from this due to time-outs will mean the child is receiving less food, which is likely to increase drive and render reinforcement on subsequent meals more effective for correct responses. If you find that the child is not receiving a substantial amount of food during this time, it means your behavioral requirements are too stringent—you are trying to teach too much, too soon.

3. For spontaneously correct responses, and those elicited under supervision and positive practice, the child should be socially reinforced and encouraged to continue eating with these two conditions serving as reinforcers. The program must be graduated so that one is first demanding only a few correct responses, and as these reach a criterion of reliable performance, then a new response expectancy is added to the program. It is not advisable to demand too many responses concurrently, lest the program will acquire a pervasively negative aura with the child receiving a minimum of reinforcement.

4. For error responses that are to be decelerated by time-outs, it is recommended that the child merely push his or her chair back from the table and sit there for one or two minutes. To illustrate, if a child ate potatoes with his or her hands in noncompliance to the instructions of using a utensil, *which the child is capable of,* he or she may receive a time-out for that behavior. After the time-out, the child is given instructions on how to use the utensil, and positive practice on that response until it is more reliable. The message is clear: inappropriate responses do not receive food nor social reinforcement; correct responses and those positively rehearsed are reinforced. You would not time-out a child for eating with hands if he or she did not know how to use a utensil, but you would if the child noncomplied to the command to use the utensil which he or she was trained to use. Just as with the responses being trained, when inappropriate responses are brought under more reliable control, new inappropriate behaviors are added to the list and subjected to deceleration. It is not recommended to have a

massive number of responses under extinction at the same time simply because the child will be on a time-out condition almost continuously, which may render meals to be noxious. As mentioned with other programs, there must be a balance so that the child is learning, yet under control, and is on a predominantly positive training program.

5. The simplest task is to arrange the table manners you wish to teach in a hierarchy. A list of these is not offered here since it will vary with each child. In preparing such a list, begin rehearsing responses which the child is capable of to assure that the training is a reinforcing success experience, and begin with responses that result in food, for example, holding a spoon rather than how to use a napkin. When a new behavior is added to the list, be sure to continue reinforcement of the previously trained behaviors. Consultation with the parents is indicated to assure that the response expectancies are comparable to those in the home.

TOILET TRAINING

Behavior Taught

Two programs are presented as guidelines for toilet training severely handicapped children. These programs are ones in which alterations are easily made to suit the particular problems of the youngster being trained. It should be recognized in reviewing these programs that each child may begin at a different level in the shaping hierarchies presented; it is not necessary to start all children at the first step. The programs are designed for children who adamantly refuse to use the toilet. They may defecate or urinate in their clothing, in bed, smear fecal matter, and may have had a history of these behaviors for several years. It is not uncommon for these children to have no history of successful much less reliable toileting. Often, parental reports indicate there were intervals of time in which the child used the toilet appropriately, but this skill dropped from his or her repertoire. These programs are neither recommended for normal children, nor are they indicated where simple toilet training problems could be rectified quite quickly with more preferred techniques such as modeling with dolls, using soda pop to assure urination, and providing reinforcers when urination occurs as appropriately modeled. Youngsters who may respond to this latter program are likely to acquire the correct toileting behavior in a very few trials. These programs are ones for whom a massive number of trials are required for learning any new behavior, regardless of whether it is learning to eat appropriately, to toilet, to dress, and so on.

Toileting problems with severely handicapped children may have quite divergent origins, some of which may be due to organic factors. This is not to say that they necessarily lack sphincter controls, but rather represents the effects of retardation on conditioning any behavior, and correct utilization of the toilet does involve numerous complex discriminations. The problem of training becomes further compounded in difficulty when inappropriate defecation receives its own reinforcement by its very completion.

We have often hypothesized that, with some children, inappropriate defecation, and smearing and urinating in strange places has an aggressive component attached to it. This becomes a popular hypothesis with children who have minimal communicative skills, such as ones who resort to temper tantrums and aggressions to make known their needs, or to avoid situations which in the past did not provide much reinforcement. In earlier studies, we tried punishment procedures, such as time-outs, requiring the child to clean up the fecal matter, and scoldings, all of which met with complete failure insofar as teaching the new behavior. We surmised that this failure was primarily due to the complex, verbally mediated punishment procedure in which the children were unable to associate the contingency with inappropriate defecation.

There is also the hypothesis that this inappropriate toileting acquired a counteraggressive component. Inappropriate toileting for some of these children appears to be a form of aggression, but the only credence for this argument is your reaction of repugnance and the fact that punishment exacerbates the behavior. You find yourself concluding from the inconvenience of the behavior that the children are simply being perverse. It may be more realistic to hypothesize that these children have simply not learned the behavior, and that on occasions where punishment accelerates the behavior it is likely that you engendered a fear response, which in turn elicited defecation or urination. These children are not so verbal as to be likely to think, "I'm going to mess the floor, and that will really make them mad." But many clinicians ascribe such complex thinking to these children. This presumes some rather complex verbal skills for these children, which is ludicrous considering that they are unable to tell you their own name. The hypothesis of counteraggression in reference to inappropriate toileting is usually more descriptive of the staff members' feelings.

We have noticed that many of these children are terrified of the enclosure of the bathroom and the sound of the toilet flushing. When you consider the avoidance of the bathroom, the ineffectual training, and the fear responses elicited by the punishment techniques, it is no surprise that the behavior persists and becomes more variant in its form. Assuming this hypothesis to be correct, it is recommended that toilet training be entirely positive, with all precautions taken to make it less likely that the avoidance and fear responses will occur.

The programs suggested here are based on making toileting a positive behavior for the child. There are programs that have a certain desensitization aspect to them, ones that progress from heavy to less supervision, and ones that pair reinforcement with appropriate use of the toilet. In consideration of this discussion, one may anticipate that successful toilet training is directly related to the child's verbal skills.

One simply cannot overlook the necessity of appropriate toileting with disturbed children if one of the tentative goals is to return the child to the home and eventually to a special education classroom in the public school. Children who soil themselves in public schools are very liable to be excluded from the programs. If it is a feasible goal to train the child to adapt to the school environment, and to make home life a more pleasant one for the entire family, one should ensure that toilet training has been accomplished. Even if the eventual disposition for the child will be custodial care, his or her adaptation to that environment will be facilitated by appropriate toileting habits. It allows the child to be a more enjoyable youngster for the staff to interact with in that facility, which means he or she will receive better care.

Data to Monitor Program

Two related behavioral counts are used to measure the effectiveness of the toileting programs. One is accelerative data in the form of the child's correct use of the toilet. Decelerative data are accumulated in the form of the diminution of inappropriate soiling, smearing, enuresis, etc. These counts are performed on an all-day basis. Since the frequency of these behaviors is likely to be low rate, periodic sample days are less likely to be sensitive to the treatment effect than if the child is monitored continuously across all days. As low rate data, it is easy to record and is inexpensive since it does not involve much staff time.

Typical Status of Child

The first level to toilet training is for the very severely disturbed child, who is exceptionally avoidant of the toilet and whose intellectual limitations preclude imitative training as a useful technique. This youngster may smear, or even become frantic by the sounds and sights associated with the toilet. It may be necessary to countercondition these fear responses by successively approximating closer distances to the bathroom with a shaping program. This is simply accomplished with many specified times during the day in which he or she is taken gradually closer to the toilet and profusely rewarded for success. When the child learns to approach and enter the bathroom, then the program may begin. This kind of youngster requires massive trials during the day to implement the program—six trials would be insufficient, sixty would be realistic. To compound the problem, it is probable that these children also have constipation problems because of their poor eating habits, which seems to be characteristic of many low-level children. A subsidiary program for that deficit is attached to this curriculum.

The second level of children for whom these programs are recommended will require fewer trials. These are children who seem to respond fairly quickly to associative training, are responsive to a variety of reinforcers, do not require counterconditioning of fears relative to the bathroom, but whose main problem is to pair defecation with the appropriate place. The second program is for youngsters who do not demonstrate the more deviant behaviors of smearing, but have a history which is totally devoid of appropriate use of toilet. Both programs suggested are indicated for children whom you cannot expect to follow instructions. All of these children require a very structured training program to acquire any new behavior.

Where Implemented

If the child's inappropriate toileting is variable and unscheduled, he or she may have to be retained in the cottage. Here, the child can be continually observed to assure that he or she is ready to toilet when taken to the bathroom. This schedule is obtained by recording when the child defecates and urinates each day, for at least one week. If there is sufficient supervision in the school, this program may be maintained there also, which is dependent upon the number of staff available to work in the school in collaboration with the cottage. If the child is scheduled in toileting, which is ascertained through baseline studies, he or she is taken to the toilet for the various steps of the training program at those times he or she normally defecates or urinates. As the program progresses, it is hoped that the child will acquire a more scheduled use of the toilet, which allows the program to be expanded throughout his or her environment. Regardless of what the child's schedule is found to be during the baseline interval, this information should be assessed separately in the home before the toilet training program is initiated there. It is not uncommon to find that the child's schedule at home will be different than that at the treatment facility. This requires that the preferred schedule for the training sessions will have to be altered for when he or she is on home visits.

Staff Required

A 1:1 ratio is required for training sessions. As either program progresses satisfactorily, a diminution in staff supervision is possible, perhaps allowing several children to be trained as a group. For example, at one stage in our studies, we had three youngsters, two of whom were verbal schizophrenic twins. They were not toilet trained but were predictably scheduled in their inappropriate defecation. The other child, who required a highly structured program, was receiving considerable reinforcement for his success in toilet training. The twins demonstrated skill in imitating others, so their program was comprised of observing the other child, and when they modeled him correctly, they were reinforced equally. This program was accomplished with one staff member during each of the training sessions throughout the day, allowing a 1:3 ratio, which is a considerable savings.

Reinforcers Required

Social reinforcements should always be used throughout this program. We often initiate the program with preferred foods, often in the form of dry fruit and similar kinds of food that are likely to facilitate the child whose defecation problems are compounded by constipation.

General Management Order

Several concurrent goals are pursued in this program. First and most obvious is to overcome the child's fear of the toilet. This is performed concurrently while improving the child's diet and exercise so that he or she is more likely to have normal bowel movements and scheduled urination. The dominant goal of the entire program is to make correct elimination highly positive and bring inappropriate elimination under extinction by ignoring those errors while teaching the child an alternate and correct response.

Counteraggressive responses by the staff directed to the child who defecates inappropriately may have the unfortunate consequence of reinforcing that behavior by accidentally being comparable to prior training history. We have tried to make it a rule that if a child is frequent in smearing, the staff remove the child from the place where it occurred. In this way, the staff who cleans the fecal matter is not in close proximity to the child, so that he or she is less likely to convey disgust by glances or comments. It is unrealistic to expect staff to perform such a task devoid of emotion.

Specific Shaping Steps

Program 1: This first program begins with successive approximations to the bathroom to overcome the child's fear of that room and the toilet. As previously mentioned, this may be accomplished by having numerous occasions during the day, perhaps hourly, in which the child is gradually walked closer to the toilet on each successive trial and given a reinforcer for his or her approach. If you progress too quickly in moving closer to the bathroom, you may need to back-up on the shaping steps and move more slowly. Inappropriate defecations and urinations occurring during these times are simply ignored and cleaned. This phase of the program progresses until the child is being rewarded for simply being seated for increasing time intervals on the toilet, and on more frequent occasions during the day.

Supervision should be correspondingly diminished during the program. This is accomplished by establishing a schedule to suit the child, designed to be close to those times during the day in which baseline studies have shown he or she is most likely to defecate. We have often had programs where every hour the child would spend ten minutes in the bathroom. With some children, the time was reduced to every thirty minutes in which the child would spend ten minutes in the bathroom. The child is reinforced for sitting or standing appropriately, and reinforced excessively if he or she urinates or defecates at those times in the receptacle. This dimension of the program often fails to be satisfied. Toilet training requires massive numbers of trials to interrupt the history of inappropriate defecation the child has acquired. One should not be hesitant to establish a program for several weeks in which twenty minutes out of every hour in the child's waking day is spent in the bathroom. The long-range dividends more than justify the time spent in this arduous training.

As one achieves success with the child using the toilet without fear, then the number of trials may be diminished. This decision depends upon scrutinizing the decelerative data, namely in the form of inappropriate defecation or urination. If it becomes obvious the child is using the toilet appropriately, that he or she is becoming more scheduled at the times during the day in which he or she will produce, one may then diminish trials so that they correspond with these times. This effect is likely to be a function not only of the training sequence, but also of the diet, improved eating behaviors, exercise, and general routinizing of the child's day.

Toward the conclusion of this program, all spontaneous use of the toilet, even if there is no defecation or urination, should be reinforced with primary and social reinforcers. As the program advances, primary rewards may be reserved only for occasion of correct defecation, but social reinforcement should probably be maintained for the duration of the six-month interval for all approaches to the bathroom, particularly at home. In other words, the child may initiate a training trial whenever the child wishes, in addition to those which have been established for him or her. If this effect is accomplished, the child is now operating independently for the toilet, and for the reinforcement which comes for doing so. One of the major goals of this program is to train the child to use the toilet without supervision. If he or she begins to acquire the skill without being directed, the behavior is more likely to be maintained in the home and school.

There are arbitrary steps involved in establishing this program. One is that the frequency of trials used during the day is roughly guided by the baseline studies and coordinated with the other daily routines. It will certainly be a trial and error proposition in determining the duration of time the child will spend on the toilet. This may be gradually expanded at first, but as training is achieved the time is diminished. Regardless of the schedule, you want to assure that as long as the child is seated on the toilet, it is pleasantly rewarding, even if it necessitates placing the TV in the bathroom, or eating meals at that place, both of which we have done with success.

Program 2: This program is identical to program 1, with the exception that the trials are less frequent, and a counterconditioning program is unnecessary to desensitize the child's fear of the bathroom. It is a program in which shaping steps of times going to the bathroom are replete with positive reinforcement. Again, supervision in the bathroom will diminish and all of the child's spontaneous approaches to the toilet will be rewarded. Initially, you reinforce when the child simply approaches the bathroom alone, regardless of whether he or she used it. Later, withhold that reinforcement unless the child actually used it correctly on those spontaneous occasions. Any combination of the above two shaping steps may be arranged for the particular needs of the child.

Learning Theory Involved

The learning theory is rather simplistic. The program is one of positive practice, massive trials for approaching the toilet, and counterconditioning the child's negative reactions to the toilet by teaching the alternate response of appropriate use of the toilet and extinction by ignoring inappropriate defecation. The purpose of the program is to associate bowel and bladder elimination with being seated on the toilet. This simple association, followed by tangible reinforcers in conjunction with any inherent reinforcement effects defecation may have with the child, will foster training. A subsidiary goal is to interrupt the parent-child battle which may have been a vicious cycle for years by consistently reinforcing increasingly more appropriate use of the toilet and ignoring any possible aggressive or fear components of inappropriate defecation.

Supporting variables in this program include the extent of these chilren's language comprehension, if their compliance has progressed so that they are likely to follow the command to approach the toilet, if their diet has improved due to the meal program, if they are able to be in a more expanded environment so that they are receiving more exercise each day, and if they have acquired more scheduled routines. All of these variables will interact with the effectiveness of the shaping program. We have not researched each of the separate effects of these variables; we are simply capitalizing on conditions likely to produce more routine defecation and urination.

Ancillary Program: Controlling Constipation

Children with severe handicaps in toileting frequently have a long history of constipation. This handicap is often associated with poor eating habits, lack of exercise as reflected in their restricted play repertoire, and possibly organic factors related to their retardation. When the food preference program and expanded daily activities fail to rectify this problem, we have used Dulcolax (Geigy Pharmaceutical Corporation) as an unconditioned stimulus to elicit defecation. This is effected by using the suppository to initiate the bowel movement prior to taking the child to the toilet. As the Dulcolax is effective, it is gradually diminished in size and thereby in its chemical effectiveness as an unconditioned stimulus. The intention is to associate the entire defecation response with being seated on the toilet. We usually begin with a suppository length necessary to reliably initiate the response, which is seldom 100 percent. This length is then shaved at 1/16-inch intervals on successive days to the extent that it remains successful in stimulating defecation. Eventually, its use may also be faded so that it is at first used daily, then every other day, then every third day, etc., until it is no longer necessary. This fading schedule depends on the success in which the conditioning effect carries over from one day to the next.

In some cases it is necessary to always use the suppository and maintain a schedule diminishing its size. We arbitrarily established the 1/16-inch interval of decreasing the length. When the Dulcolax is diminished to approximately ¼-inch, it is then replaced by a glycerine suppository (Squibb Pharmaceutical Corporation), which again is subjected to a similar fading program as used for the Dulcolax. At this state, defecation is not dependent upon chemical facilitation, but rather mechanically assisted with the glycerin, which is a less intense, unconditional stimulus. Again, this suppository may be either gradually eliminated in its length, and/or its occurrence on successive days. The choice of either fading program depends on the success you are achieving with the child. It is recommended that staff administering such medication be under medical supervision, and that it be performed in a skillful manner not traumatic to the child. Administration of the suppository can be stressful for the child; primary reinforcement may be used to make this more pleasant.

CHAPTER

4
Case Studies

INTRODUCTION

The case studies cited here represent multiple response programs involving acquisition of new responses, controlling or decelerating existing ones, and accentuating preferred habits already available to the child. Academically, the data are contaminated experimentally; in fact, very few replications are performed to demonstrate control conditions. The value of behavior modification is most amply demonstrated through multiple response studies on the same subject and using very stringent experimental controls. These case studies demonstrate the first prerequisite, but do not satisfy the second.

The cases presented here are diverse, no two of which are comparable. A number of these children have dominant autistic features which allowed them a common diagnosis, but the behaviors for which they were specifically treated were not always identical nor were the treatment programs. Many of these youngsters progressed through the same treatment hierarchy of conditioning food as a reinforcer, social reinforcers, attention, etc., but other concurrent programs distinguish these cases from each other. It may be speculated that these youngsters have comparable predisposing organic features, as suggested more precisely by Ornitz and Ritvo (Ornitz et al. 1968; Ornitz and Ritvo

1968). And, it is probable that these children will acquire and retrieve the prevocal adaptive skills which give them and their instructors so much difficulty.

A number of these children had measurable intellectual skills as assessed by pretreatment test scores; some were untestable at initiation of treatment. All, however, were ineligible for school because of behavioral and intellectual reasons. As a group, these children had been through the "clinic shuffle," and thereby had experienced a variety of outpatient experiences. There is considerable variance among the children presented here; they were not all obviously psychotic or autistic, some were referred simply because of their ineligibility for school.

There may appear to be a message of redundancy in the psychotic children cases to the extent that the same treatment orders were replicated with several children. The treatment program has not been compared against a group of similar youngsters where no treatment was provided during the same time interval. Rather, we are comparing each child against himself or herself, using a similar treatment system, for these case studies cannot be lumped together as evidence of a group study. Furthermore, these children all began on the treatment hierarchy at different points dependent upon the skills they had and the extent of their noncompliance and attention. There was simply too much diversity within these children to group them together; we are still emphasizing the experimental-clinical approach even though a comparable treatment system may be used.

The most saliant features in these children's treatment programs are presented in the case studies. It should be noted that there were a multitude of other management orders in effect for each child, all of which are not reported in these case studies because it would be too voluminous, and many of those programs were not data oriented. These cases are not presented as an exposition of success, but as a demonstration of the varying degrees of progress we made with each child and the reality of the child's disposition that emerged from the data. Some of the programs may serve as a source for treating similar kinds of youngsters and also to impart the message of an objective, treatment-based, disposition for each child.

The format in which the cases are presented is intended to describe the treatment programs in such a manner that when retrieval occurs one knows the most necessary programs to reinstate. The case studies are not intended to be presented as a series of unrelated observations about the child with speculations based exclusively upon a preponderance of clinical judgment, but to be an objective explanation of the major techniques performed, the behaviors measured, and the results relative to time intervals. The case studies are intended to stem the drift toward the oversimplified notions of behavior modification as being composed of candies and praise, praise, praise; it sounds nice, but it does not coordinate sufficiently with the deficit the child may have at admission. Succinctly stated, one may praise a child endlessly for academic performance, but if that child does not have the prerequisite responses necessary for performance in the classroom setting, such as attention to task, control over deviant behaviors, etc., the praise will be a waste of time. These case studies show the sequence of programs progressing from simple to most difficult and include the prerequisite steps necessary for determining if these children can be returned to a classroom, or if custodial care may be the final decision. We also emphasize the point of responsible treatment with these children, which takes into consideration their general health, their eating, and being on a routinized schedule; these points unfortunately are omitted in case studies with children using behavior modification procedures.

CASE STUDY: PAUL

Admission Age: 6 years, 3 months.

Duration of Residency: 6 months.

Diagnosis: Childhood autism.

Background: Initially, Paul was referred to a local clinic near his farm home after he was discharged from his first two days of kindergarten because of his noncompliance, aggression, bizarre mannerisms, and random motor behavior. When first seen by the local clinic psychiatrist, Paul immediately walked into the room, picked up the *American Journal of Psychiatry,* and began to read from it perfectly. Despite this, he was a youngster who was incapable of telling you his own name, much less where he currently was, what he was doing, or what he had done. His spontaneous language was confined to a conglomerate of loose associations which seemed to be used randomly with neither logical sequence and meaning nor use as functional language. He did demonstrate this unusual skill of hyperlexia (Mehegan 1969), which led some professionals to think that Paul was a very bright child beneath this facade of bizarre behavior.

Since there were no facilities available where he resided, he was eventually referred to the Children's Treatment Center 250 miles away. It was questionable whether to accept Paul for treatment because of this distance. However, he demonstrated many of the classic behaviors of the autistic child, and his unusual skill for reading with

total absence of comprehension portrayed him as an interesting youngster to treat since one seldom locates an autistic child who demonstrates an island of proficiency such as Paul's sight reading. Also,
since the family was so willing to cooperate in parent training, even
at such a distance, he was accepted for admission.

Paul's developmental history was inconsistent with that of a
normal child. He did not learn to respond to verbal commands nor
interchange at a verbal level like other youngsters, because, in part,
he simply did not comprehend the meaning of the commands at the
same rate of acquisition as other children. This was confusing to his
family since he learned to parrot language, blocks of words, TV commercials, and written statements exceptionally well. He was not
formally instructed how to read and it was always an enigma to the
family how he acquired such a skill. It was conceivable that he was
receiving some vicarious training from the other older sibs when they
were doing their homework, as well as from the TV commercials he
avidly watched. However, it was our impression that he did not
acquire such information through direct instruction by another person.
He was asocial with other peers, he twirled objects, and demonstrated
many mannerisms and posturing responses that he seemed to acquire
on his own. He seemed to be oblivious of danger and had to be
watched constantly for fear that he would injure himself. There were
some routines which he had acquired within the home, but typically
he had to be watched constantly.

His unusual skill for word recall was very heartening to the parents. For example, he could name all thirty cows in the barn by name
with his unusually pitched voice. Interestingly, he would walk around
the barn kicking the cows, yet they never moved suddenly to hurt
him, which was not the case for others. This became a philosophical
debacle for Paul's father and me. Like many autistic children, he had
that wide-eyed vacant look that can be mistaken for alertness, but in
actuality he seems to be devoid of responding consistently to external
stimuli. Actually, he had very few habits or complexity to his behavior.
It was deceiving to observe his reading ability or to hear his rambling
bizarre speech which had led many professionals to believe that this
was a severely emotionally disturbed child. This assumption blinded
them to feasible organic limitations or specific handicaps which may
have been primarily responsible for the acquisition of the peculiar
responses typical of Paul.

A contractual arrangement was made with the family and the
referring agency to implement and maintain Paul's treatment program.
The goal was to enroll him in the treatment regimen, train the parents
to perform those programs, and have the local clinic personnel monitor
Paul after he returned to his home, and hopefully, public school. A

social worker from the referring agency came to the Center for intensive training on the parent training curriculum prior to Paul's admission. During the course of treatment, the social worker administered our parent training program to the family through video and audio tapes. The social worker performed this packaged training program and returned an audio tape of each presentation, which we critiqued and returned to him. Thus, we were training and monitoring the social worker's effectiveness of conducting our parent training with the family 250 miles away.

Since it was necessary to teach the mother the specific skills necessary for working with her child, as well as to keep her informed of Paul's progress, she came to the Center for a one-week visit at the second, fourth, and sixth months. She was treated as one of the staff, and instructed very directly on how to initiate and maintain the programs currently in use at that time. She worked with Paul and other children at the Center. After each visit, she returned home with Paul for a weekend with one of our staff who ascertained if she was able to maintain Paul's programs at home and if the father was also capable of acquiring these same skills.

It was possible to engage this family in such an intense contract because it was nonthreatening to them, and it was made clear that we in no way suspected that Paul was an emotionally disturbed child for whom they were responsible for the behaviors he demonstrated. This was an unusually bright and intact family which probably accounted for their success in profiting from this training and treatment arangement. Phone calls were made weekly to the parents to keep them informed of Paul's progress, as well as the little details of his daily life so that they kept in touch with him as their child.

Admission IQ: At date of admission Paul was untestable at our facility, as had been the experience of the referring agency. One month prior to admission, we arranged for a home visit and administered the Vineland Social Maturity Scale to the mother, with her demonstrating items she claimed he was capable of performing so that we would have realistic estimates of his performance in the home. On this testing he received a chronological age of 6 years, 3 months, with a social age equivalency of 3 years, 7 months.

Discharge IQ: After four months' inclusion in the treatment program, Paul was administered the Stanford Binet, Form L-M. He was 6 years, 8 months of age at this time. On that examination, he received a Mental Age of 4 years, 0 months, yielding a tabled IQ score of 56. At date of discharge, he was again administered the Stanford Binet and at chronological age 6 years, 10 months he received a mental age of 5 years, 1 month, which yielded a tabled IQ score of 71. He was also assessed on the Vineland Social Maturity Scale and received a social age equivalency of 8 years, 3 months, which was a 4-year, 6-month increment during the six-month treatment interval. It is recognized that the administration of the same intelligence test after a two-month period is questionable for retest effects. However, the items on which he was receiving additional credit for further mental age equivalence were items which he had not received during the first examination.

Specified Referral Problems: The primary problem was Paul's failure to be included profitably in a public school curriculum. Our task was to prepare him behaviorally and academically to be available for special education instruction in his local public school. The referral behaviors which were disruptive to the home as well as school included the following:

1. Random motor activity
2. Echolalic speech
3. Eating problems
4. Noncompliance
5. Temper tantrums
6. Aggression
7. Mannerisms and posturing
8. Unusual sight reading skills without comprehension
9. Oblivious to people and events transpiring about him
10. Nonaffectionate
11. Inattentive
12. Absence of goal-directed work skills
13. No constructive play
14. Failure to respond socially with peers

Teaching Paul to Take an Appropriate Time-Out

Behavior Counted: The data in figure 4–1 represent the accumulation of times in which Paul received a correct time-out as well as frequency of time-outs in the quiet room for all behaviors under deceleration during the course of treatment, such as noncompliance, aggression, and bizarre mannerisms.

Treatment A: Under treatment A, illustrated in figure 4–1, the program was begun by his taking time-outs in the quiet room for two minutes for the behaviors under this punishment/extinction procedure. On all such occasions he was told why he was taken to the quiet room. The proposed treatment succession was intended to gradually move him out of the quiet room by first requiring him to sit

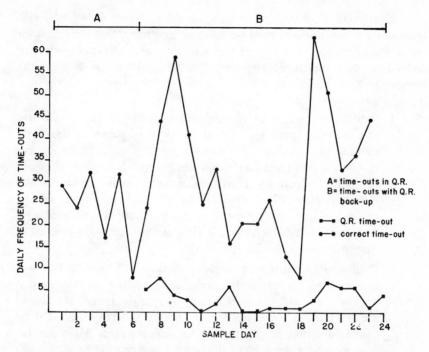

FIGURE 4–1 *Teaching Paul to Take an Appropriate Time-Out*

quietly with the door closed, then having the quiet room door open, followed by seating him outside the door, then down the hall, and finally generalizing everywhere with each successive step dependent upon 80 percent success on the prior step. We judged that the initial step of requiring him to sit still in the quiet room for two minutes was not being acquired rapidly enough. He was spending numerous periods of time in the quiet room, unable to understand the expectancy and therefore overloading the punishment/extinction side of the program. We decided to change the management order to teach him how to take a time-out in places other than the quiet room, but using the quiet room as a back-up for occasions when he did not take an appropriate time-out. This management order would hopefully make the contingency more discriminative for him.

Referring to figure 4–1 under condition A, it was noticed that there was a deceleration in the frequencies of time-outs he was receiving at that time. This reflects the total number of times he was being timed-out in the quiet room for all behaviors at the beginning of the program, and as these behaviors came under control, new ones were added to his program. For this reason, there is considerable variance in the number of times he receives a time-out during the course of the program since new behaviors were being added.

Treatment B: Referring to condition B in figure 4–1, a new curriculum was established. Paul would continue to receive time-outs for noncompliance, aggression, temper tantrums and any new behavior added to that treatment regimen. The program progressed in the following four steps:

1. Paul would receive a two-minute time-out at the location where the behavior occurred, even if he required some assistance returning to that place. He would go to the quiet room for five minutes if he raised his seat off the ground during the time-out he was taking at the place where the behavior occurred. All other behaviors that occurred during this time-out would be ignored. Thus, the time-out in the quiet room was used as a punishment for not taking a time-out on the spot where the inappropriate behavior occurred.

2. Paul would continue to receive time-outs as before, but he was now to keep his seat on the floor, and go to the spot designated by the staff without assistance and remain there. He would receive a quiet room time-out as before for five minutes if he failed in either of the two above expectations. All other behaviors would be ignored. He would not be able to slide away along the floor, but could still talk and wiggle while sitting.

3. The expectations for taking an appropriate time-out advanced to sitting with his seat on the floor, going there by himself as directed by staff, and sitting still, cross-legged with his hands on his lap and without wiggling. He would receive a time-out of five minutes in the quiet room for failing in any of these behavioral requirements during the time-out.

4. Paul was now required to follow all requirements of step 3, and in addition to remain silent for the two minutes. This was the desired time-out criterion and was used thereafter. The five-minute quiet room back-up was continued as necessary.

The criteria for progressing to each successive step was 85 percent success for two consecutive days of taking time-outs with no back-up time-outs in the quiet room. These data were obtained by counting the total number of time-outs he received and the number of time-outs which were unsuccessful.

As may be seen in figure 4–1 under condition B, the frequency of requiring him to take a back-up time-out in the quiet room remained low and constant with some variance. Also, there was an acceleration in actual number of time-outs given as new behaviors were placed under this regimen. One variable which accounted for the excessive high spike toward the end of the curriculum was the introduction of the management order for decelerating bizarre mannerisms, the data of which are reported later in this case study.

Results: This program was rather successful in teaching Paul to take a time-out in circumstances similar to his home and school settings. It was obvious by the low but steady rate of requiring a quiet room back-up that there would be the inevitable retrieval of old behaviors which would necessitate more time-outs for controlling their rate, and therefore a necessity for having a quiet room as a back-up when he returned home. This requirement was continued in the home, but was difficult to achieve in the school setting. It required almost two months for school officials to provide a quiet room to maintain his training of taking correct time-outs. And, of course, there was a corresponding retrieval of inappropriate behaviors occurring during that interval and a diminution of effectiveness of the time-outs in the school setting.

Accelerating Paul's Compliance to Verbal Commands

Behavior Counted: Typical of all compliance programs, the behavior counted was the number of commands given him during the sample days and the success to which he responded appropriately to those commands. If he would start initiating the response correctly within ten seconds, it was counted as a success. If he failed to initiate the response by that time interval, it would be a noncompliance. The command would typically be repeated. It was attempted to have commands at a level which he would comprehend throughout the course of the program advancing from simple to complex. However, if he initiated a response correctly, he could be given additional direction to continue that response in the event that he was unable to recall the whole sequence of the response expected of him.

Treatment A: Figure 4–2 shows the treatment program for compliance, with the A interval representing the controlled baseline period. If Paul did not respond to the command successfully during the baseline condition, it would be repeated up to three times if necessary. If the command was really not essential, it was dropped after three trials. If it was essential that he do what was commanded of him, then he would be "walked through" the command following the three trials.

Treatment B: During treatment B, the management order was very simple and typical of that used in compliance training. Com-

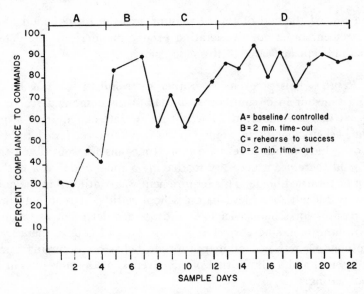

FIGURE 4-2 *Comparative Effects of a Two-Minute Time-Out and "Rehearse to Success," Both With Social Reinforcement, on Compliance to Verbal Commands*

mands were expected to be monitored and increased in complexity during the course of the program. Each time he was given a command he had ten seconds to initiate the correct command given of him. In the beginning stages of the program we alternately provided primary and social reinforcers, and gradually deleted the former. If he failed to initiate the response within the required time interval, he would receive a two-minute time-out in the quiet room. Figure 4-2 should be compared to the graphs for temper tantrums and aggressions in order to show that there was a diminutive reliance upon the quiet room to produce desired deceleration effects on these behaviors. During the course of Paul's compliance training he was receiving fewer time-outs and relatively less occasions of using the quiet room to support the effectiveness of the time-outs. In figure 4-2, under treatment condition B, both the two-minute time-out and positive reinforcement were used for treating noncompliant responses.

Treatment C: Under condition C, we attempted to rely exclusively upon "rehearse to success" or positive practice, and delete the time-outs for noncompliance. As may be seen in figure 4-2, compliance dropped, but then rose. The reason for the improvement was that we began making fewer expectations of Paul, i.e., his diminution in compliance was training staff to only make commands which were simple, rather than increasingly complex ones, which is not reflected in these data. We therefore reinstated the two-minute time-out in condition D, and regained Paul's compliance to more varied and complex commands.

Decelerating Temper Tantrums

Behavior Counted: The behavior counted throughout the sequence illustrated in figure 4–3 was always each incident of a temper tantrum occurring on the sampled days. A temper tantrum was defined as a combination of the behaviors of screaming, lying on the floor and hitting, scratching, biting, or kicking—typically after being told to do something. On occasions there were isolated incidents of the above combination of behaviors when there were no apparent antecedents, but this would still be counted as a tantrum. Aggressions occurring during a temper tantrum were logged under a separate count for that behavior. Temper tantrums had to be separated by a time interval of at least thirty seconds to receive individual counts. During that thirty-second time, there could be no occurrences of those behaviors which resulted in the definition of a tantrum.

Treatment A: This was a four-day controlled baseline condition in which staff counted the frequency of the behavior, without intervening physically, but waited for a short period of time and then repeated the expectation which may have eventuated the tantrum. All staff reacted the same way to tantrums: they simply kept repeating the commands. The baseline interval on figure 4–3 shows that the

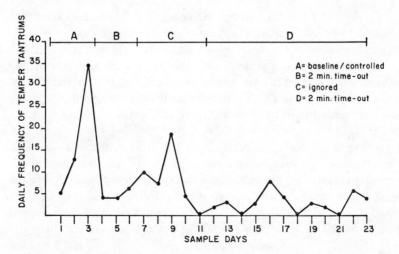

FIGURE 4–3 *Comparative Effects of a Two-Minute Time-Out and Ignoring on Temper Tantrums*

frequency of tantrums was quite variable, ranging from five to thirty-five per day. The entirety of this graph does not include the qualitative shift in tantrums during the course of treatment. As stated previously, it may be expected that the duration and kinds of behaviors composing a tantrum would correspondingly change along with the diminution of tantrums.

Treatment B: During treatment B, Paul would receive a two-minute time-out in the quiet room for each occurrence of a tantrum. The remaining data points on the graph represent samples obtained one day for each week. The treatment interval of B in which he was receiving a two-minute time-out represents four weeks of treatment. During that four weeks, there appeared to be a gradual increase in Paul's tantrums. During the last two weeks of that interval, staff were reporting that he seemed to enjoy taking a time-out, as evidenced by his laughing, smiling, running to the quiet room spontaneously by himself, repeating a behavior which would eventuate a time-out, and then say, "Take a time-out, take a time-out," running there by himself. We were under the misguided impression that he was operating for the isolation of the quiet room as an avoidance behavior. The same effect was noticed for other behaviors such as aggression and compliance also under a time-out contingency. So, as we had changed those programs, the time-out was deleted from his program for an interval of time to determine if another program would work, on the presumption that the time-out was actually facilitating the behavior it was intended to decelerate.

Treatment C: Under treatment condition C, the tantrums were subjected to an ostensible extinction program whereby in each occurrence the staff would simply ignore Paul's deviant behavior entirely until he had ceased that behavior and then they would continue working with him. This treatment program initially spiked the behavior, but there was a definite deceleration as the program progressed. However, with his other behaviors, in which the time-out had also been deleted, it was observed that simply ignoring the behavior was ineffectual. Therefore, we decided on the treatment condition D of reinstating the two-minute time-out, since it also corresponded to the shaping program for training him to take a time-out. Furthermore, we were becoming aware that we were avoiding Paul, making fewer demands of him, which meant that his tantrums retained their operant value of avoidance and we were not in control of teaching this child.

Treatment D: As mentioned, a two-minute time-out in the quiet room was utilized for this treatment interval. If he did not take an appropriate time-out for each occurrence of a temper tantrum, he would receive a five-minute back-up in the quiet room. That program succeeded in reducing the frequency of tantrums to a rather stable, low rate. However, it was evident in this program, as in others, that by the end of the six-month treatment interval the behavior was still present and the treatment programs would have to be continued at home and in the school to which he was discharged.

We hypothesized that his operating for a time-out, even delivering them to himself, was Paul's first understanding of the contingency which he would gleefully rehearse. We had noticed this in other autistic children, and it appeared that it was their new comprehension of a cause-effect relationship between a behavior (the tantrum), and a contingency (the time-out). Furthermore, we observed with these children that if we maintained the time-out condition, it would gradually show a deceleration effect on the behavior. These are children who cannot comprehend many verbal explanations, and it is only by repeated experiences that they acquire the behavior.

Controlling Aggressive Behavior

Behavior Counted: Aggression was defined as including any of the following behaviors: pushing, shoving, biting, kicking, hitting, scratching, or spitting. We also included attempted aggressions, which are interrupted before being completed. For example, if he attempted to bite a staff member who pulled away before he had completed contact, this would still be counted as an aggressive response. Those aggressive responses which occurred during temper tantrums or other behaviors under a separate program were also included in the total counts for aggression.

Treatment A: The baseline, shown in figure 4–4, began with a count of the aggressive responses. Staff members did not respond differentially to these behaviors. They tried to ignore them, unless it was likely to be physically harmful to them, at which time they would remove themselves from the situation. Since there was a stipulated management order on how to respond to the aggressive behavior, i.e., by ignoring or removing yourself, this would be considered a controlled baseline condition.

Treatment B: During this treatment condition, Paul received a two-minute time-out which was coordinated with the program for training him to take an appropriate time-out without use of the quiet room.

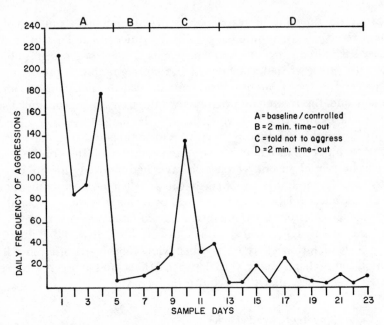

FIGURE 4–4 *Comparative Effects of a Two-Minute Time-Out and Being Told "to Stop" on Frequency of Aggressions*

Treatment C: Treatment C represented the reversal that we had used in all of Paul's programs designed to decelerate behaviors which had been timed-out. It was at this time, as for temper tantrums, that it appeared he was working for a time-out as an escape response. We began the program in treatment interval C in which a time-out in the quiet room was no longer utilized, but he was simply told, "Don't do that," verbally indicating the particular response which was defined as aggression. As may be seen in treatment interval C, this indeed facilitated the behavior, and it rose spectacularly back to its baseline status. However, there was a diminution in that behavior toward the end of treatment interval C. We suspect, as with some of the other programs, that this represented our not making as many demands on Paul, which meant there were fewer occasions for him to avoid by aggression.

Treatment D: With the experience of this and other programs, we had decided to reinstate the time-out condition, during which we would continue Paul's training of taking an appropriate time-out so that it could be utilized back in the school and home. As may be seen in treatment interval D, this treatment regimen was successful in controlling aggressive behaviors down to a low rate although they still remained evident by termination of treatment. Again, as with the other deceleration programs, it indicated that the six-month interval was not sufficient to completely control these behaviors; the programs would have to be maintained at home.

Teaching Paul Five-Second Eye Contact at Fifteen Feet

Behavior Counted: The data to monitor the sequence of programs for teaching Paul increasing duration and distance of eye contact as a prerequisite for language training and academic work were the number of trials and successes within training sessions of that behavior.

Treatment Sequence: Eight shaping steps were used to teach Paul eye contact which were as follows:

Shaping Steps for Training Eye Contact

	Steps			*Steps*
A	one second at one foot		E	five seconds at one foot
B	two seconds at one foot		F	five seconds at five feet
C	three seconds at one foot		G	five seconds at ten feet
D	four seconds at one foot		H	five seconds at fifteen feet

The eye contact training sessions of Steps A–F were taught in three ten-minute training sessions during the day by cottage staff, as well as two meals during the day in which the food was used as the reinforcer. During the specific training sessions, cereal, candy, or raisin reinforcements were used in conjunction with social reinforcement. At the meals, he would receive one bite of his meal for each successful eye contact response meeting the criteria at the level which we were currently training. The criteria for moving to the next step of the shaping program was 85 percent success for two consecutive sessions. This eye contact training was continued in session and also in other academic programs in the school. During the first few weeks of meal-times, staff typically gave Paul the bite of food as a reinforcer, but as the program progressed, he was able to take the bite himself at their command after a successful response for which he would always be socially reinforced. During this part of the program, which preceded the training of preferred foods, if he did not like a certain food it would not be offered; it was our choice to use the most preferred foods at the meal for reinforcers for successful eye contacts. The meal programs always lasted for thirty minutes, and the third meal which re-

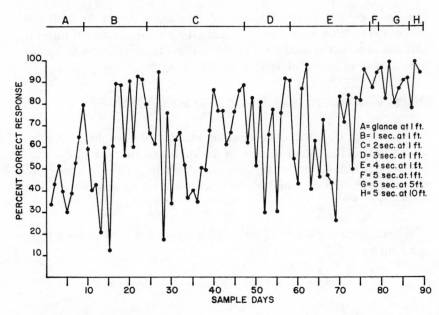

FIGURE 4–5 *Shaping Program for Teaching Paul to Maintain Eye Contact for Five Seconds, at Ten Feet*

mained at the end of the day was offered on a cafeteria basis to assure that he was receiving adequate nutrition in case he was not so successful on the preceding meals.

The data in figure 4–5 show the successive treatment steps and show that there was within each step an acquisition of the response, and when he proceeded to the next step there would be diminution in success, followed by an acceleration, which continued throughout the course of training until five seconds success was reached. Eventually his performance was high and steady without a great deal of variance in achieving the successive steps. During steps G and H, eye contact training was conducted only in sessions and not during mealtimes.

Teaching Paul to Control Bizarre Mannerisms

Behavior Counted: Bizarre mannerisms were a series of responses which contributed to the diagnosis of childhood autism, which we did not begin treatment with until the last month of treatment. We wanted to determine if these responses would decelerate spontaneously. These behaviors did not diminish without treatment, and the following combinations of behaviors were grouped together for a combined count of bizarre mannerisms: hand flapping, twirling, finger spelling, shaking hands up and down or making circular motions with his fingers. These latter responses occurred most frequently when he was running and/or excited. Three seconds had to elapse between mannerisms for separate counts. For example, if he was continuously flapping his hands, he would receive a count of only one until he had ceased flapping for a three-second interval and then started the response again in order to receive a count of two. These counts were not taken when Paul was in his room unstructured, such as during rest period. They were counted if he was in his room during a structured speech or working time.

Treatment A: Figure 4–6 shows the baseline and treatment condition for bizarre mannerisms with Paul. Baseline was sampled on a Thursday/Friday/Saturday/and Sunday series on all-day counts. Successive samples were taken one day each week, and there was not a long interval of time in which the behavior was under treatment. However, the controlled baseline (staff ignored him) interval did show that Paul had a high rate of these bizarre mannerisms, which had not been affected by other treatment programs during the six-month residency.

Treatment B: This treatment condition was a simple two-minute time-out for each occurrence of bizarre mannerisms. It should be recalled, since this was the sixth month of treatment, that he was taking

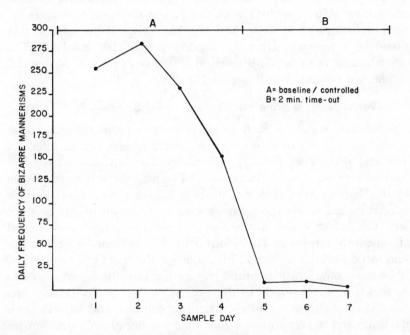

FIGURE 4–6 *Effect of a Two-Minute Time-Out on Bizarre Mannerisms*

a time-out in places other than in a quiet room. The time-outs he received for these behaviors were consistent with the management orders on the time-out shaping program.

When Paul was given a time-out for bizarre mannerisms, he was told why, e.g., "Paul, no finger spelling, take a time-out." After the time-out, he would be structured back into the same activity and required to rehearse not displaying the bizarre response, e.g., "Paul, walk down the hall with your hands at your side." If he succeeded with this positive practice routine by following staff's directions, he would be praised considerably. If he failed, it was taken as a non-compliance, perhaps accompanied by another bizarre mannerism, and he would receive another time-out. In structuring Paul after a time-out, he was returned to the same activity in which the bizarre behavior occurred. If he was finger spelling during a meal, after the time-out he would begin eating the same food again but without finger spelling. There was also a general management order that if Paul was observed not to be bizarre in situations where he usually demonstrated these mannerisms, he would be praised very highly. After three weeks of this treatment, the effect of which is shown in treatment B of figure 4–6, the management order for finger spelling was changed. This was an unusual response in which, as Paul spoke, he would spell out the letters of the words he was saying. These were not the same rate as the spoken words, of course, but they did represent some form of communication. After the third week of time-out for bizarre mannerisms, when he was finger spelling, he was told to stop. If he did not, that would be a noncompliance for which he would be timed-out. The other bizarre behaviors still received a time-out for each occurrence, but he was reminded with one trial for finger spelling.

Teaching Paul to Remain in his Room during Rest Period

Behavior Counted: Staff members were to count the number of times Paul left his room during the prescribed rest period intervals. The rest periods were thirty minutes in duration and occurred at least once or occasionally twice a day. The program was accomplished by the shaping steps shown in figure 4–7. Five pieces of plastic tape were stretched across the open door to a maximum height of three feet. The first tape was on the floor; the remaining tapes were spaced at nine-inch intervals. The continuous management order was for him to be directed to stay in his room for the half-hour rest period. If he came out, which required tearing the tape, he was directed to go back into his room. If he did not, he was physically taken there, the tapes were returned to the original positions, and he was given the command to remain in his room. He was not given a time-out for having left his room. At the end of successful rest periods, when he

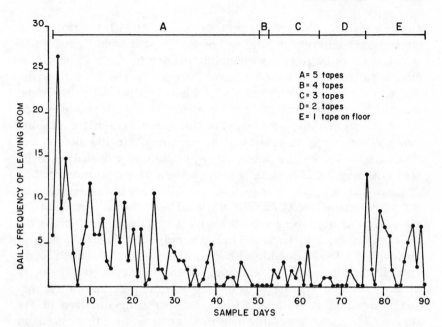

FIGURE 4–7 *Shaping Program for Teaching Paul to Stay in Room During Rest Period*

did not attempt to leave his room, he was verbally reinforced. This program progressed so that when he had two consecutive days of rest periods without leaving his room, the top tape was removed. As shown in figure 4–7, these tapes were gradually removed. At the conclusion of the program in step E, there was an acceleration in the frequency of his coming out of his room when there was only a tape on the floor. Staff were not unduly concerned about this change, although it was recorded. He was now coming out of his room for more appropriate reasons, such as making requests to staff for certain items, or speaking to them. However, this qualitative shift in his behavior when leaving the room is not shown on the graph.

This is an unusual program; it requires that the child is sufficiently compliant to stay in his room much of the time, with the tapes serving as a visual reminder of the expectation. The tapes were not a physical barrier; Paul could walk through them. But with his limited verbal memory for directions, the visual presence of the tape was useful and could be gradually faded.

General Management Orders for Which Data Was Not Accumulated

1. Mealtime: At the beginning of the program several expectations were established for Paul's mealtime behavior. Some of these expectations were on a compliance basis; some were not available responses and were taught. Prior to the meal he had to sit with the rest of the group before entering the dining room. The staff would cue him to ask for food to be passed, withholding it until he did ask; providing models for him if it appeared that there was a particular food he wanted; and praising him heavily for his succeeding with that imitation, with no time-outs for failure. Staff taught him to stay seated for the duration of the meal by redirecting him to his seat and praising him for remaining there as well as returning. He did not receive time-outs for leaving the table. Heavy praise was provided when he said, "Excuse me." If he did not say this, the staff would intervene and demand such a response from him. Initially he was not required to eat a portion of everything although all foods were placed on his plate. He did not have to finish his meal to have dessert; it was his discretion to eat if he wished. Thus, the meal was primarily a positive one, with the food available without pressure to eat prescribed foods. Later in the program, Paul was taught to enjoy eating a greater variety of foods. Some of the meals, as indicated in the program for eye contact, were used as training sessions for increasing duration of eye contact. The above general management order was for those meals in which eye contact training was not performed.

2. *Bathtime:* Bathtime was trained to be a "fun" time for Paul. The staff would sing nursery songs to him (e.g., "This is the way we wash our arm,") making the bathing as enjoyable for him as possible. He was initially quite fearful of the tub, but with this positive approach, he soon learned to enjoy bathing.

3. *Limitations:* The nursing station and the director's office were "off grounds" for Paul unless he specifically asked permission. He was on a program in which staff would model for him to ask to enter. He would be praised in so doing, regardless of whether this was done either spontaneously or following staff's model. After he had learned to model relatively well, it was then a compliance issue: he would have to ask to come in or else he would receive a time-out. If he asked, he would receive social reinforcement.

4. *Modeling:* Modeling was used extensively with Paul. In physical activities, such as tying his shoes or zipping his coat, the staff would provide the model by demonstrating how to do it and assisting him with the routines while diminishing their assistance and cues. Time-outs were never used in the modeling procedure; only positive reinforcement was used. Diminishing cues were used throughout the course of the program so that he was being reinforced for spontane-

ously making the request for assistance, which decreased as the skills were acquired.

5. *Work and Play Sessions:* A play box was assembled containing cardboard materials, chalk board, projector, Peabody Language Series, Peabody Body parts and clothing, and Peabody fruits and shapes cards. He had two twenty-minute work and play sessions during the day. They were designed to help structure him at times as well as to provide staff with activities to teach Paul that could be fun and eventually become spontaneous. It was acceptable to have more than two sessions per day, particularly on weekends, but he was always scheduled for at least two sessions. He had ten instruction cards in an envelope with detailed instructions of how to handle each activity which lasted for approximately ten minutes. There were two matching-type activities which provided him with enjoyment, and also coordinated with the kinds of academic materials he was learning in school. Praise and primary reinforcements were used for success on engaging in the activity with less and less supervision. Time-outs were not utilized; it was primarily a positive program.

6. *Ignoring/Extinction Programs:* Several responses were ignored with Paul to determine if they would extinguish by that consequence. His incessant references to TV commercials or rote recitations of "bizarre" language were ignored, and staff would not respond to them. This was difficult since some of his commentaries were rather humorous, such as when he referred to "the dragon who lived across the green moat in the castle." Also, he was reinforced socially and with primaries when he would ask appropriate questions so that he would learn the discrimination between correct and incorrect spontaneous language.

On various occasions he would decide to take his own time-outs. We ignored this behavior when it would occur. As we later learned, this appeared to be his comprehension of the sequence of an inappropriate behavior and taking a time-out. At some times he would just repeat, "Take a time-out, take a time-out, take a time-out," and run in the quiet room and shut the door. On these occasions staff would simply ignore this behavior; they would not go to the quiet room after him but waited for him to return on his own.

7. *Preferred Foods:* Two months after admission, we began training Paul to eat a greater variety of foods. Up to this time, we had used the already known preferred foods to condition attention, eye contact, and the beginnings of language. Now that these programs had progressed beyond the need for food, we wished to teach Paul to

eat a greater variety of foods that would be typically available in his home. The three daily thirty-minute mealtimes, plus snacks, were used for this program. He was to eat with everyone at the same table. Staff regulated the food intake with meals lasting a maximum of thirty minutes. If he finished prior to that time and excused himself properly, he could leave the table. To make the meal progress evenly, staff began with the most preferred foods, then the next least preferred, and followed by the next least preferred food. A preferred food was used for rewarding eating other nonpreferred foods in the meal. If there was nothing in the meal that was apparently reinforcing, potato chips from the kitchen were utilized for reinforcing him for eating the other foods. The general methodology required using two bowls; one containing the preferred and the other the nonpreferred food. Paul was to feed himself all bites of food. He was told to take a bite of the nonpreferred food after which he would receive the preferred. He was sufficiently intact to follow this regimen on his own without requiring our feeding him directly, which simplified the procedure. We found that quite often the initially nonpreferred food at the beginning of the meal would shift and actually become a preferred one during the meal. In such an event, it would then be used as a reinforcer for eating less preferred foods. He was not coaxed or prodded during this regimen. The offer of the nonpreferred food was made to him and then staff would wait for him to eat that food, after which he would then be given the preferred food as the reinforcer for having done so. No time-outs were used for this program so that eating remained on a positive program. This program was in effect for only one month. By the end of that month he was eating just about all foods offered at mealtime. He would occasionally vomit when he had taken a food which in the past had been an unpreferred one. A management order was then established at the conclusion of this program in which he would eat with everyone else as usual. Staff would still serve his food to him, but if there was something that was definitely unpreferred this would be given to him first in a reasonable portion which he would have to eat before progressing to the other foods. It was apparent that sometimes he would vomit quite purposely, and in such instances the same kind of food that he had rejected would again be given so that he would learn that vomiting was not a useful avoidance mechanism. Some foods he definitely did not like, and as with all children, we can expect at least three to six foods where we simply did not press the issue. During the general mealtime management order, if he ate something of everything, he was allowed to have dessert. If he asked appropriately he was allowed to have seconds on food of his choice.

8. Transition Change Program: As with many autistic children, Paul was quite resistent to any changes in his schedule. He would learn a definite routine or sequence of events in his day, but was rather intolerant of changes in that sequence. The goal was to teach Paul to be able to tolerate chances in his routine, since this would be expected behavior when he would be returned to the public school setting. The procedure was to establish a baseline of situations which were changed to ascertain how he would respond, and which would be reassessed after treatment. The behaviors he would demonstrate when there would be a transition different from the usual routine were crying, temper tantrums, tearing or running aimlessly about, refusing to comply, aggressing, spitting, and verbally explaining what he thought should have been occurring. Ten situations were tested at the beginning of treatment. These activity changes or transitions were: going to school instead of activity therapy, taking the dishes to the kitchen instead of the cart at conclusion of the meal, getting out his math book instead of his reading book in the classroom, and so on. These items were scored as either a plus or minus. A plus meant he would perform the new transition without demonstrating any of the above mentioned behaviors; a minus meant that he exhibited one or more of the above avoidance responses. Prior to treatment he was successful on seven of these transitions, and after treatment he was able to do eight of them without demonstrating any of the above behaviors. This certainly was not a phenomenal success, but there was some qualitative shift in his response to the transitions. Actually, staff felt that we had a poor pretest of these activities since he was in an unusually compliant mood that particular day. Regardless, he was trained on a program in which there was a change in his routine at least four times every day. Staff wrote ideas of different activities which would be changed so that they could vary on successive days. Although that data did not represent an ideal change, staff felt by clinical impression there was a difference in his responding to changes in routine by the conclusion of that program, but unfortunately there are no substantial data to validate that impression.

9. Bizarre Responses: When Paul was observed masturbating in public, he was informed simply that if he wished to do this he would have to do so in his room. No punishment was given for that response; ːt was only redirected to a more appropriate place, and the redirection given until he had ceased the activity in the public place or went to his own room.

Also, when he was observed running bizarrely up and down the hall in his unusual gate, he was redirected to walk appropriately and praised for having done so. Changes in both bizarre movements were reinforced socially.

10. *Meal Manners:* This management order began approximately one month before discharge. Food was no longer being used at meal-times for a reinforcer; he was eating most foods, but his table manners definitely needed improvement. A plate was provided having sections at first, in which the various foods were placed. Staff modeled how to hold a spoon and fork in eating separate foods in succession. Social praise was used for success. When he took unusually large bites of food, or resorted to eating with his fingers, he was redirected to the use of proper utensils and amount. By modeling and direct assistance, he was taught how to use the knife to cut foods into smaller portions. Direct physical help was given to the extent needed and gradually faded by staff. He was timed-out in this program if he refused to follow the models or assistance provided. We did have a generalization problem at mealtime of his persisting to raise his hand as taught in school. It was necessary at meals to teach Paul to wait for a time interval to speak and to do so without raising his hand. This was done by modeling and redirecting. Staff would say, "That's only for school. Put your hand down." He was also modeling two other children's speech patterns, which was very atypical at this time, particularly during meals. Staff would not admonish him for this; they would redirect him to an appropriate form of speech and have him rehearse this for which he would be praised.

11. *Expression of Feelings:* By the last month of treatment, Paul was expressing definite emotions he had regarding home visits, mail, and the prospects of seeing his family. Two staff were primarily responsible for caring for Paul at times when he would become distraught in his feelings about his family. He had difficulty expressing his feelings; it was usually shown diffusely accompanied by aggression, tears, and obvious remorse. This mixed emotion was handled by staff comforting him physically until he calmed which we hoped would establish the appropriate feeling of depression regarding homesickness. This program was in effect one month prior to his discharge, and it did not succeed in separating out the confused initial aggression and then depression which occurred at these times. It was gratifying, however, to see a child for the first time in his life express such complex and personal emotions.

12. *Provoking:* By the sixth month, time-outs were reduced to thirty seconds. If he did not take an appropriate thirty-second time-out,

he would receive a two-minute time-out in the quiet room. The objective of this general management order was to have control with a very short time interval, which would be implemented in the school room and home. At this stage of the program, aggression had almost disappeared, but we were observing low-level approximations of this behavior which we defined as provoking. This would be in the form of his teasing or taunting another child but without touching him, whereas aggression had been defined by physical contact. This teasing was also in the form of continually repeating statements, waving his hands in front of another child's face, getting very close to a person and then asking a nonsensible question, and also just getting as close to another youngster as he could without touching him. Each instance of this kind of behavior received a thirty-second time-out preceded by the staff telling him very pointedly, "No teasing." After the time-out had transpired, the staff requested and assisted Paul to say some verbal response as an alternative to the provoking or teasing he had previously demonstrated. A staff would model that alternative response for him and then have him positively rehearse it. When occasions were appropriate, staff assisted him in talking with some of the other children so to rehearse the correct behavior before provoking actually occurred.

CASE STUDY: BRET

Admission Age: 6 years, 10 months.

Duration of Residency: 1 year.

Diagnosis: Childhood autism; unequivocally agreed on among all referring agencies and our staff.

Admission IQ: Untestable on Stanford Binet; Vineland Social Maturity Scale: 1 year, 2 months.

Discharge IQ: Administered at chronological age 7 years, 7 months; mental age 3 years, 1 month; IQ = 37, Vineland Social Maturity Scale: 5 years, 0 months.

Specified Referral Problems: Bret was referred after numerous outpatient trials ranging from day care centers to psychiatric consultation. He was a wildly impulsive child who was minimally compliant to very simple commands. His language was composed of a few words which he used functionally but infrequently. His social aloofness and failure to respond to parental training was apparent to the parents by the time Bret was eighteen months old. Prior to his admission, he had made a shambles of the interior of their new home. He dismantled furniture and appliances with the most primitive tools, e.g., he once removed all screws from the bannister, which was discovered by the father one evening while going to the bathroom— a rather disconcerting experience in the dark to say the least. Electric cords and wires were a major obsession with Bret; he cut and tore them into small pieces.

His behavior also contained numerous tics and mannerisms that appeared regardless of whether he was alone or with other persons. Bret was tantrumous when compliance was insisted upon and often darted away. His darting behavior was occasionally of this avoidance form, but more often was an approach response to some preferred activity, such as wires, climbing, or dismantling some object. Bret was oblivious to the presence of other peers, and a little less so with adults. Eye contact was virtually absent and he was unable to remain seated and work on a supervised task as expected in a special-education classroom.

He was described by referring personnel as hyperactive; it was our impression that this overpopularized description actually resulted from his often irritating aimless wandering and darting. Lack of social control was a more apt description. Bret was an autistic child with a very limited response repertoire whose retardation and massive language comprehension handicap caused his social uncontrol. Toilet training was incomplete; he had severe food preferences; fecal smearing was frequent; and he would invariably strip off all his clothes in a wink in the most embarrassing places.

The family had been "saints" in their endless endeavors to train and tolerate Bret. His wild, unpatterned behavior had essentially eliminated the parents' social life, yet they persisted and cooperated with any service agency who would offer some help for their child. Unfortunately, they only experienced the usual "clinic shuffle," accumulated a variety of diagnostic reports, and were made to feel responsible for Bret's condition. Fortunately, they were sufficiently intact to withstand all this and felt that the professionals were at as much a loss as they were.

Bret was admitted on a research basis. We counseled the parents on the recent research on autistic children so that their expectancies of Bret and us would not be unreasonable. At the three-month evaluation we spoke very directly with the family of giving up and locating a custodial facility for Bret. But, he began to show gradual adaptation to the program and, in fact, looked so encouraging that we retained

him an entire year to strengthen his new habits and arrange placement in an appropriate setting.

As a preamble to this case study, we continuously stressed to the
family the tenuous nature of our treatment effects, the high probability
of retrieval, and the available alternatives should maintenance of his
program become too consuming of the family interactions.

Accelerating Bret's Compliance to Verbal Commands

Behavior Counted: Each command delivered to Bret was counted
as a trial. A success was his attempt to comply within ten seconds;
there two counts yielded a percent compliance to commands.

Treatment A: This was a four-day baseline during which each
command was repeated up to five times, and then dropped. If it was
essential that he comply, such as going to a meal, he was assisted
with as little intervention as possible. Figure 4–8 shows that his compliance to simple commands at this time ranged between 30 and 35
percent.

Treatment B: Bret had ten seconds to start a compliance. If he
was successful in attempting to comply, he would receive social praise

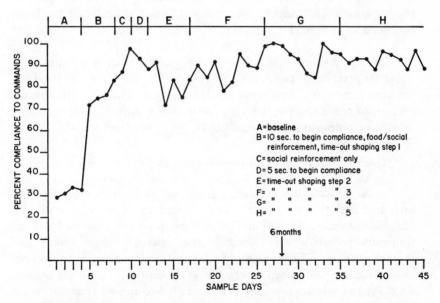

FIGURE 4–8 *Accelerating Bret's Compliance to Verbal Commands With Time-
Out Shaping*

plus small pieces of preferred foods, and a short statement of what he had done correctly. On occasion with new and difficult commands, staff explained that when he complied he would receive a reward (food) which they would show to him, and then deliver the command.

Noncompliance received a time-out according to the current steps he was on in the time-out shaping program. Those steps are shown on figure 4–8 and detailed in the "time-out shaping" section of this case study.

Treatment C: The time-out condition remained the same for this step, but only social praise constituted reinforcement; primaries were deleted from the program. Also, all commands were now restricted to four words, as it had become apparent that numerous noncompliant responses could be attributable to his simply not comprehending what he was told.

Treatment D: All conditions remained the same as above, with the exception that he was required to begin compliance within five seconds when the command was given.

Treatments E–H: All conditions remained the same as in treatment D with the exception that the manner in which a time-out was delivered changed according to the data on the time-out shaping program. Those steps were always an immediate two-minute time-out followed by a five-minute quiet room time-out if he failed to sit according to the behavioral expectancies of that time.

Results: As seen in figure 4–8, Bret's compliance was maintained above 90 percent for the duration of treatment. We always had to keep the commands to simple one- and two-step commands with the exception of some routines which had become habitual, such as getting dressed or going to school unassisted.

Teaching Bret a Time-Out Shaping Program

Behavior Counted: The daily frequency of both two-minute time-outs and five-minute time-outs in the quiet room were tabulated on each sample day. This time-out shaping program was used for all time-outs occurring for noncompliance, darting, aggresssions, and temper tantrums. Thus, when he received a time-out for noncompliance, staff had four possible counts: (1) compliance trial, (2) compliance, (3) two-minute time-out trial, and (4) five-minute time-out in the quiet room. The training progression of this program is shown numerically in figure 4–9.

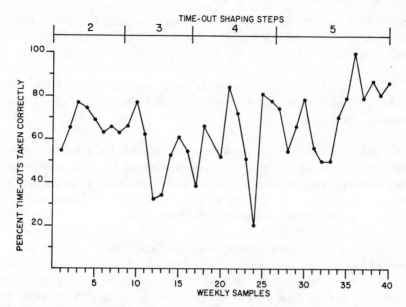

FIGURE 4–9 *Teaching Bret to Take an Appropriate Time-Out*

Treatment A Step 1: For the occurrence of each behavior to be timed-out, Bret received a two-minute time-out in the quiet room which was preceded by a brief statement of what he had done to warrant this punishment procedure. This time-out procedure was continued until his compliance count was 85 percent or higher for two consecutive days. This indicated that the quiet room had a known decelerative effect on behavior, in this case his noncompliance. With this effect established, we had confidence in using the quiet room as a back-up condition for training him to take correct time-outs. Five weeks were required for Bret to attain the 85 percent criterion and advance to Step 2. The data of this first step are not shown in figure 4–9, but the remaining steps of teaching Bret to take a time-out are included.

Step 2: Advancement from this to successive steps was dependent on 85 percent success for two consecutive days in taking two-minute time-outs according to the behavioral requirements at each step. The time-out/quiet room data were recorded daily, and are shown as weekly averages in figure 4–9, which usually masks the last two days when he did receive 85 percent success and was able to progress to the next step. On Step 2, his two-minute time-out was delivered at the spot where the behavior under deceleration occurred. Staff could offer assistance in directing him where to sit down. He received a five-minute time-out in the quiet room only if during this two-minute time-out he raised off his seat. He was allowed to make noises, scoot, and wiggle.

Step 3: The behavioral criteria for a correct time-out was his going unassisted to the place designated by the staff, otherwise it was identical to Step 2.

Step 4: The expectations were more difficult for a correct time-out. He had to go to the time-out place unassisted, keep his seat on the floor without wiggling or scooting, and sit cross-legged with his hands on his legs. Infractions of any of these behavioral requirements resulted in a five-minute time-out in the quiet room.

Step 5: The above expectations were continued with the addition of no talking or noises during the two-minute time-out. Upon attainment of Step 5, the data were only taken in weekly samples since this was the final goal of the program. Seven months transpired before Bret adapted to this shaping step of the program. Perhaps this provides some idea of the massive learning handicaps which characterize these children, and is typical for many autistic children.

Results: We were able to train Bret to take an appropriate time-out, but not without hundreds of trials, performed daily and consistently, including during weekends at home. Bret never achieved continuous errorless performance. We suspect that for children with such discrimination handicaps, sequences of responses are acquired simply by their being rehearsed repetitively, and the reinforcement or punishment conditions may not have the contributing effect we would like to believe. For example, Bret's data in general show that time-outs, be they two-minute or five-minute quiet room ones, served to decelerate a variety of behaviors. Yet his errors in taking two-minute time-outs remained. We suspect that he learned two habits here, by rote recitation: (1) to be seated quietly for two minutes, and (2) to get up from the two-minute time-out and go to the quiet room. In other words, the quiet room succeeded in part to teach him to take a correct time-out, most of this time. But by its frequent administration, he learned the second habit of darting or scooting, and then going to the quiet room.

Decelerating Bret's Aggressive Behavior

Behavior Counted: Aggressions were defined as spitting, kicking, throwing things, hitting, biting, grabbing, or walking on other persons. Aggressions occurring during temper tantrums were included in this count.

Baseline: During this baseline interval of four consecutive days, staff counted these behaviors all day until 8:00 P.M. and did not intervene other than remove themselves or another child from Bret's presence if physical harm was obviously eminent.

Treatment: During treatment he always received a two-minute time-out for each aggression; the time-out was performed according to the current management order previously described for training him to take a correct time-out. Those time-out shaping step intervals are superimposed on figure 4–10. Each time Bret received a time-out he would receive a simple explanation of why, such as, "You hit me. You take a time-out." Upon completion of the time-out, the command would be given again in addition to rehearsing back in the original situation the correct behavior, for example, "Bret, you had a time-out because you hit me. Now go to school and don't hit."

Results: Figure 4–10 shows that aggressive behaviors were responsive to the decelerative effects of the time-out shaping program. It wasn't until the twenty-sixth sampling period that we achieved the

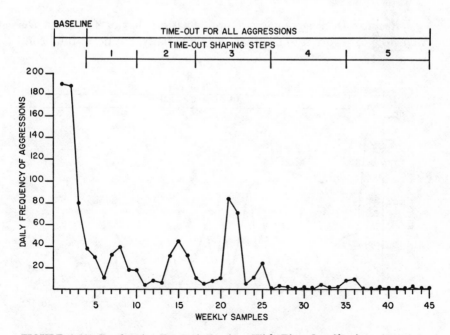

FIGURE 4-10 *Decelerating Bret's Aggressions With Time-Out Shaping*

first zero count for a given sample day: this represented five and one-half months of treatment. Again, the training for an autistic child is a long, arduous one for very simple effects.

Decelerating Bret's Darting Response

Behavior Counted: Darting was defined as Bret's running away while in a structured activity or when walking with staff, on a time-out, or when given a compliance command.

Treatment A: The four-day baseline required that staff lock the door in the cottage since he repeatedly ran out of the building. They allowed him to dart, and gave up to five compliance commands to return. If after this he still did not return, and it was mandatory because of scheduled activities or potentially physically harmful, they would physically retrieve him; the latter was done only when absolutely necessary since we suspected that "the chase" was one of the few reinforcing games Bret had.

Treatment B: This behavior received a two-minute time-out according to the time-out shaping program, which is also shown on the treatment B interval of figure 4–11. This program was conducted all days, but sampled only weekly.

Results: Darting remains a problematic behavior for Bret. We were able to reduce it to less than ten times daily, but never fully con-

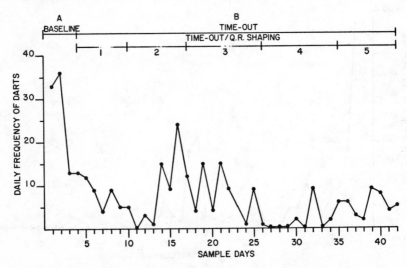

FIGURE 4-11 *Decelerating Bret's Darting Responses With Time-Out Shaping*

trolled the behavior. Two conditions seemed to be responsible for this absence of control. One was that many of these "darts" occurred during time-outs and represented his routine of then going to the quiet room, which had been discussed as a habit pattern he acquired rotely by the training conditions of teaching him how to take an appropriate time-out. Secondly, Bret became increasingly obsessed about wires, any kind of electrical wires, which he would race to, grab, and tear at. He routinely tore the telephone from the wall at home, worked his way through two TV sets in the cottage, cut telephone lines, and shorted out the electrical circuits numerous times in the cottage and home. He even severed a 220-volt line to the home water pump with a pair of scissors, with no greater injury than a momentary dazed look when he emerged from the room. We suspect that he was incredibly pain insensitive. Regardless, this obsession with wires persisted to account for much of his darting; the program to control his concern for wires is described later.

Decelerating Bret's Temper Tantrums

Behavior Counted: Bret's tantrums consisted of any or all of the following: screaming, lying on the floor and kicking or crying, tearing things apart or throwing things (typically his clothes or bedding), and stripping off his clothes.

Treatment A: During this baseline period staff counted the daily frequency of tantrums; each behavior(s) constituting a tantrum had to be separated by an interval of two minutes to receive separate counts. Tantrums in response to commands were allowed to persist, although the command would be delivered up to five times and then discontinued unless it was imperative that he comply, in which case he would be physically assisted. If he was screaming for something which staff could not discern, it was ignored. If they knew what he was tantruming for, he was given that item. This was a controlled baseline designed to replicate those conditions which we suspected maintained this behavior in his natural environment.

Treatment B: This was a two-minute time-out program for all occurrences of tantrums. The shaping steps of the time-out training program are superimposed on figure 4–12.

Results: Tantrums were reasonably limited after the initial controlled baseline. We suspect that staff ignored more tantrums than we intended by our facsimile of his home environment contingency during the baseline, which may have been responsible for the diminu-

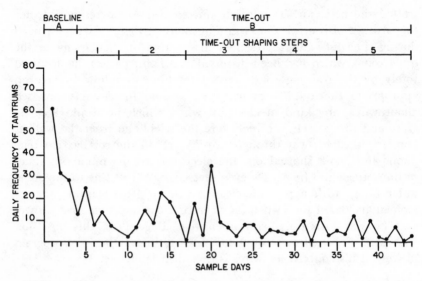

FIGURE 4-12 *Decelerating Bret's Temper Tantrums With Time-Out Shaping*

tion of the behavior at that time. But again, a four-day baseline is not a reasonable time interval to which one may attribute a treatment effect with such a retarded child.

It should be noted that these data encompass eleven months of treatment, and tantrums were still occurring. This indicates a high risk of retrieval after discharge, which the parents and school personnel were appraised of.

Training Bret Appropriate Toileting

Behavior Counted: Staff counted each time Bret defecated or urinated in places other than in the toilet. This was exclusive of nocturnal enuresis. Bret had a habit of urinating in corners, bureau drawers, defecating in closets, and beneath furniture, all of which was disconcerting in its ingenuity of new places.

Treatment A: A four-day baseline was accumulated to discern how frequent this repeated behavior was likely to be. As can be seen in figure 4–13, one could expect three to eight occasions of this behavior daily, during which time he was almost totally avoidant of the group bathroom. It was reported and observed in the home that when he was seated on the toilet he would have to be alone, lights off, stripped of all clothes, and seated backwards on the toilet with a bath towel draped over his head.

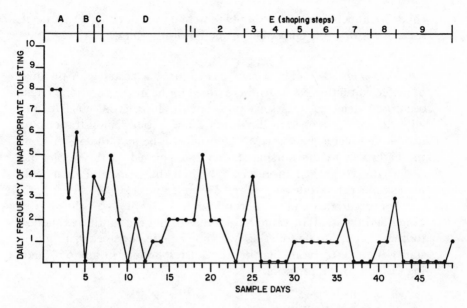

FIGURE 4-13 *Shaping Progression for Teaching Bret Appropriate Toileting*

Bret smeared fecal matter when alone in his room or in the quiet room, and staff bathed him after these episodes. We decided against any "retribution therapy" in which he would be required to clean up his mess. The reason was that this appeared to be in part an aggressive response for Bret, and our forcing him to clean it would exacerbate the aggressive and counteraggressive interaction between him and the accompanying staff member. We decided to make this a positive program to teach him an appropriate and rewarded response, and to extinguish all potential reinforcement of the inappropriate toileting. He was not present when staff cleaned up, so to prevent vicarious reinforcement from their inevitable facial grimaces and utterances of disgust.

Treatment B: This step represents our testing several approaches for developing a toileting program for a child whose inappropriate behavior was in existence for at least five years. His learning handicaps negated our using a simplified priming, modeling, and reinforcing paradigm. The data do not reflect an experimental regimen demonstrating the salient features responsible for eventual control, rather it served as a monitoring device to indicate when we should modify or hold steady with his program. The development of this program was a very real utilization of an experimental-clinical approach with a child. Treatment interval B simply represents our devising a treatment sequence which was embodied in the following steps.

Treatment C: Our first step was to make a poster with pictures of preferred reinforcers which were stored in the nursing station. These comprised items such as soda pop, potato chips, gum, etc. He was allowed, on a free operant basis after a few initial demonstrations, to utilize the toilet as he wished. If he produced, he took the poster from the bathroom to the nursing station and pointed to the reward he preferred. We praised profusely, gave him the item, and then with joy examined the toilet with Bret. He never flushed it.

For occurrences of inappropriate toileting he was shown the poster and the items he could have received, and the routine explained to him. Inappropriate toileting was sampled one day weekly, although staff were able to recall that he was not responding in any outstanding fashion to the program.

Treatment D: This was a pilot study of a modification of the above procedure, which staff felt was too complex to leave on a free operant basis, i.e., to allow Bret to decide when he wished to enter the bathroom. This was wise, since he never demonstrated very complex operant behavior that involved acquisition of new, socially appropriate responses.

This pilot study required that each hour Bret be taken to the bathroom, and shown numerous candies and preferred foods contained in a box. He was first told to stand before the toilet and urinate, for which he was rewarded socially and with primaries, regardless of whether he urinated. After this he would be prompted to sit (no time-outs for noncompliance—this was considered a new response to be acquired) and reinforced with praise and primaries for doing so. He was to be cued continuously for five minutes to remain seated, and reinforced socially as well as with primaries each minute he remained there. He was encouraged to have a bowel movement, which again would be reinforced. He was permitted to strip off his clothing if he wished; it was not recorded as a tantrum when it occurred in the bathroom. Stripping outside of the bathroom was timed-out, however. He was not required to flush the toilet; he was terrified of the noise. Staff checked and initialed the data book when they completed this trial each hour.

After one week we formally adopted the above program which we had "de-bugged" by training all staff to perform it correctly. We also added to this management order that each time Bret wished to go to the bathroom in addition to each hour, it would be done with all the reinforcers made available. However, we were not observing any obvious effects, so a modification was made.

Treatment E: Staff observed that Bret was not showing noticeable interest in the program as a rewarding routine. The daily counts did reflect a diminution in his inappropriate defecation, but it seemed to stabilize to at least twice daily as shown in figure 4–13. In reviewing our effects thus far, three toileting habit patterns were now apparent with Bret: (1) the inappropriate behavior of defecating and urinating in unusual places; (2) using the toilet under the conditions stipulated in treatment D, which implied to us that the reinforcement system was slightly beneficial; and (3) on weekends his use of the toilet, upon occasion, in the bizarre manner of sitting backwards with a towel on his head, in the dark and naked. It was decided to combine the two habit patterns of using the toilet, however strange he may appear, in hopes that we could have a higher frequency per day of using the toilet, and less likelihood of toileting outside of the bathroom. If we could teach him to use the toilet consistently, however bizarrely, we could gradually delete the bizarre mannerisms. Nine steps comprised this program.

1. This was a one-week pilot study which comprised the following:
   a. Bret was taken to the bathroom each half-hour all day, including school.
   b. He was placed in the single toilet bathroom by himself with lights off and permitted to sit naked, backwards on the toilet with a towel draped over his head.
   c. Preferred fruits and candies rewarded defecation and social praise without primaries for urination.
   d. If he disrobed before he could leave the bathroom, he would have to dress again. This was handled as a compliance issue in which he would receive a time-out for refusing to dress.
2. Identical to Step 1, except that he was taken to the bathroom only once each hour.
3. Same as Step 1, except that he had to ask for the towel for his head while seated on the toilet. During the previous step we offered the towel to him when he entered the bathroom.
4. At this step, all conditions of Step 1 remained in effect except that he was not given the towel even when he remembered to ask. In this step, it seemed feasible to no longer give the towel since he had all but ceased asking for it on the preceding step.
5. The program was now altered so that the light would be left on in the bathroom. Since his inappropriate toileting remained

relatively suppressed, and he tolerated this additional change to his program, we advanced to the next step.

6. Bret was now required to sit correctly on the toilet, i.e., not backwards.

7. Bret was now to keep all his clothes on while in the toilet, and to keep his pajamas on in the morning for the first trial. Even if his pajamas were off, which was usually the case when he awoke, he had to put the pajama trousers on before leaving the room.

8. The above conditions remained constant except that staff now reminded him every two hours to use the toilet. The frequency of bathroom visits in the school was every one-half to one hour. He retrieved much of his inappropriate toileting specifically in the school, whereas he continued to respond correctly in the cottage. Thus, we "backed-up" in the classroom and had him go more frequently, although the behavioral criteria remained the same as in the cottage, i.e., being dressed, sitting correctly, etc. During the remaining weeks of his residence this time interval was expanded to hourly visits to the toilet while in school, and remained at that time interval when he was discharged.

9. All bowel movements continued to be reinforced socially and at this time with preferred fruits. Urination was socially reinforced only. He was now just reminded to use the toilet before each meal and evening snacks. He was of course allowed to use the toilet as frequently as possible, with the same reinforcement conditions being maintained.

Results: All of these steps were performed by the parents on the weekends and vacation time in the summer. The data were reasonable; Bret now used the toilet frequently and correctly. However, his inappropriate toileting was only recently controlled and the data stop just prior to his discharge. It would be predictable that this behavior was very likely to be retrieved upon his discharge to the school system, but at least there was a viable shaping hierarchy which could be reinstated, and with sufficient consistency and replication could reinstate correct toileting.

Decreasing Bret's Self-Mutilation

Behavior Counted: The following behaviors were grouped as evidence of self-mutilation, and if two or more occurred simultaneously, they would all be counted.

1. biting himself
2. hitting himself
3. scratching himself
4. banging head on anything

5. hitting himself with some object
6. pulling his own hair
7. kicking himself

We did not count these behaviors during rest period or when he was receiving a time-out. The counts began when he arose in the morning, and continued until 10:00 P.M. He would often demonstrate these behaviors during bedtime settling.

Treatment A-1: This was the first baseline, taken four months after treatment. We did not expose these responses to time-outs initially since it would overload the program in the negative side, and we were also interested to see if they would diminish spontaneously as a general function of the entire program. The data in figure 4–14 certainly indicates the behaviors continued to be present, and rather variable. However, we persisted in not treating these responses for the same above reasons, and we waited another five months and resampled to determine if they would eventually decline.

Treatment A-2: This represents the second baseline, and the variance in Bret's self-mutilation was as great as in the first baseline. It

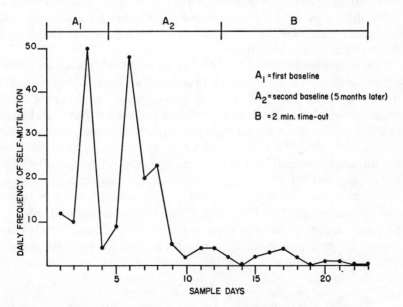

FIGURE 4–14 *Treatment Sequence for Decreasing Bret's Self-Mutilation*

seemed to be in decline at the conclusion of this baseline, but there were no conditions which would lend us to believe that some spurious treatment effect was occurring. Staff were responding to these behaviors the same as always, i.e., ignoring them with what was likely to be no appreciable effect. As for many of Bret's behaviors, and perhaps for other autistic children, the absence of social reinforcement does not have much effect on behavior due to their social aloofness and self-stimulating repertoire. However, the presence of contingencies can have an effect if they are imposed very directly and persistently.

Treatment B: Time-outs had been demonstrated to be effective with Bret, so the two-minute time-out was imposed on each occurrence of these responses. The data show a continued deceleration of self-mutilation so we kept this program in effect.

Teaching Bret to Eat Appropriate Quantities and Varieties of Foods

Behavior Counted: This was one of the more exacerbating habits we tried to train. For years Bret had eaten highly preferred foods; the family fed him separately because he was so disruptive; he had all varieties of histories of unusual eating habits, whose retrievals had disastrous effects on our efforts to train him to eat normally. He had not taken white milk out of a glass for two years before treatment, and for Bret to touch that glass was like asking him to pick up a snake. Such strong preferences dominated his eating, and he had numerous trials of persons withholding food as a contingency for him to eat, and eventually relinquishing this contingency in recognition that a five-day fast was a lark for Bret.

It would be an exercise in futility to review all eleven meal programs we devised and revised for Bret over the course of eight months until the ninth program began to have a stable effect. This ninth program, which was gradually altered to train appropriate and independent eating, was a refinement of an earlier attempted program that almost succeeded. This final meal program represents fairly uniform treatment procedures for conditioning a variety of foods to be reinforcing as outlined in the earlier chapter on treatment techniques. We suspect that the reason the first programs failed was due to the high frequency of asocial behaviors which were so disruptive to the meals. Attempts to control these behaviors while concurrently reinforcing his eating in a situation which had been historically plagued with avoidance behavior made for a confusing situation which usually spiralled Bret.

Baseline A: The first step was to accumulate a list of foods ranging from most preferred to nonpreferred. For all three meals for one week, staff would offer his food during meals, one bite at a time, by placing the utensil with the food on his plate. They offered this food on a one bite per item in a round-robin fashion until the meal was completed or a thirty-minute time period had expired. Staff were to indicate by a plus or minus if he ate each spoonful, this data being marked beside each food listed on the menu. If he ate an entire portion, this would also be noted. The menu was fairly representative of the varieties of foods usually served, so this information allowed us to collate a hierarchy of preferred foods. The empirical evidence indicated he would eat 0 percent of eggs but 100 percent of bites of broccoli, which was then placed near the top of the list of preferred foods. As an average, 52.7 percent of all food trials were successful during this baseline week. Eighty-two foods and dishes were collated into a hierarchy from most to least preferred. It was clear on the extremes of this hierarchy which were the preferred and unpreferred foods, but less distinguishable in the center of the list.

Pilot Program B: This phase of the program lasted one week. At each meal a menu would be posted which indicated the preferred and unpreferred foods. The twelve most unpreferred foods as determined by the baseline were deleted from these meals, and substituted with items Bret was more likely to eat. Each meal then was composed of preferred and not-too-unpreferred foods. Bret would be offered a bite of unpreferred food, which when eaten would be reinforced with a preferred bite. The meal continued in the "round-robin" fashion until all portions were completed. If he refused a nonpreferred food, staff would provide five trials, offering different preferred foods as reinforcers, to induce him to take that bite. If he continued to refuse, the meal would stop, and that food would be saved as the first bite on the next meal. This necessitated our reheating, or cooking anew, that particular dish of food, which fortunately was an infrequent event.

Treatment Program C
Step 1: The above pilot program was then implemented for one month, with the following modifications:

a. If the meal was composed of almost all preferred foods, they were still offered as if some were unpreferred on alternate bites just to maintain the routine of the training. We felt that maintaining set routines was just as important as the reinforcers used in teaching Bret new habits.

b. Instead of counting bites taken of each dish or item on the meal, we relied on an easier rating system, which was:
0 = ate none of meal
1 = ate 1/4 of meal

2 = ate ½ of meal

3 = ate ¾ of meal

4 = ate all of meal

We recognized that ratings 1–3 had considerable subjective judgment involved, which was tolerable, since we were concerned primarily with the frequency of Number 4 rating, which did not require much judgment.

c. The same meal would be prepared for the next time if Bret received a rating of zero.

d. When his weekly average ratings of the amount consumed was 3.8 out of a possible 4.0, we would advance to the next shaping step.

Within twenty-seven days, Bret achieved the 3.8 criteria; in fact, during this entire time interval he succeeded in eating 94 percent of all meals.

Step 2: Since Bret was now eating just about all meals completely, we decided to begin adding foods which were of the twelve most unpreferred. We added cocoa, hot cereals with milk, meat loaf, Swedish meatballs, and potatoes in any form. The same criteria was maintained before proceeding to the next step; it was attained in thirteen days, and he ate 97 percent of all his meals.

Step 3: The very unpreferred foods of pork and beef dishes were now included in Bret's meals. In twenty-one days he reached the 3.8 criteria and his average for the entire three weeks was 94 percent of all meals.

Treatment D: This last step in the meal program commenced one month prior to discharge. We did not require Bret to learn to eat eggs and bread (no child should be required to eat everything!) yet he was eating sandwiches and french toast. We decided that we would now reduce the supervision of the meal, but maintain the routine on which he was successfully trained: that routine was to eat one bite of each food in a clockwise fashion around the plate, until the meal was completed or the thirty-minute mealtime had expired. We dished his food so that preferred and unpreferred foods alternated in their arrangement around his plate. So, everything was the same as in treatment C, except that Bret received a full plate before him, and was supervised with only occasional verbal direction. During this time he achieved 100 percent success in eating all meals, i.e., he always received a rating of 4.0 for all meals.

Results: Bret finally learned to eat exceptionally well when we finally organized a methodical shaping program. We also felt that the eventual success of this program was due to considerable structure being incorporated in the mealtime, and their being performed in a very routinized fashion. This meant that for each step in a meal, Bret had a specific available response. There was very little decision-making involved for him in eating his food sequentially in a clockwise fashion. In previous programs when he would be confronted with deciding to take a bite of potatoes, meat, or vegetables, he would become disorganized as evidenced by throwing food, tantrums, etc.

Teaching Bret Control of Bizarre Mannerisms

Behavior Counted: Bret had a plethora of motor tics, jerks, and contortions which we grouped under the rubric of bizarre mannerisms. These behaviors included: flipping of his earlobes; masturbating; contorted facial expressions; tic-like touching of his lips, ears, arms, or legs in an inappropriate manner; touching other persons or objects in this same unusual way; plugging ears; and repetitively wrinkling and picking his nose. Each response would receive a count of one, except when he would go through the routine of tapping his nose, ears, arms, and legs in one quick motion, which would receive only a count of one. Some of these tic-like responses were so quick that it was almost impossible to notate each one. Each response had to be separated by at least two seconds to receive separate counts; this criterion made it much simpler for staff to decide upon separate bizarre mannerisms. These responses were not counted during rest periods.

Treatment A: This was the first baseline as shown in figure 4–15 and was run for five consecutive days one month after his admission. Staff ignored these mannerisms at all times.

Treatment B: One month later, we began counting but not treating these behaviors. Again, we wanted to determine if bizarre responses would decline when other atypical responses were being treated, such as his aggressions, darting and noncompliance. As shown in figure 4–15, daily frequency of bizarre responses, which were sampled one day every two weeks, did not diminish. The biweekly sampling periods were continued for six months; Bret did not generalize from other controlled behaviors to his bizarre mannerisms.

Treatment C: We decided to control Bret's mannerisms sequentially, beginning with those performed on other people. At this step each time he licked or touched another person in his peculiar way, he received a two-minute time-out in accordance with the shaping

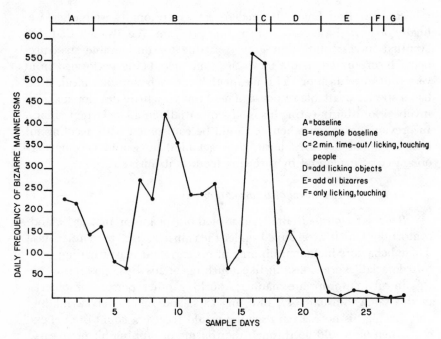

FIGURE 4-15 *Teaching Bret Control of Bizarre Mannerisms*

step he was on. Staff would demonstrate and explain to him what he had done; we questioned him to make him very aware of these mannerisms. They would not lick him in their demonstration, but would extend their tongues, point to theirs and say, "No licking." The data in figure 4–15 were one sample day during the one week of treatment C, and the continued responses of bizarre mannerisms spiked during this treatment.

Treatment D: It was decided to continue with the addition of a new response—licking or kissing other objects, such as the floor, were now also subjected to the time-outs. We were not concerned about the initial acceleration of bizarres during treatment C, since exacerbation of a response usually precedes deceleration as the individual operates more frantically for the old, preferred, contingencies. Figure 4–15 illustrates that during D we were beginning to realize a stabilization of this behavior.

Treatment E: In the third step to eliminate bizarres we added all of his bizarre mannerisms. This was risky, since it is preferred to approach such multiple responses in a more sequential order so the child is not being exposed to an excessively punitive program. We took the risk in this instance because we were fast approaching the discharge date. To clarify figure 4–15, treatments C–G were sampled weekly, as contrasted to B, which was every two weeks. Fortunately, during treatment E, Bret was adapting to the program and demonstrating fewer of all of his bizarre mannerisms.

Treatment F: Typical of so many decelerated behaviors in these children, low level approximations began to emerge in Bret. His head tic had become a movement of tilting his head toward either shoulder. If he moved his head greater than one-half this distance, he would receive a time-out. Low level facial grimaces appeared in the form of slightly extending his lips and/or wrinkling his nose. These were not timed-out, but he was told not to do that expression, which if necessary was demonstrated to him. These low-level facial grimaces were not included in the combined bizarre mannerism count, so there is no evidence to conclude this was a useful procedure.

Treatment G: This was the final step of the program in which we now only timed-out the original licking and touching responses, which were observed to be most resilient to the time-out condition.

Results: Figure 4–15 shows that appreciable control had been gained over these varied mannerisms, which when unchecked for a six-month period did not diminish spontaneously. It is predictable that Bret has a high risk of retrieving these behaviors, and that if the program is not implemented consistently, for all responses, they will quickly attain this pretreatment status. Bret's pattern during the baseline is another example which does not support the contention that deviant behaviors will "go away" when a number of others are exposed to treatment. Each response has to be treated specifically, and one never hopes for spontaneous generalization effects, but does anticipate retrieval.

Non-Data Programs

Destructiveness: Bret's affinity for destroying any appliance with a wire, plus furniture and mechanical objects, was unbelievable. If there were any planful pursuits for Bret, it was in this behavior—the channeling and control of which plagued us. A series of programs were designed to modify this behavior to an appropriate form and eventually to control his apparent impervious habits of destroying objects— none of which met with appreciable success. He routinely tore the telephone from the wall on weekends, and eventually ruined two televisions in the cottage by rushing up and pushing them on the floor.

Short circuits, telephones out of order, doors that fell from their hinges could always be traced to Bret's manipulation of these things.

The program that we placed the greatest emphasis on was teaching him an alternate response. In collaboration with the family, we accumulated a large box of mechanical and electrical objects (e.g., old appliances, tools, Erector set, etc.). We scheduled two fifteen-minute daily sessions at a designated place in close proximity to objects, such as the TV which he typically destroyed. He was reinforced socially and with primaries for increasing time intervals of playing with these objects and not bolting to the TV, etc. Failures to remain at the place and attempting to destroy anything not in his special box received a time-out. We were successful in teaching Bret to play at these times with his special toys with minimal supervision and reinforcement. However, the counts of his succeeding, or attempting, to tear wires from the walls, upset the TV, etc., were totally unaffected by this program. We began to time-out his destructive responses and eventually had to time-out his staring at these objects (other than watching a TV show), which was the invariable precursor to his destroying that object. This program was in effect up his discharge at which time there was no convincing evidence that we had achieved any definite diminuation of this behavior.

In hindsight, we suspected that the program of his playing with wires and appliances only served to reinforce this kind of behavior. We thought we were teaching him to play with permitted items, in a structured setting, and that this would substitute for those inappropriate occasions when he would attack a light switch, fire alarm, etc. He obviously learned to do both things, each being reinforced.

Conclusion: There were numerous other programs for specific behaviors for Bret which were composed of rehearsal and reinforcement in sessions and in vivo. Language was the most important of these, in which specific responses were taught in sessions, assessed for accuracy in school to determine when he could advance to more difficult items, with continual reinforcement of spontaneous language. To illustrate the difficulty of Bret's language acquisition, eight months' training were required to progress through the following questions, trained in two daily ten-minute sessions in cottage and school: (1) "What is it?" (2) "What color?" (3) "Who is it?" (4) "Where is it?" and (5) "Yes or no" questions.

Other specific phrases were taught, such as "Please help me," "Excuse me," "Toothpaste please," etc. Staff would continually attempt to stimulate speech rehearsing and reinforce it socially and with primaries during the day. His daily frequency (we accumulated a bi-weekly total day word count) of words remained stable, but were more varied in content. The new words and phrases were always ones which had been specifically trained. As with Bret's other behaviors, he learned to do just exactly what he was taught, and new, spontaneous combinations of habits did not emerge. Low-level approximations of decelerated responses were considered to be more of the same behavior.

In conclusion we predict that Bret will always require a highly structured environment, capable of maintaining this training. To expect that of a family, however well trained, is questionable. The amount of constant supervision to support their treatment effects would very likely be destructive to a home. Residential care is questionable. How many facilities are prepared to deal with the many behaviors required for Bret? The current alternative is usually massive sedation under the disguise of chemotherapy to simply eliminate all behavior. During the course of Bret's treatment he never received medication. His appearance from admission to discharge was like a Mr. Hyde and Dr. Jekyl; reliance on drug intervention would have a similar destructive effect on Bret. We continue to maintain that Bret's most grievous problem is his retardation. We know that he can be programmed to be a very compliant child, but we correspondingly know the energy and planning required to perform those programs. So, at the conclusion of Bret's study we are once again faced with the dilemma that at this stage of educational and mental health programming, it is unlikely that the treatment effects will be sustained.

CASE STUDY: DAVID

Admission Age: 6 years, 9 months.

Duration of Residency: 6 months.

Diagnosis: Moderate retardation, emotionally disturbed, considered borderline psychotic; had normal neurological and EEG, but had accumulated a diversity of diagnoses through several evaluations which bridged the entire diagnostic range from brain damage to psychosis to simple retardation.

Admission IQ: Untestable.

Discharge IQ: Stanford-Binet, Form L-M; IQ = 53.

Specified Referral Problems: David could not be retained a special-education class available in his home community because: (1) no available comprehensible speech; (2) whined and cried in group setting when attempted to be taught; (3) absence of peer interaction; (4) low compliance; (5) oblivious to people and learning materials; (6) gross- and fine-motor coordination were unusually poor, which also raised the question of neurological involvement, although this was not substantiated by evaluation.

David's superficially pensive appearance in combination with his bizarre mannerisms prompted the diagnosis of psychosis from referring professionals, rather than emphasizing the reality of his retardation.

Teaching Eye Contact for Two-Second Duration

Behavior Counted: The percent of training trials in which David successfully maintained at least two-second eye contact.

Treatment A: Staff would be seated facing David and deliver the verbal cue of "Look." He was provided social praise plus tokens for each trial if he looked directly at the staff within one second and held that eye contact for two consecutive seconds. At least five seconds would intervene between trials. Staff did not have him look longer than two seconds before rewarding, even though he may have seemed capable of doing so. The tokens were redeemable for preferred candies, but we actually doubted that he comprehended this contingency. In fact, staff would have to remind him to exchange them for candies.

Treatment B: Staff would be seated facing David, the same as above. The verbal cue of "David" was now provided instead of "Look." Social praise was provided for every correct trial, and tokens also for every third correct trial. He had to initiate eye contact within one second of the cue, and had to hold that eye contact for two consecutive seconds. Five seconds also intervened between trials.

Results: Figure 4–16 illustrates the progress of this treatment. This program was first conducted concurrently with attention training in the school. The results were satisfactory; 85 percent criteria was achieved for responding to his name with at least two-second eye contact. This eye contact program was extended in the school for the purpose of teaching attention-to-teacher commands and his responding to the teacher. The eye contact duration of two seconds was considered sufficient in the cottage for speech training sessions.

Teaching David to Remain in His Seat During School

Behavior Counted: We recorded the frequency of David's getting up from his seat in the classroom; his time out of the seat was not

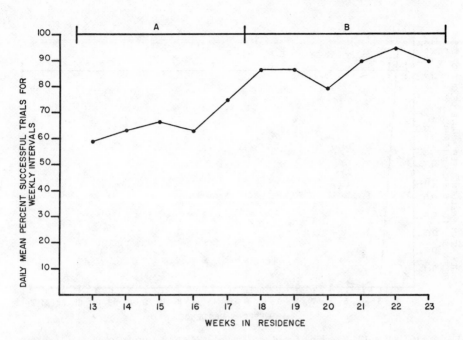

FIGURE 4–16   *Training David to Maintain a Two-Second Eye Contact*

measured in this program. We were concerned with an "all or none" effect, i.e., he was to remain in a regular classroom until instructed to do otherwise, which is a predictable requirement for his retainment in a public school. Being out of his seat at a high frequency even for extremely short intervals of time would be disruptive to any classroom. He had to either be up or down as instructed by the teacher.

Treatment A: Figure 4–17 shows the baseline of the number of times per minute David was out of his seat during class time. Neither reprimand nor instruction was given to return David until a reasonable period of time had passed and the instructional materials required the teacher to command him to be seated again so there would be some semblance of classroom instruction during the baseline period. Consistency of instructions to return to his seat was not maintained during this time. Thus, the teacher had freedom in how she wished to return David to his seat. If he returned shortly by himself, nothing was said whatsoever.

Treatment B: While seated, and on a variable time schedule, the teacher would socially praise David for remaining seated. This was expanded gradually so that a greater time period intervened between

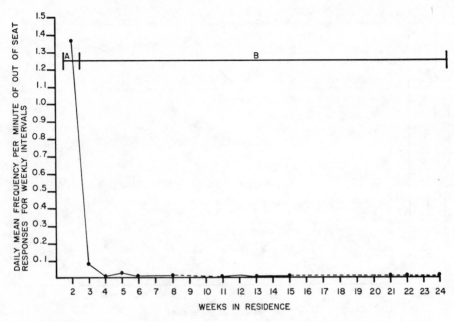

FIGURE 4–17 *Teaching David to Remain in His Seat During School*

praises as the program progressed. Each time he began to rise from his seat, the teacher, in anticipation of his leaving, would tap his desk, with a firm look that commenced the unmistakable message of "sit down." Thus, positive reinforcement for the correct response, and a cue which signaled some implied social punishment for the inappropriate behavior comprised the program.

Results: This was a satisfactory program in which the reinforcement schedule was thinned by discharge time so that it was readily manageable in the public school classroom. Also, this program met the condition of reinforcing an alternate response, with a minimum punishment effect involved in controlling the undesirable behavior. In fact, he was never directly punished; there was only an implied social punishment by the teacher tapping his desk.

Teaching David to Attend to Teacher Instruction and Maintain Attention while Responding for up to Ten Seconds Duration

Behavior Counted: The total number of training trials and the number of successful trials at the response criterion level were counted. This yielded a percent success measure for successive levels of the training program. When an 85 percent criterion was established we progressed to the next shaping step.

Treatment A: Staff counted the number of the successful trials in which he looked at the teacher to her cue: "David, look at me," for the criterion level of a one-second eye contact. This program ran concurrently with the eye contact training in the cottage, which accounts for the rather high initial rate of training. The rewards used were social praise for each correct response plus a star that was redeemable for preferred candies. This token system was unusual in that he collected the stars and redeemed them for candies which he hoarded and seldom ate, yet the entire system seemed to be effective as a reinforcing procedure. Perhaps the social reinforcement was responsible for the treatment effect.

Treatment B: Same as treatment A, but the response criterion was raised to two seconds.

Treatment C: Same as treatment A, but the response criterion was raised to three seconds.

Treatment D: Same as treatment A, but the response criterion was raised to five seconds.

Treatment E: Same as treatment A, but the response criterion was raised to eight seconds.

Treatment F: Same as treatment A, but the response criterion was raised to ten seconds.

Results: In this shaping program, depicted in figure 4–18, David learned to maintain 90 percent of the total commands directed to him by his teacher for at least ten seconds of eye contact. Thus, he was available for instructional commands, as well as for giving responses in which he would attend to the person he was talking to for that predictable time duration. This ten-second criterion was necessary for academic materials, group instruction, and group classroom participation. This time period is usually not required for the acquisition of speech responses, but David had such difficulty with language acquisition it was considered necessary.

Decelerating David's Whining in Both the Cottage and School

Behavior Counted: Total number of times David whined in the form of a whimpering cry.

Treatment A: The baseline was accumulated by counting the daily frequency of whining in the cottage and school. Duration was

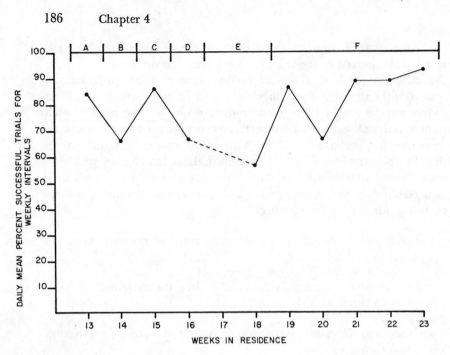

FIGURE 4–18 *Teaching David to Maintain a Ten-Second Eye Contact in School*

not recorded for these data. We were concerned with completely controlling the whining behavior; we did not want a treatment effect of partially decelerating the duration, but rather, a complete effect since this behavior had such a long and pervasive history.

Treatment B: Each time David whined, he received a one-minute time-out where the behavior occurred. He had been trained to take a time-out in other programs and if he did not take a silent time-out at the spot commanded, he was placed in the quiet room for a two-minute back-up as punishment. After his time-out had transpired, he had to tell the staff member what he had wanted, or what caused him to whine or cry. Thus, we were asking for an alternate response to replace his whining, and it was to be initiated by him. We were extinguishing the cycle of whining to make known his needs, however diffuse they may be, in which people anticipated his wishes and thereby reinforced his whining. Staff cued David as much as necessary for him to produce a simple explanation of his problem, which was congruent with the current level of his language training. Social reinforcement was used exclusively in this program.

Results: As shown in figure 4–19, whining in the cottage was not as effectively controlled as it had been in the school. The more con-

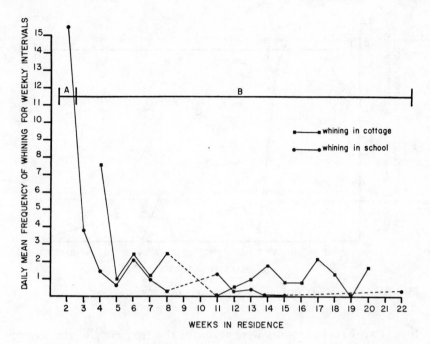

FIGURE 4–19   *Daily Frequency of David's Whining in Cottage and School*

sistent structuring available in the school contrasted to the more spontaneous social interactions in the cottage and may have been partially responsible for this difference in the program. The prognosis is that to maintain or reinstate this level of communicative skill in place of whining would require the consistent structure we had available in the school. Unfortunately, that criterion was never optimally satisfied, and every six to twelve months after his discharge, the family and school had to be retrained as he retrieved this whining as an alternate to the sparse and very difficult-to-produce language he acquired.

Decelerating Inappropriate Mealtime Behavior in David

Behavior Counted: The following behaviors occurring at mealtimes were counted for David and sampled periodically during the course of this treatment program: licking his plate, giggling inappropriately, wiggling in his chair, grabbing food, fingering food, and lying over on the table during the meal.

Treatment Baseline: The data shown in figure 4–20 only contain results of the treatment condition itself without reference to a base-

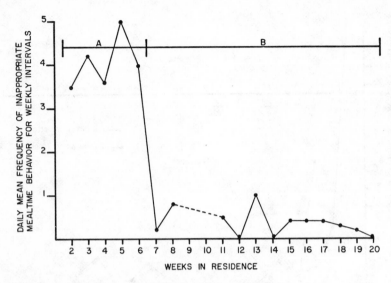

FIGURE 4–20   *David's Inappropriate Mealtime Behavior*

line. Two baseline counts were taken of the frequency of the above
behaviors several days before commencement of the program. On the
first day, he made sixty-nine inappropriate manners, and on the
second day staff observed fifty-eight occurrences of these behaviors
during the course of the three meals.

Treatment A: This treatment condition was held constant
throughout this program. Each time that David demonstrated any of
the above behaviors that he was forewarned of before each meal, he
received a two-minute time-out. He took this two-minute time-out on
the bench in the hall outside the dining room. If he did not sit quietly
and take a correct time-out, he received a thirty-second time-out in
the quiet room installed in the hallway for this purpose. Just before
David received his time-out, staff told him what he had done wrong,
for example, "You do not lie on the table at meals, and you do not
finger your food."

Results: Satisfactory, since the daily rate of sixty or more inappropriate mealtime behaviors was decelerated close to one or zero
per day. This did not mean that he was holding his fork perfectly,
or sitting straight in his chair. He was able to talk during meals at the
end of this program rather than slouching excessively over the table.
At the inception of the program, when he finished eating the few preferred foods he would avoid by playing with the food or similar
inappropriate behaviors which others took as a cue that he was
finished eating. At the termination of this program, he was able to

complete his meal appropriately, with language occurring as indicated by his speech program and ask to be excused. Needless to say, he would still be obvious in a restaurant.

Improving David's Speech Articulation and Comprehension

Behavior Counted: Total number of correct training trials occurring in each speech session in the cottage were recorded.

Treatment A: This treatment, as indicated in figure 4–21, refers to the use of social reinforcement for correct or approximately correct responses. This contingency was maintained throughout the course of the training procedure.

Treatment B: This treatment refers to the initial comprehension training program. This program was composed of trials progressing from simple to more difficult, by training responses to the following hierarchy of questions: (1) What is this? (2) Yes and No games. (3) How many? (4) What color? (5) What does this do (or what is it used for)? (6) What is the _____ doing?

These trials were ones in which positive practice was implemented when he did not have a correct or acceptable and reinforceable response. Then, the staff provided him with an acceptable response, had him repeat it, and then reinforced him for that extent of success. With particularly difficult responses, several rehearsals occurred.

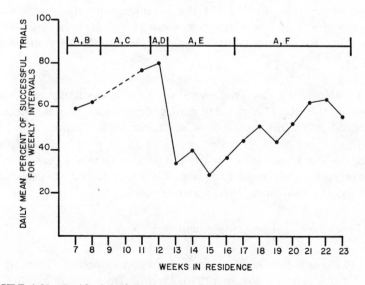

FIGURE 4–21 *David's Speech Program in the Cottage*

The articulation training during this treatment step was that of training him to use the "b" and "p" sounds at the beginning, middle, and ending positions of words. This training session was conducted once a day in the cottage for approximately twenty minutes, and practiced in vivo frequently during the day whenever David was expected to speak.

Treatment C: This treatment was a comprehension and articulation program which was an extension of the B treatment step. The comprehension program was composed of training sessions in which staff would demand phrases or sentences for questions regarding "yes and no questions" and "what color is something."

During Step B, he was taught to fill in words of statements staff provided him, such as: "The ball is _____," whereas in Step C, he had to give an entire phrase or sentence by himself in order to be reinforced. Articulation training in treatment Step C involved practicing the sounds "m" and "h" at the beginning, middle, and ending positions of words; training was also maintained for the previously acquired responses indicated in Step B.

Treatment D: The comprehension items trained at this time were questions regarding time and self-concept, i.e., questions regarding himself. These questions replaced items 3 and 4 in treatment condition B. The remainder of those items in B were used, and at this step we now required a full sentence for a reinforceable response. Articulation training was a continuance of the above trained sounds, but adding sounds "k" and "g" at the beginning, middle, and ending positions of words. The management orders had detailed instructions on how to elicit each particular sound from David which was unusually difficult for him.

Treatment E: Comprehension training in sessions was discontinued at this stage. A general management order was in effect in which staff asked him questions as in a normal conversation, for which he received positive practice and assistance in learning how to respond correctly. The articulation training at this stage was a repetition of those sounds already acquired in steps B through E, and was performed on errors elicited during this in vivo training.

Treatment F: The management order was as follows:

1. Do not let David rehearse incorrect responses. Thus, if he says *gair* for *fair*, say, "No, David." Do not just ask him to

repeat, but rather make him position his tongue, teeth and lips correctly and then ask for the correct response.

2. Make sure he is looking and sitting quietly first.

3. Rehearse correct response several times; do not stop with just one correct trial.

4. Let him know specifically what he has done wrong, and the same when he has done something right. Thus, if he has said *cat* for *cake*, say, "No 't' David, 'k'." Then have him repeat, *cake*. The same if he says *goodbye;* make sure to praise him for a good "b" sound.

5. Break down into syllables and separate sounds of those words which he has a lot of difficulty with. Thus: wa ter mel on; even: w-w-w- a-a-a- if that is necessary to break it down that minutely.

6. If he gets fixed on a sound or word such as *wat* for *rat,* then change and have him say, *row, ra* and *re.* Then *ra* and finally *rat.* Then have him repeat it.

7. Again, if he says part of a word correctly and the rest incorrectly, make sure to let him know what part is incorrect; thus, you are not punishing the entire response as incorrect.

8. He should be able to say the sounds of letters b, p, g, m, n, t, c, d, j, and k correctly with no prompting, especially in beginning positions.

9. Sounds of letters f, h, l, q, r, s, v, w, x, and z still need work as far as helping him position his teeth, tongue, and lips and rehearsing correct responses.

10. Short "i" sounds such as in *milk* still need work as to blends. The other vowel sounds are good.

11. Exaggerate sounds to get them: "ee-yes"

12. Exaggerate your lip, tongue and teeth movements.

13. Try looking in the mirror at the way you do make sounds.

14. Try helping him position his teeth, tongue, and lips with your hands and helping him hold his hands there as well.

This represents a typical speech management order, which for David all staff had to be capable of performing.

Extension of Results: Example of Organizational Plan of Treatment

The degree of success achieved with David was in part a function of the organizational groundwork established for him during his residency and after discharge. In his residential program, he was trained at the very low level of how to attend to another human being as a prerequisite to teaching him the majority of the other behaviors. As the program progressed, this training approach was converged to: his community teacher to whom he was discharged, the social worker from the referring agency, and most important, his mother. At the time of discharge, David was a talking child eligible for placement in a special classroom in his community and capable of functioning in a small group. By that date, the teacher, speech therapist, and parent had all been trained by our special-education teacher and David's special staff so they could maintain his treatment programs. At the conclusion of the school year in his community, his progress had been satisfactory to the teacher and family. At the next autumn when he began school, we performed a follow-up on his adjustment which was in the same school, with the same teacher. A typical change had occurred that we had noted in many other children similar to David. During the summer he had gradually retrieved old behaviors, characteristically his isolation and mutism. He retrieved very gradually and the mother never realized the growing silence and isolation surrounding David each successive day during the summer. She was retrieving her old behaviors of dealing with David, of talking for him, of anticipating his needs, and simply forgetting the level of achievement he was capable of and maintaining such standards. When he returned to school, his teacher was rather chagrined by his mutism but accepted it as her problem and did not immediately call us for assistance. The speech therapist accepted this reversion with similar disconcern. In our follow-up, we were not surprised by the change, but we were amazed at the rate in which it occurred and how other adults were so slow to react to the significance of retrieval.

Our organizational outline was for our special-education teacher to retrain the teacher, teacher's aide, and the speech therapist. This was achieved by (1) showing them what David had done, (2) describing what prior adjustment had been accomplished in their school, (3) explaining the programs necessary for reinstating his behaviors, and (4) demonstrating these programs to them. Several visits were necessary to reteach everyone these skills. The programs taught were the most simple ones: attention, articulation and comprehension problems, compliance, and not allowing him to avoid but retaining him in a work situation until he makes the correct response. His avoidance would receive a time-out in an out-of-the-way place in the classroom. These professionals were taught that they had to push David rather hard to initiate his performance, but that after performance was achieved to some extent he was available for positive reinforcement and more enjoyable to teach. At that time, the family trainer of the group began retraining the mother one night a week at the Treatment Center. We scheduled a home visit where we analyzed what the mother was doing with David to reinstate his behavior and also arranged for her to work with other professionals teaching her son so that she could become more aware of his level of performance. After six weeks of retraining, she could maintain his behavior, and the improvement of his language and performance at school merited our intervention.

The value of this program is that we were able to program for a problem which is typical with many youngsters after residential care. It is normal to expect that they will reacquire many of the referral behaviors and lose the treatment gains you had achieved with them. This has no reflection upon the value of the residential program itself. The program, in this case, for example, was quite successful in teaching him the kinds of behavior necessary for school. But, he had seven years of the behaviors which rejected him from school, and six months of our training, so it is no surprise that the habit strength was the dominant with the old abnormal behaviors. In this example, the mental-health clinic social worker did have sessions with the mother to determine if there were any personal problems which may have been in part responsible for her inability to perform the program. We learned this was not the case; rather, that she had gradually retrieved her habit patterns of seven years in contrast to the six months of our parent training, and at such a gradual rate that she was never aware of David's retrieval of his old behavior. This follow-up will have to be maintained with David for years, and his adjustment to society will always be problematic. It may be that his old behaviors will eventually never be reacquired, but because of his limited intellectual resources, it is expected that he will always have difficulty in coping with many new expectancies as he approaches the adult world.

CASE STUDY: GEORGE

Admission Age: 5 years, 7 months.

Duration of Residency: 6 months.

Diagnosis: Referral diagnosis of childhood schizophrenia, accepted.

Admission IQ: Two months prior to admission George was administered the Stanford-Binet Form L-M and received a mental age of 4 years, 6 months, with an equivalency IQ of 83.

Discharge IQ: Chronological age of 6 years, 2 months; on a Stanford-Binet Form L-M he received a mental age equivalency of 5 years, 10 months, and an IQ of 94.

Specified Referral Problems: George and his twin brother, John, were not acceptable for a public school placement because of their incomprehensible language, noncompliance to commands, obliviousness to peers and hyperactivity. An outstanding characteristic of the twins was their obliviousness to other persons. They did have daily routines at home that were very simple. However, they did require supervision in these routines. Their bedrooms were almost devoid of furniture and decor because they would demolish them if left unsupervised. If not observed when outside, they would wander off into the village. It was our impression that these children had received very little child-rearing: essentially they had raised each other, acquiring their own crude language which was an approximation of what they were imitating from other persons. It was almost impossible to understand what the twins were saying unless you had worked with them for a long period of time. It was our suspicion that these children had definite handicaps at birth, but they had since been accentuated by the lack of training they received in the home.

Training Compliance to Verbal Commands

Behavior Counted: The behavior counted was the daily frequency of commands directed towards George on sample days and the number of compliant responses to those commands. This information led to a percent compliance to commands as shown in figure 4–22 for the baseline and treatment condition.

Treatment A: This treatment, the baseline, was five consecutive days in which staff counted the compliances to their commands. For each command given, ten seconds was allowed for him to begin compliance which was tabulated as a success. They repeated the command up to five times if necessary. The command was discontinued unless it were mandatory that he complied, such as coming inside, whereby they physically moved him through that command, but without admonishment. During the baseline he was not praised for compliance; the behavior was on a controlled baseline.

Treatment B: This treatment required that if he initiated a compliant response within ten seconds after the command was given, he was reinforced and it was counted as a success. If he did not initiate the response within that ten seconds, he received a time-out. If he

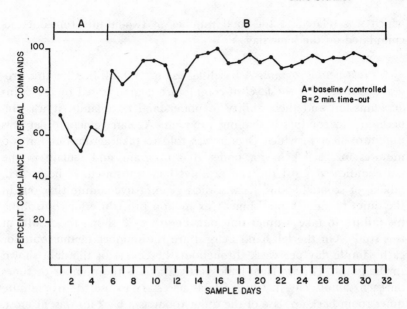

FIGURE 4–22   *Accelerating George's Compliance to Verbal Commands*

ceased the response after he had begun, he was given another trial with the same ten-second interval and the procedure would be repeated. After receiving a time-out for noncompliance, he was taken back to the same situation, and on a positive practice basis he was given the same expectation again with the alternative of either social reinforcement with random primary reinforcement or a time-out for noncompliance. The commands given were simple and at a verbal level he could comprehend; all compliance was reinforced on a 100 percent schedule socially.

The time-outs he received coordinated with the program of training him to take an appropriate time-out. This program required that for each two-minute time-out that he did not take correctly, he would receive a five-minute time-out in the quiet room. The program was considered to be successful as shown in figure 4–22, in that the compliance progressed to greater than 95 percent and remained steady. Furthermore, he was not required to receive time-outs in a quiet room at an unusual rate during the course of this program as described below.

Training George to Take an Appropriate Time-Out

Behavior Counted: This count consisted of daily frequency on sample days when he received a five-minute time-out in the quiet room, which was related to the total number of two-minute time-outs accumulated on the same day.

   Treatment Program: A baseline was not established for this program. Considering the level of compliance demonstrated by the twins at admission and their ability to understand commands, it was unnecessary to conduct a shaping program. A management order was put into effect in which George was told to take a time-out for two minutes for each behavior under that program, and remain in the place indicated until the two minutes had transpired. If he moved, talked, or scooted about, he was then given a five-minute time-out in the quiet room as a punishment/extinction procedure for controlling his failure to take a quiet time-out. Figure 4–23 shows the results of this study. On the left-hand margin are the number of time-outs for each sample day per week throughout the course of the data shown in the graph. On the right-hand vertical axis is the number of times on each sample day in which it was necessary to use the five-minute quiet room back-up. Use of the quiet room as a back-up was, at most, once a day even when he received seven or more time-outs; most of the time it was unnecessary to use the five-minute quiet room time-out. This program was considered successful in teaching George to take

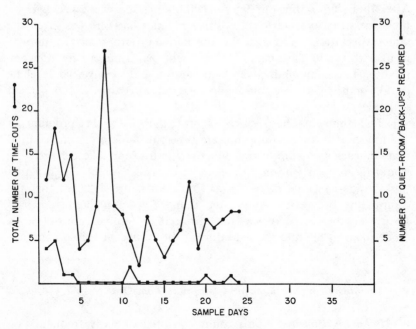

FIGURE 4–23   *Time-Out Shaping Program for George*

an appropriate time-out, unsupervised in a form that could be utilized in a public school classroom when the behaviors emerged after discharge.

Controlling Aggressive Behavior

Behavior Counted: On the successive five-day baseline, and for the weekly samples taken thereafter, the total number of aggressive behaviors occurring on those days were counted as shown in figure 4–24. Aggression was defined as making physical contact with another youngster—usually in the form of hitting, pushing, shoving, and tripping. These were usually very subtle maneuvers, and transpired between the twins quite regularly as well as toward other children. Frequency of that behavior is shown on the baseline which had a range from twenty to over fifty per day.

Treatment B: The treatment sequence was a two-minute time-out for each occurrence of aggressive behavior. The two-minute time-out was coordinated with the time-out shaping program. Thus, George or John would receive a two-minute time-out for aggressive behavior and be seated at the spot where the behavior occurred or in a corner. If they moved, talked, or scooted, they had a five-minute back-up time-out in the quiet room. This two-minute time-out was effective in decelerating the behavior, as shown in figure 4–24. However, there was a frequency of zero to three aggressions per day which persisted during the course of treatment. A positive practice regimen was performed in conjunction with each time-out. After the time-out had terminated, the child was taken back to the situation where the aggressive behavior occurred, and made to apologize to that person. He usually needed verbal cues to articulate an appropriate apology, and upon completion he was verbally reinforced.

A few weeks before discharge, it was observed that the twins were both showing taunting as well as an occasional aggressive response toward other children. Their aggressiveness had changed in quality, having a more verbal character to it now, but still was of a provocative nature that would be difficult in the public school. We were very concerned that if this behavior of verbal aggression and teasing were to accelerate and persist after their discharge back into the public school, it would contribute to their being rejected from that facility. Furthermore, these were children could not tease like a normal child. If another youngster countered they would be liable to retrieve their more physical aggression which would be intolerable in the classroom. These were youngsters who had been trained to apologize upon command, who had been controlled for their frequency of physical aggres-

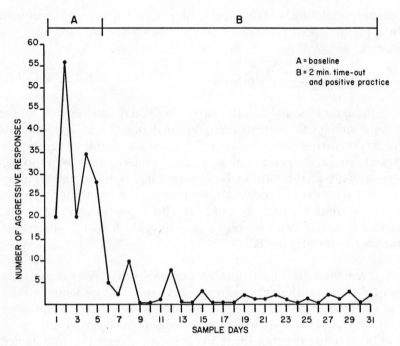

FIGURE 4-24   *Deceleration of George's Aggressive Behavior*

sion, and who were now acquiring verbal aggression. They had been trained to interact in a variety of complex situations, but they were not prepared for consequences for taunting and teasing normal peers. Thus, we decided to control this behavior very rapidly. This was accomplished by a program used with other children where it is imperative to control new low-level responses acquired just prior to an impending discharge (case of "Will" in Browning and Stover 1971). For each occurrence of these verbal aggressions, the child received a one-half hour interval of time in his room whereby he had to put on his pajamas and climb into bed. When the one-half hour was completed, he dressed and began his day over again with all the positive reinforcement available for commencing correctly and continuing to perform appropriately thereafter. He was informed very clearly why he had to take this time-out in his room in pajamas to start the day over. Verbal admonishment was not utilized, and staff responses were very straightforward and explanatory. Verbal aggression was of a very low rate, usually once or twice a day. The program did succeed in controlling this behavior at our facility, but it was not transferred successfully to the home, and there were occasions when this behavior was observed back in the school after discharge. The program may have been successful if the parents had adapted its implementation in the home at discharge.

Training Eye Contact as a Prerequisite to Language Articulation Training

Behavior Counted: The trials and successful responses elicited for the two eye contact programs in the school and cottage are represented in figures 4–25 and 4–26 as the percent correct responses occurring during the sampled training trial days.

Eye Contact Training—School: For the first two months, eye contact training was conducted in sessions in school. This delay for training in the cottage was due to the difficulty in scheduling.

In the school program, a baseline was taken of all anticipated training steps before they began. These data are shown in figure 4–25, contained under the five successive days of the "A" interval on the graph. The five days of the baseline sequentially represent the testing of eye contact at increasing distances. During the baseline, he received ten trials with the teacher attempting to elicit eye contact for one second at one, three, four, five, and ten feet. From this baseline data

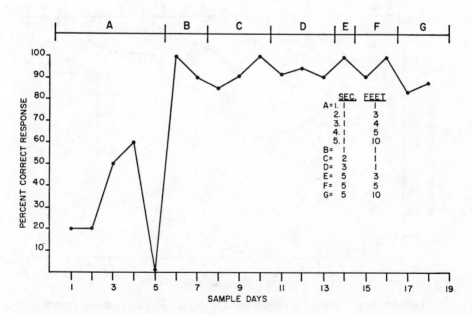

FIGURE 4–25 *Training a Five-Second Eye Contact at Ten Feet as a Prerequisite to Language Training in School*

it appeared that his performance was optimal between four and five feet, but with greater distances it dropped off precipitously. However, the pretreatment data indicated that he would require training for all distances.

Treatment Sequence: The treatment sequences of B–G represent training according to the following order which is outlined in figure 4–26. Food reinforcement was used intermittently and faded during the succession of treatment steps. Social reinforcement was used on a 100 percent schedule throughout the program. It is apparent that George acquired the response set quite quickly by attending to his name cue for increasing time and distance. The program was considered successful in the school, and appeared to facilitate acquisition of the same steps in that setting.

Eye Contact Training—Cottage: George's eye contact program in the cottage prescribed three ten-minute training sessions per day. Cereal, candy, and raisins were used as primaries in addition to social reinforcement. The procedure was identical to that employed in the school. Staff sat in the chair across from him and stated his name with the command, "Look at me." If he held the eye contact necessary for the

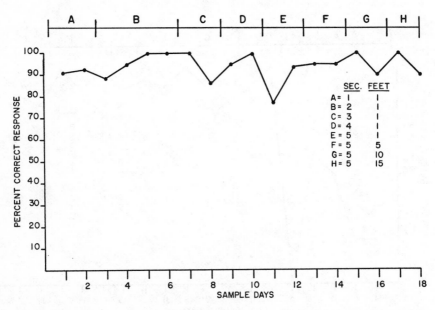

FIGURE 4–26 *Training a Five-Second Eye Contact at Ten Feet as a Prerequisite to Language Training in Cottage*

criterion of success at that time, he was praised and offered the primary reinforcement. Staff recorded trials and successes within each training session. It was necessary, as within the school, that he achieve 85 percent success on two successive training sessions before moving to the next shaping step. The data in figure 4–26 portray that he advanced rapidly through this treatment sequence. At the beginning of some steps, there would be an initial drop in performance but followed by acquisition of the response at the criterion distance and time.

Treatment Progression of Articulation Training

George was tested on eighty-eight of the basic items on the Templin Darley Articulation Test. He scored 6 on this test. Because of this low score an additional pretest, or baseline, was established for the sounds that would be trained in the course of treatment. This is shown in the baseline of figure 4–27 for the sounds of b, c, d, f, g, h, j, k, l, and m. Rationale for this baseline was to ascertain whether George could imitate verbal cues since he was not able to produce from visual cues on the Darley test. George's skill in imitating these sounds cued to him under the ten or greater trials given varied from 80 to 0 percent. The treatment sequence which follows progressed alphabetically for no specific reason other than it would be more convenient in communication across staff. Training sessions of ten minutes in length, four times a day, were conducted in the cottage and school. The staff produced the sounds in training at that time, and had George imitate that sound, using primary and social reinforcement for correct responses. Incorrect responses were identified by saying, "No," but not in an admonishing way, but rather to separate out the error response followed by providing him further cues and assisting him to imitate the response successfully. When George was able to imitate the sounds successfully, he was then required to imitate sounds with a visual cue rather than the verbal cue. Objects in the environment were used for this part of treatment. Thus, George was taken on walks, etc., and asked to produce the sounds in words of familiar objects. The sounds, when acquired with visual cues, would then be utilized in word lists provided by the teacher which used these sounds in frontal, terminal, and medial positions of words. He was assessed on usage of these sounds in words in the classroom at each step to determine when he was eligible to progress to the next shaping step. Some of these steps were acquired very rapidly, as shown in figure 4–27, and some required considerably more training for acquisition of the 90 percent criterion. All responses were acquired, and were also trained in vivo and positively practiced for error responses oc-

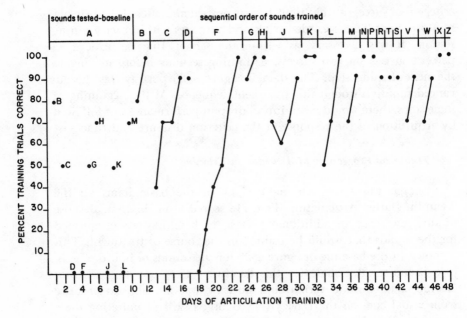

FIGURE 4-27 *Articulation Training Sequence*

curring spontaneously in the school and cottage. At discharge, George scored 88 out of the 88 basic items on the Templin Darley Articulation Test.

General Management Orders in Effect during the Six-Month Program

General management orders were initiated immediately or at most two months after admission, and included the following:

A. *Bizarre Behaviors:* These behaviors were identified as hand and facial movements which both twins used in communicating with each other. It had the unfortunate effect of spiraling them into very silly behavior which removed them from social control. Occurrences of these responses were timed-out, and by clinical impression were reasonably controlled, although data was not accumulated to demonstrate this conclusion.

B. When the twins fought, which occurred quite often, they would both be given a time-out at the same time with instructions, "No fighting." These occurrences were not included in their aggression count depicted in figure 4-24. Time-outs were considered to be successful in controlling this behavior toward each other as it was in their interaction with other children.

C. *Clinging Behavior:* These youngsters were provided considerable affection during the program, and responded pleasantly to this. However, they would be over-responsive, and it was necessary to restrict them to one hug and a verbal good-bye when leaving. This behavior had to be curbed because they would hug by hanging on one's leg or arm with a clutch that would not cease until they were literally pried off.

This particular affectionate behavior would degenerate to a very bizarre, if not an aggressive response. Thus, they would be told and instructed on how to say good-bye more appropriately. They would receive a time-out for clinging and clutching a person. Repetitive verbalizations of "good-bye" were ignored.

D. At date of admission a management order was issued in which the twins would positively practice using one's name to elicit his attention. When they reacted erroneously, they were instructed to rehearse stating the person's name appropriately for at least two correct trials, for which they would be socially reinforced.

E. At date of admission a mealtime management order was begun for inappropriate mealtime behavior. They were given a compliance command to rehearse the correct response which they were known to be capable of performing. If, on command, they did not cease the incorrect behavior or comply with rehearsal of the correct response, they received a two-minute time-out; social reinforcement was provided for response correction. These mealtime behavioral requirements included sitting still rather than wiggling about and climbing on the chairs and table. They had to use the correct utensils, and they needed numerous cues during the beginning of the program to perform this correctly. They could not eat with their hands. They had to use staff names when asking to be excused and also to ask for the food with appropriate words or by pointing if they did not know the word. They had to sit still at the table when they were finished with their meal prior to being excused.

F. A management order for swearing was issued on the last month of their residency. They were now imitating language quite well, and acquiring at the same time numerous inappropriate responses from other children, and apparently on some home visits. Each time they were heard swearing, they had to positively rehearse in the same situation using words other than the profanity. They received social reinforcement for correct rehearsals. Time-outs were not used for swearing; it was entirely a positive practice program.

G. Four months after admission, a management order was begun for appropriate bathroom behavior for both twins. Whenever either of the twins entered the bathroom, they were accompanied by a staff member. The twins had to stop at the nursing station or to find a staff member and have them accompany them to the bathroom. Staff members were present to assure that the children used appropriate bathroom behaviors. This included elimination and urination, hand washing for meals and after using the facilities, tooth-brushing, and hair combing. This degree of structure and positive practive was necessary since they would urinate indiscriminately about the room, fail to clean themselves, play in the water, and in general, render the bathroom a disaster area. Social reinforcement followed their correct responses regardless of whether they were spontaneous or required verbal direction. The program was considered successful at our facility. After discharge, during the first two days of public school, one of the twins urinated in the hall of the school, suggesting again the reality of behavioral retrieval.

CASE STUDY: JOHN

Admission Age: 5 years, 7 months.

Duration of Residency: 6 months.

Diagnosis: Childhood schizophrenia was the accepted referral diagnosis as it was for his twin brother, George. A primary goal of the treatment program was to determine the extent of retardation or special learning handicaps. We were also concerned with the etiological question as to whether the unusual behaviors acquired by these youngsters may have been attributable to under-stimulation and faulty training by the parents. Both twins were unplanned; obviously rejected by the parents; and aside from minimal parental supervision, they had almost raised themselves.

Admission IQ: The Stanford-Binet Form L-M was administered three months prior to admission. At that time he received a mental age of 3 years, 8 months, with an IQ score of 65. At date of discharge, his chronological age was 6 years, 2 months, and on the Stanford-Binet Form L-M he received a mental age equivalency of 5 years, 1 month, with an IQ of 81.

Specified Referral Problems: The referral behaviors were very similar to those indicated previously for his twin brother, George. It was suggested at the beginning of treatment that John's performance would be less than George's, which proved to be true. It became apparent that John was not the preferred twin, as evidenced in the manner in which the parents followed the programs at home and their general attitude toward him in contrast to his twin brother. However, the major referral problems were comparable for both children, ranging from language to social training to prepare them for classroom interaction and free play with peers. The treatment curriculum was similar for both children, although many aspects of it were conducted independently.

Acceleration of John's Compliance to Verbal Commands

Behavior Counted: The behavior depicted in figure 4–28 is the trial and success to commands for compliance during the five successive days of the baseline and for the one day per week samples recorded throughout the course of the six-month treatment program.

Treatment A: This was the baseline interval of five consecutive days in which staff counted the number of commands delivered to John and the occasions in which he successfully complied. As shown in figure 4–28, his compliance was not severely limited; staff were confident that the commands made to him were at a level that he could comprehend and perform. His baseline compliance ranged from 56 percent to 65 percent.

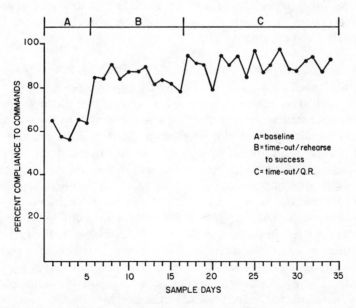

FIGURE 4–28   *Accelerating John's Compliance to Verbal Commands*

Treatment B: Under treatment B he received a time-out for each occurrence of noncompliance, with the time-out condition being consistent with the management order of training him to take an appropriate time-out. After each time-out he rehearsed the response to success. This was to make it more likely that he would have the correct response available at a later date.

Treatment C: During treatment interval C, he was at the stage in the program where he received a five-minute back-up time-out in the quiet room if he did not take an appropriate time-out. In the first step of his compliance training program (indicated as "B" in figure 4–28), if he did not take an appropriate time-out during that time period, he was taken back to the time-out spot and reminded to take it appropriately (a rehearse to success program). This was in contrast to his brother's time-out shaping program in which George always received a five-minute back-up time-out when he failed on the two-minute time-out. During treatment condition C, it was decided to utilize the program used for his brother, George, since it seemed to be more successful. John's variance in compliance then declined, although with either time-out condition there was a satisfactory progression in compliance as shown in figure 4–28.

Teaching John to Take an Appropriate Time-Out

Behavior Counted: Ratio between number of time-outs and number of occasions in which the quiet room was utilized to punish/ extinguish incorrect time-outs.

Treatment: Figure 4–29 depicts the effectiveness of the program which was in effect for four and one-half months. For the first two months, each time John was given a time-out and he did not remain seated but scooted about or talked, he was taken back to the situation and told to take the time-out over again. This positive practice approach was repeated until he completed a correct time-out. This initial program was discontinued because he was not learning to take an appropriate time-out as consistently as his twin brother. John was then placed on the same program as George in which inappropriate time-outs were backed up with a five-minute time-out in the quiet room. These data, illustrated in figure 4–29, display that the variance in the number of time-outs remained the same and the occasions when the quiet room was necessary to back-up the time-out varied proportionately. The program was considered to be useful for John, but it was unfortunate that we did not have the program in effect earlier as

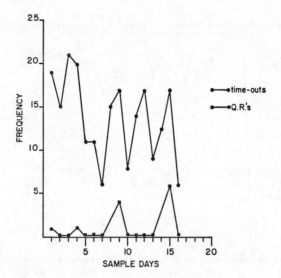

FIGURE 4-29   *Teaching John to Take an Appropriate Time-Out*

we had for his brother. The data seemed to indicate that positively practicing the time-out was not as effective as using a time-out in the quiet room as a back-up.

Training Eye Contact as a Prerequisite for Language Training

Behavior Counted: The data recorded throughout the course of eye contact training were the number of trials and the percent correct responses of those trials during each step of the training program.

Baseline: The eye contact training for John, as with his brother George, was initiated first in the school and afterwards in the cottage. As illustrated in figure 4–30, the baseline condition was sampled in school on five successive days for one-second eye contact, but at the increasing distances of two-, three-, four-, five-, and ten-foot steps. As shown in figure 4–30, his performance dropped precipitously after five-foot distance, and at all distances his eye contact was exceedingly poor.

Treatment Sequence: The treatment sequence progressed in accordance with the table on figure 4–30; time increased from two to five seconds, and distance from one to ten feet, with progression to a new training step dependent upon achieving a criterion of 90 percent

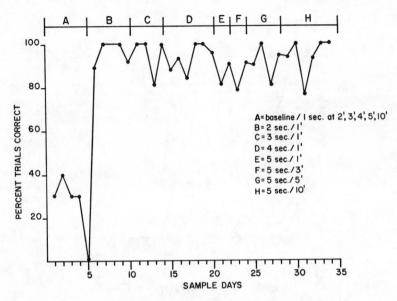

FIGURE 4–30 *Treatment Sequence for Training Eye Contact in School*

accuracy for two successive training intervals. John moved quickly through this treatment sequence. Generalization training was conducted in the cottage, the acceptable results of which are shown in figure 4–31.

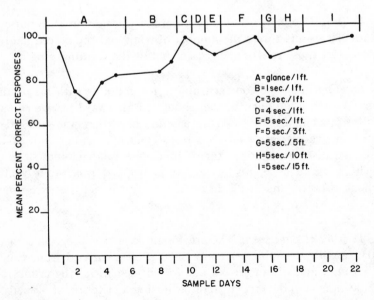

FIGURE 4–31 *Treatment Sequence for Training Eye Contact in Cottage*

Controlling John's Aggressive Behavior

Behavior Counted: Aggressive behavior was defined as his making physical contact by hitting, kicking, pushing, or shoving another child. An aggressive response occurring between John and his twin brother, George, was not included in this total count. They were handled under a general management order which is described in George's program.

Treatment A: In figure 4–32 treatment A was a controlled baseline, as defined by staff ignoring the behavior and counting it as discreetly as possible. The behavior was actually accelerative during this five-day baseline, which may have represented an early extinction effect.

Treatment B: This treatment represents the one-day-per-week samples for the remainder of treatment. For each aggressive response, John would receive a two-minute time-out. However, during this phase of the program he was receiving a time-out training sequence that was changing and it is not indicated on the graph. At the first stage of condition B, if he did not take an appropriate two-minute time-out, he was taken back to the spot and told again to take an appropriate time-out with the staff repeating this until he did take the correct two-minute time-out. After a few weeks, this program was dropped in favor of using a five-minute back-up in the quiet room.

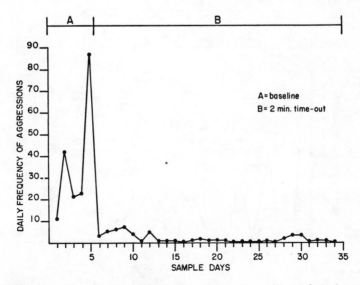

FIGURE 4-32 *Effect of a Two-Minute Time-Out in Controlling John's Aggressions*

The time-out condition, regardless of the two training effects, showed that aggressive behavior was under good control for John, with aggression seldom occurring during the remainder of the program.

Teaching John Appropriate Toilet Behavior

Behavior Counted: John had a fairly high rate of inappropriate toilet behavior, characterized by urinating and defecating on the floor close to the toilet, or urinating in places other than the bathroom. Staff simply counted the frequency of this behavior occurring on the consecutive days of the baseline, and the weekly sample periods thereafter.

Treatment A: During this baseline John was not required to do anything; staff simply counted the frequency of his urinating or defecating in an inappropriate place, including in his pants. Staff had to be certain that it was John's urination they discovered, or else it would not be counted.

Treatment B: Under this treatment condition, John was simply required to clean up the urine or feces with as little staff supervision as possible. Staff supervision was in the form of verbal direction; he was not receiving time-outs for this behavior, but if he refused to follow a command given to him to clean up his mess, he was timed-out for that noncompliance. Upon termination of the time-out, he was returned to the same situation and began the cleaning under

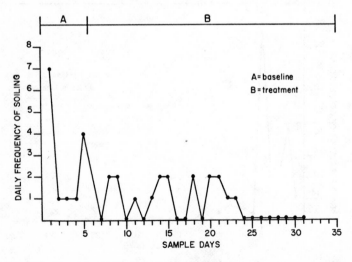

FIGURE 4-33 *Teaching John Appropriate Toileting*

supervision by staff. The frequency of inappropriate toilet behavior, figure 4–33, shows that it ranged from zero to two times per day, and eventually did drop to a zero level for the last eight weeks of treatment.

Teaching John Appropriate Articulation

Behavior Counted: The behavior counted was the percent successful trials occurring during each of the training steps.

Treatment Sequence: The baseline interval, indicated as A in figure 4–34, shows the pre-testing on the b, c, d, e, f, g, h, j, k, l, and m sounds, and revealed that his proficiency in imitating these sounds on command varied from 80 to zero percent.

The treatment steps are also contained in figure 4–34. These were training sessions occurring each day: two ten-minute sessions in the cottage and two ten-minute sessions in the classroom. The teacher tested for the correct use of these sounds and indicated when staff should move to the next step in the training hierarchy. Typically, but not always, this required 90 percent proficiency on two successive training sessions to move on to the next step. The sample points on the graph represent several days. Training was composed of positive practice on the sounds, followed by the use of these sounds in the frontal, terminal, and medial positions on words provided to the staff

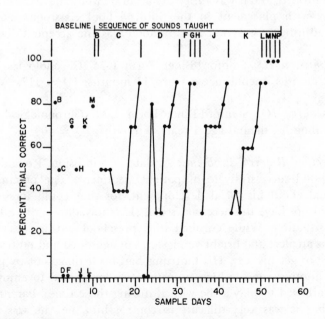

FIGURE 4–34 *John's Articulation Training Program*

by the school teacher. It is beyond the scope of this case to include all the words used, but such lists are easily contrived. The program was successful in teaching John 95 percent correct articulation of all sounds taught. After acquisition of these sounds, he was on a positive practice program in his spontaneous language that occurred during the day when he utilized these sounds. Both John and his brother demonstrated retrieval of many of their early error responses following discharge, which seemed to be a function of the parents' inability to maintain the programs.

CASE STUDY: RONALD

Admission Age: 4 years, 2 months.

Duration of Residency: 5 months.

Diagnosis: The question of brain damage had been raised primarily on the basis of this child's hyperactivity and the difficulty in controlling his impulsive behavior, but had never been formally substantiated by neurological evaluations. Most realistically, he appeared to be an unpatterned, untrained aggressive youngster with very few social skills. He was not adaptive to the preschool setting in which he was enrolled, and it was anticipated that he would have considerable difficulty with placement in the public school classroom. Formally stated, adjustment reaction to childhood was the accepted diagnosis.

Admission IQ: Stanford-Binet Form L-M. Chronological age 4 years, 2 months; mental age 4 years, 11 months; IQ = 117.

Discharge IQ: Stanford-Binet Form L-M. Chronological age 4 years, 7 months; mental age 5 years, 0 months; IQ = 109.

Specified Referral Problems: At date of admission, Ronald could not respond successfully to outpatient treatment. The parents were concerned about his social development, for they could foresee that he would not have the necessary social skills for adapting to a kindergarten situation. While enrolled in a preschool setting, he was observed as an alert and bright youngster, but aggressed and tantrummed in order to get his way. His tantrums had been timed-out by placing him in another room, which unfortunately he seemed to enjoy since he was allowed to play as he wished during those times. Parents indicated that it was very difficult to control him, i.e., he was almost consistently noncompliant to their verbal commands, particularly the mother's. His speech was characteristic of a whiny, pleading nature, but when crossed, he could "swear like a trooper." He was not an independent child by any means; he was always operating to have an adult do something for him, which was hopeful since seeking out the attention of adults meant that such attention could be used contingently for appropriate behaviors. He did not seem able to persevere with a task assigned to him to the extent expected of most four-year-old children; his play with other children was eventually interrupted by aggressive behaviors and attempts to verbally dominate them. There was variable occurrence of nocturnal enuresis. He was dependent upon his "maxi," or his security blanket, which he was still dragging around pressing to the side of his face. If he became jealous of other kids for the attentions they obtained from adults or peers, this would provoke his aggressive behavior toward them. He was sufficiently alert to know when to provoke his peers in such a manner that he would seldom be observed. His innocent appearance was not altogether deceiving, but his angelic face could quickly turn into a rather angry, snarling look that was often punctuated by a rather direct, profane comment.

Ronald's behavior program was not considered to be a very complex one. Most simply stated, we did not perceive him as being severely emotionally disturbed. To us, Ronald was a child who had been unpatterned, uncontrolled, and this behavior had dominated his repertoire. His use of tantrums, aggression, and similar asocial behaviors served to compensate for slightly impaired language development. He did not have the prerequisite skills for placement in a regular classroom since he competed so persistently in a group situation for all of the teacher's attention, and in ways which were disruptive to that kind of group setting. Ronald was obviously of normal intelligence, quite alert, and the parents were willing to collaborate with the parent training project. His school program had focused upon his paying attention, delivering eye contact, and using these two prerequisite skills to facilitate speech and preschool training which would be conducted in our classroom. This, in conjunction with compliance training, was continuous throughout the school and cottage programs.

Control of Ronald's Tantrums and Aggressive Behaviors

Behavior Counted: Samples with a hand-tally counter were taken throughout the day on the sample days both in the cottage and in school for both physical aggression and tantrums. Physical aggression was defined as hitting, kicking, throwing things at persons, and biting, usually while lying on the ground. We defined tantrums as screaming and throwing things, which were often accompanied by his hitting, kicking, biting, pinching, spitting, and pulling away from staff members, often while lying on the ground and refusing to move. This occurred usually in situations where he was denied having what he preferred.

Treatment A: This treatment was the baseline for tantrums and aggression. We had some ideas regarding the kinds of contingencies which may have been maintaining his tantrums and aggressive behaviors since these responses seemed to be related, as indicated above. Apparently tantrums did allow him to have his way, but perhaps not as effectively as aggression. If one simply asked him to stop in a nice way, this would only facilitate the aggressive behavior which would continue until he obtained what he wished. We studied tantrums for a short period of time since they dropped out rather quickly. First, we wished to have a controlled baseline which we would consider to be a close representation of what had been occurring in the home and preschool setting. There usually was some situation in which he was denied having what he preferred that would precipitate these behaviors. We had a controlled baseline in which the staff did nothing in particular about the tantrums involving peers except to say, matter-of-factly, "You're not supposed to do that," as he was aggressing on that peer. If the staff asked Ronald to perform something to which he responded by tantrums so as to avoid compliance, they took him, physically if necessary, and continued assisting him to follow the request so long as the tantrum remained at the screaming and hollering stage. But, as soon as it progressed to physical aggression, which it invariably did, they gave in to him and let him have his way. For example, if staff told Ronald to come inside and stop riding on his tricycle, he would lie down on the ground and start screaming and rolling around; they were to physically bring him inside, paying no particular attention to the tantrum behavior. However, as soon as he hit staff, they were to give in to him and allow him to stay outside. There were situations during the day in which he did go from one activity to another and these transitions would precipitate tantrums and aggressive behavior. At these times, if just the tantrums occurred and aggression did not, staff left him alone; they waited five minutes and repeated the expectancy again. If aggression then occurred, they waited five more minutes and then physically took him, aggression or no aggression, into the next activity. This had to be done, otherwise he would have avoided the entire treatment program and baseline with his aggressive behavior. We also took a baseline count of the aggressive behaviors which occurred at these times. This was a controlled baseline in which the staff were to respond rather matter-of-factly when this occurred, "You're not supposed to do that." If the aggressive behavior occurred during a temper tantrum, we were to

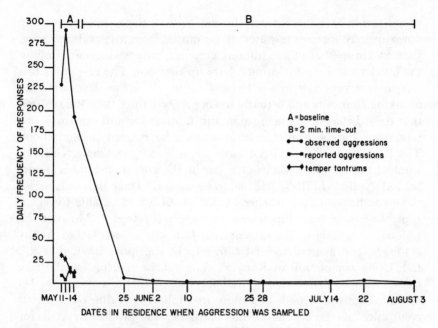

FIGURE 4-35 *Treatment Sequence for Control of Ronald's Tantrums and Aggressions*

count both separately. Since he seemed to be rather "tuned-in" to aggressing when he would least likely be apprehended, we required staff to also count separately the reported incidents of aggression by other children in the cottage. The staff were instructed not to respond in any way to reported aggression occurring under these conditions during the baseline.

Figure 4-35 shows the baselines for these counts. Temper tantrums essentially dropped out during this time; reported aggressions rose slightly, but aggressive behavior itself was exceptionally high. His tantrums were not really low, since they were occurring between fifteen and thirty times daily, which is high for a four-year old child. His aggressive behavior was inordinately high, as evidenced by almost 300 occurrences daily.

Treatment B: The treatment program was initiated following the baseline. Ronald was given a two-minute time-out for every occurrence of aggression and temper tantrum. Tantrum behavior was not sampled thereafter, since it simply dropped out of his repertoire during the first week of treatment, and it did not occur significantly thereafter to warrant resampling. Again, when these aggressive and tantrum behaviors occurred, staff would say, "You're not supposed to . . . ," and then inform him he was to take a time-out at the location where the behavior occurred. He had to take these time-outs sitting down quietly for two minutes. If he moved, wiggled, said anything, sneered, frowned at other children, etc., he was moved immediately to the quiet room for a five-minute back-up time-out. The reason for this was to interrupt the habits he had acquired in the daycare center of taking time-outs and actually having a good time at it. We realized that these behaviors of aggression and tantrums would remain in his repertoire and be available to him when he entered public school. The public school would not have a quiet room available; children would have to take a time-out there in the corner, behind a piano, behind another child, etc. He had to be trained to take time-outs under those conditions so the teacher in the school would be able to regain control of these behaviors whenever there was retrieval. This was the rationale for having a stringent time-out which was backed up by a longer, and a more secured time-out, in the quiet room if it did fail. Upon completion of Ronald's time-out, he returned to the task from which he had been removed for the assaultive, tantrumous behavior. After five seconds had transpired following a time-out without recurrence of aggressions or tantrums, he was praised by staff for behaving so appropriately and differently than before when he was removed from that situation. In addition, staff were alerted to praise Ronald, whenever they would think of it, for not demonstrating aggressive behavior at various times throughout the day. Actually, a management order of this kind is seldom effective since staff habituate to the child and rapidly forget to praise him for not aggressing. Management orders are contingent for staff also, and they are alerted to providing a contingency when the behaviors occur which reminds them of what they are supposed to do. Staff did not act on aggressions reported by other peers, since by this time Ronald had acquired a reputation whereby his "enemies" would capitalize upon their revenge by reporting false aggressions.

Results: The results were considered satisfactory in that the time-out conditions in conjunction with positive reinforcement for incompatible behavior was successful in controlling his aggressive and tantrumous behaviors. His parents and teachers were taught how to perform the treatment program.

Teaching Ronald Compliance to Verbal Commands

Behavior Counted: A count was obtained on four consecutive days of the baseline and the successive sample days thereafter for the ratio of his compliance and noncompliance to verbal commands occurring all day both in the cottage and school.

Treatment A: This treatment was a controlled baseline established for the percent of verbal commands to which he complied. The control conditions under which this was attained was that the staff issued a command to him, and if he did not comply within a ten-second interval, using the 1001, 1002, etc., method of counting to oneself, they matter-of-factly repeated the expectation again, and repeated the cycle for up to four times if necessary. If he did comply, he was not praised on these occasions, since it appeared from our rather cursory observations that historically there was very little praise for compliance to verbal commands for Ronald. Each time the command was redelivered, it was counted as a new count, since we were interested in the percent of all commands made to which he responded. As shown in the baseline data in figure 4–36, there was stable compliance to verbal requests right around 40 percent.

Treatment B: One week after inception of the baseline, a treatment program was begun which was simply a two-minute time-out, the same as for aggressive and tantrum behaviors. These time-outs were taken immediately at the spot where he noncomplied. Every time he complied with a command, he received social praise. If he did not comply to the command to take a time-out, he would receive a five-minute back-up time-out in the quiet room. In the second week of the program, the management order was made more stringent since it had become apparent that he knew how to take a time-out perfectly. At

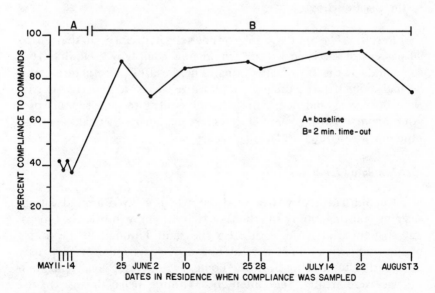

FIGURE 4-36 *Accelerating Ronald's Compliance to Verbal Commands*

that time it was decided that if he did not take the time-out within five seconds after he was told to, and perform correctly thereafter for the remainder of the two minutes, he would then have a five-minute time-out in the quiet room. We were realizing that during his time-outs, he was becoming increasingly verbally provocative to staff. His provocations were usually in the form of questioning their reason for giving him a time-out or making derisive statements. We then decided that his time-outs not only had to be performed by sitting still in that same place, but with no speaking whatsoever. He was not cued or argued to be quiet, since this seemed to be what he was operating for. It had become apparent from home observations that the verbal battles between Ronald and his mother sustained his noncompliance, so we wished to interrupt that interaction. Each time he was given a time-out and was not silent, staff did not inform him why he was receiving a quiet room time-out. He adjusted very rapidly to this contingency. As shown in figure 4–36, the compliance count dropped on the last sampling day. At this time just prior to discharge, he was spending the majority of his week at home with the parents. It is not unusual at date of discharge to see a diminution of treatment effects occurring. This usually means several things. For example, a child may be retrieving more of the old referral behaviors due to a not-very-successful fading-in process to the home. It may also indicate that staff became lax in performing the treatment program because of their habituation to the child. Regardless, he was sufficiently compliant at this time to be placed in nursery school prior to admission to the public school.

Results: The results were considered satisfactory, in that 85 to 90 percent of the time Ronald would now comply with adult verbal commands at the treatment setting. This level of performance could be maintained if the program was utilized consistently. His parents were instructed and demonstrated their ability to perform this program for maintaining compliance. The remainder of Ronald's cottage program was without data.

Nondata Programs

Ronald had a very structured day which evolved around eating, sleeping, playing, going to school, activity therapy, music class, trips, and structured activities with peers and staff. Throughout the course of these activities, which were at best a weak facsimile of what may be expected to occur back in the home, aggressive behavior and compliance were treated very intensely. Whining behavior was treated with a general management order in which he had to repeat what he was requesting, but without the whining. Successful rehearsals were reinforced socially. It should be added that there was no evidence of thought disorder (i.e., language disorder) on any of his test scores, nor in his behavior in the school or cottage. He was admitted as a pre-school child whose problems of compliance and aggression and tantrums were imminent to disrupt his participation in public school. We felt that we were successful in controlling those behaviors. The purpose of his admission was to prevent rejection from public school, and equally important to enter the public school with an unblemished record in which there would be no stigma of his being an "emotionally disturbed" child and thereby treated differentially.

The parents were diligent in attending parent training. However, it was our impression that they retained their old habits, which were retrieved to a certain extent after they had him back in the home for several months. Several trips were required by our staff, as well as coordination with a school psychologist, to work with the classroom in which he was placed. Our special-education teacher and the social worker from the referring agency counselled the parents on their difficulties in maintaining Ronald's progress. Prognostically, this child was treated in a manner to prevent serious difficulty later. A variety of programs were conceived which were very simple, had positive effects, and could be implemented in the home and the school. He was not a difficult child to teach, but the prognosis is tenuous on the basis of parent training which had not been able to effectively alter the parents' habits of interacting with Ronald.

CASE STUDY: TROY

Admission Age: 9 years, 7 months.

Duration of Residency: Four and one-half months.

Diagnosis: He accumulated a variety of diagnoses ranging from a moderate degree of infantile autism (if that label may be placed on a continuum of severity), childhood schizophrenia, mild retardation, and brain damage. He was in that category of youngsters whom we treat frequently: his social development was consistently below his peers; his language and academic skills were in sufficient deficit to raise questions of retardation; and his mixture of bizarre and repetitive behaviors prompted the diagnoses of childhood psychoses. The parents' reports of Troy's developmental history revealed that his social aloofness, inordinate interest in spinning and rocking, and language handicaps were increasingly apparent since birth, and could not be reasonably ascribed to functional causes. The mother had spent many hours very consistently training Troy to speak, to comply, and to learn self-help skills. This training was definitely to his advantage; his deficits would have been much more severe at date of admission if it had not been for his mother's perseverence in educating Troy. We did observe that demands of Troy were usually minimal, but the mother demonstrated a natural reliance upon positive reinforcement, which was typical of her child-rearing techniques with all the children. The family was uniformly protective of Troy, which perhaps accounted for his acquisition of crying and whining behaviors that were only quelled when the family ceased in their demands. Troy's crying on those occasions lent support to the family's belief that the expectancies held for Troy had to be minimal or else they would unwittingly do psychological harm to him. This was a very bright, well-educated and close-knit family who were receptive to the didactic approach of parent training. The training provided was congruent with the techniques already in existence at the home such as: consistency, establishing behavioral goals known to everyone, open communication, and reliance upon positive reinforcement.

The accepted referral diagnosis was an acknowledgement that Troy historically demonstrated mild symptomatology of infantile autism, but that more importantly, there was some concomitant degree of retardation to be expected and verified. This was explained to the family and they seemed to accept, during the program as well as in follow-up, that an intellectual deficit would be a characteristic of Troy. Regardless, they were dedicated to teaching him to compensate optimally against his learning handicaps.

Admission IQ: Wechsler Intelligence Scale for Children—Verbal Scale, 61; Performance Scale, 74; Full Scale, 64.

Specified Referral Problems: Several reasons prevented Troy's placement in a special education classroom. The school system could not decide if Troy was retarded, emotionally disturbed, or brain damaged. The parents realized that Troy's achievements actually declined while in the school system because it could not provide the necessary structure and training they knew he required. They, as well as school personnel, recognized that his persistent crying tended to remove him from inclusion in a group experience, and in fact precluded his learning under individual instruction. Troy was an extremely thin youngster; although pensive and attractive in appearance (which was quite deceiving), he just did not seem to correlate with a concomitant diagnosis of retardation. His eating habits were very poor; the family had been inadvertently reinforcing his strong food preferences for years. Whenever Troy was blocked, frustrated, or did not have a quick response for some situation, his predictable action was to cry and whine and thereby avoid. He was compliant in that he would attempt to follow a command, but would soon break down into his whining and crying state. Troy avoided peers entirely, and preferred to engage in a paucity of self-play activities which were dominated by his rocking continuously on the swing in the backyard. The parents reported that his summer before admission to the treatment group had been spent exclusively on the swing in the backyard. As with many of these youngsters, this rocking behavior appeared as an extension of what was so dominant in his repertoire since infancy. Troy would seldom speak to others spontaneously, and his responses to others' questions were barely audible and extremely sparse in content. Troy had immobilized all of his previous instructors by the pity elicited by his crying and whimpering which assured them that he was a sad but bright-normal child. Troy engaged in producing unusual sounds, demonstrated several self-stimulatory patterns, and his effect was inappropriate, such as laughing when he saw other children fighting or hurt. He avoided other children, and he would ask repeated questions throughout the day which centered exclusively about his routine. Short term memory was limited, and he was unable to understand or express very simple verbal concepts. His muscular coordination was below age expectancy. He was a fairly compliant child to simple instructions, and he was primarily passive, never aggressive.

Teaching Troy to Control his Rocking

Behavior Counted: During the baseline and designated sample days to assess treatment staff recorded the accumulated time Troy was rocking. Rocking was simply defined as making a swinging motion with his back and trunk. This behavior occurred on the rocking horse in the day room; while standing or sitting on the swings; and quite often on his bed when he was alone in his room away from some structured activity.

Treatment A: This treatment was the baseline interval in which staff added the daily totaled minutes Troy was rocking. This was a controlled baseline since staff were directed not to respond in any way to this behavior, but simply record its duration. As revealed in the baseline, in figure 4–37 this accumulated time varied between 100 to 300 minutes per day, which would certainly be considered a pathological behavior for a nine-year-old child.

Treatment B: This treatment was comprised of a schedule in which Troy was allowed to rock, but on a diminishing basis. Since swinging on a swing is an appropriate kind of play activity for a child, this was decided to be the substitute activity for his rocking. Considering his previous history it was apparent that we also had to reduce total time of swinging, since this could by its duration become bizarre. The parents were in agreement to maintain this program on the weekends in which they would control the time intervals and frequencies during the day in which he would be allowed to use the swing.

The management order stipulated that each morning after he awakened, staff inform him that he could not swing or rock unless he received permission. If he was rocking, they told him that he could not do that until "swing time." He was sufficiently compliant to follow this command. According to the schedule of time periods below, he was allowed to swing on the swings for a maximum of ten-minute intervals, the frequencies of which diminished during the day on successive weeks. If he did rock he was informed that a time was reserved for "swing time" and he would now lose his next ten-minute swing time. The schedule of diminishing time on swings to replace the rocking behavior was as follows:

Week 1: Every two hours, ten minutes of swinging time.
Week 2: Every four hours, ten minutes swinging time.
Week 3: Every eight hours, ten minutes swinging time.
Week 4: Each day before bedtime, ten minutes of swinging time.

Henceforth, he was allowed only ten minutes of swinging time per day; the time period was selected at the discretion of the parents. The data for this program, indicated as interval B in figure 4–37, were recorded on sample days whereby the staff did not remind him that he was not supposed to rock. On these sample days we were testing for generalization effects without benefit of our verbally cueing him.

Results: The results were satisfactory. Troy learned to swing on the swing once a day for only ten minutes, which is not considered pathological for his age. He was no longer rocking five hours per day. Rocking had been replaced by the appropriate activity of swinging on the swing for a reasonable period of time.

Teaching Troy to Control his Crying and Whimpering both in Cottage and School

Behavior Counted: During each sample day, the staff recorded the total time Troy was engaged in crying or whimpering. These occa-

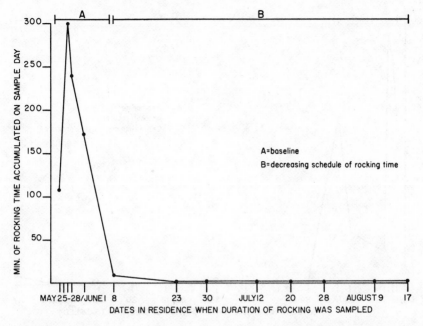

FIGURE 4–37 *Controlling Troy's Rocking by a Diminishing Time Schedule*

sions of crying had to occur in situations where there was no observable evidence of physical injury or reasonable situations with peers to induce the crying. Since the children composing the group at that time had been controlled for aggressions fairly well, there were few instances in which his crying was warranted due to aggression by another child.

Treatment A: This treatment was the baseline condition and maintained for four consecutive days. The baseline was controlled in that staff were informed to allow Troy to cry for as long as he wished on each occasion during which they would surreptitiously record the durations of that crying. As depicted in figure 4–38, duration of crying varied from twelve to eighty-seven minutes per day, which was considered to be abnormal for his age. In fact, swinging, or crying to avoid, constituted much of his day. The marked diminution of crying on the final sample days should not be construed as an extinction effect of the controlled baseline ignoring the crying and simply timing it. On the basis of our experience, four days is too quick to expect an extinguish response after so many years' duration. Rather, we have assumed that the baseline condition of these four days provides a rough sample of the high and low variance of Troy's crying. We acknowledge that this is a speculative conclusion.

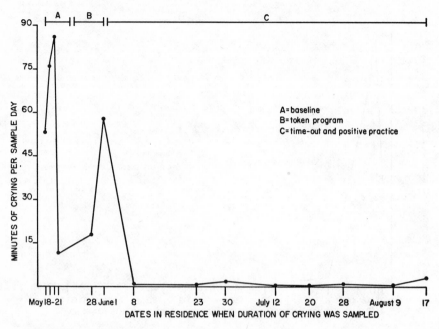

FIGURE 4–38 *Decelerating Troy's Crying in the Cottage and School*

Treatment B: A token economy was employed during this treatment condition. Twelve daily times were selected during Troy's waking hours to observe him. During these preselected observation times,
if he was not crying, Troy received a token plus verbal praise for not
crying at that time. These observation times varied so that he was
unable to predict their occurrence. These observation times occurred
both in the cottage and school to assist generalization of treatment
effects. Troy could receive up to twelve tokens during the day, which
were redeemable for his favorite food of chocolate milk at snack time;
twelve tokens yielded a full glass, six a half-glass, etc. As in figure
4–38, this treatment program was entirely ineffectual.

Treatment C: A time-out in conjunction with positive practice
of an appropriate alternate response characterized this treatment program. Each time Troy was observed crying during the scheduled daily
observation periods, he was given a time-out until he ceased crying—
the instructions were verbalized very clearly to him on each occasion.
Upon cessation of his crying, he was instructed to explain why he was
crying. Staff were permitted to use as much verbal assistance as necessary to help him explain the circumstances responsible for his crying.
They were usually simple explanations ranging from "I'm sad," to "I

miss home," to "I don't know when school starts." Throughout the duration of this treatment sequence, the staff gradually faded their verbal assistance in helping him to explain his difficulty.

Results: The results were considered satisfactory during treatment condition C, since crying was reduced to a relatively reasonable level ranging from zero to three minutes duration per day. As characteristic of many psychotic children, he was most anxious when there were changes in schedules; crying was most likely to be engendered for circumstances such as when his parents were due to take him home for the weekend and he was unsure as to exactly what moment they would appear in the door. This was not considered to be a serious handicap since we could design a program to train him to handle shifts in scheduling. His crying had now ceased as an avoidance response when he was in an expectancy situation which he was not exactly sure how to perform. The program had utilized the punishment/extinction condition of a time-out for crying, and social reinforcement for being able to verbally explain what his difficulty was. This coordinated with his speech training program of using language instead of tears to operate his social environment.

Teaching Troy to Maintain Eye Contact in the Cottage Setting

Behavior Counted: Staff counted the number of times on designated sample days they called Troy by his name and the number of times he turned and looked at them with eye contact to that command. These data yielded a percentage of the times eye contact attention was elicited by Troy's name. The rationale for this program was based on Troy's moderate obliviousness to other persons, which made him unamenable to learning many new behaviors because he did not attend sufficiently to instructions in the educational setting.

Treatment A: This treatment condition was held constant throughout his residential program. The treatment program required that at various times during the day, when deemed appropriate by the circumstances, staff would use Troy's name to demand his attention for asking or telling him something. When he responded to his name by turning toward them and maintaining eye contact, it was counted as a success and he was rewarded socially, after which a request or command was delivered by the staff. This program was conducted both in the cottage and the school, but his primary training setting was in the cottage. To test for generalization effects, samples of the program were obtained in the school setting. Figure 4–39 contains the data of this program.

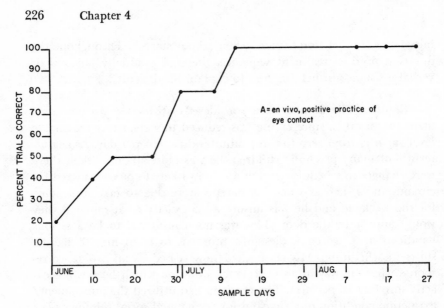

FIGURE 4–39 *Teaching Troy to Maintain Eye Contact in the Cottage Setting*

Results: The results were considered satisfactory. Within forty-five days, he was responding consistently 100 percent of the time to his name by holding eye contact, which by termination of the program was sustained for the duration of the request or command delivered to him by the staff member. Social reinforcement was considered to be effective in this program. This conclusion is based entirely on the acceleration effect shown on the graph, but was not determined experimentally to assess if this was a necessary and sufficient reinforcement condition for the training effect. It is suspected that this training effect was facilitated by the corresponding attention training which occurred in the school setting where this sampling for treatment effects was obtained. It cannot be determined from this graph whether the treatment effect was as clear in the cottage as it was in the school. One could speculate that generalization effects of the treatment condition, which were predominantly performed in the cottage, had generalized to the school setting—which was a primary goal of the program.

Troy's Eye Contact Training in the School

Behavior Counted: Two forms of data were collected for monitoring the effectiveness of eye contact training which was a prerequisite response for academic work, peer interaction, and speech training. The first form, in vivo, measured the average duration of eye contact that occurred when he was asked something by the teacher while working independently or directly with the teacher on a 1:1 basis, and also whenever she attempted to engage him in any form of conversation. The second form of data was obtained during special training sessions for eye contact. This latter data was the percent of training trials occurring during the training session in which he maintained the criterion level of eye contact. The data for this program are shown on figure 4-40.

Baseline: The baseline data obtained were to be as heuristic as possible for determining the first step of a training sequence. Ten samples of eye contacts were obtained on independent work, 1:1 work, and during in vivo conversation with the teacher. This baseline data was obtained to provide a sample of his eye contact duration to yield the point at which training should most optimally begin. During independent work, when his name was called, average eye contact was 1.4 seconds. When engaged in 1:1 direct supervised work with the teacher, average eye contact was zero seconds. When the teacher was talking directly with Troy, his eye contacts averaged 2.4 seconds. His average eye contacts for all three situations was 1.6 seconds. Considering his intellectual deficits, this was an insufficient duration for him to attend to instructions for acquisition of the academic, speech and social training to which he would be exposed. This information indicated that we commence at the two-second interval of eye contact training, and it was suspected that he would succeed at that level.

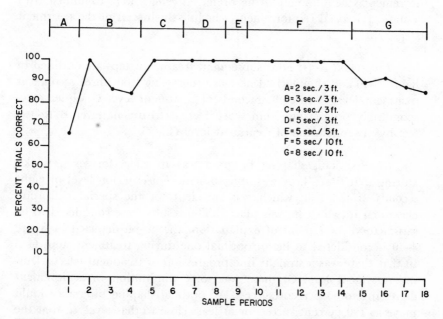

FIGURE 4-40   *Treatment Sequence for Troy's Eye Contact in the School*

Treatment A: During this treatment sequence, the teacher trained Troy to maintain two seconds' eye contact at a distance of three feet from her during the training sessions. These training sessions were conducted during the classroom setting with at least three and up to six children present during the school day. Four to six sessions were performed each class day. Daily recordings were made of the data obtained to determine when it would be necessary to move to the next longer shaping step. Thus, an in vivo sample of three kinds of eye contact occasions were used to determine where the eye contact training sessions should begin in the classroom. In the classroom, training sessions were prepared in which he was instructed and reinforced for criterion level eye contact according to the shaping steps; the data obtained from those sessions were used to determine progression to the next step. It is useful with some children to continue sampling on the three measures of eye contact to determine when to move to the next step. Generalization effects are used to determine the next training or shaping step. That is the preferred treatment regimen, but it was not used in this case.

On the successive training steps outlined below, the distance from the teacher was increased and the duration of time was correspondingly expanded. The eventual goal was to teach Troy to maintain eye contact while immersed in a group situation in a classroom for sufficient periods of time so as to receive and follow instructions. Random reinforcement schedules employing preferred cereals were combined with a static 1:1 social reinforcement schedule during all of the treatment steps.

Treatment B–G: Four subsequent treatment steps are outlined in figure 4–40 and summarized here as progressing from three seconds at treatment level B to eight seconds at treatment level G while correspondingly progressing from three feet at treatment level B to ten feet by the conclusion of treatment level G.

Results: This shaping program was in effect for seven weeks. During that time, Troy was able to achieve a criterion level of eight seconds at ten feet, which was sufficient for the special education classroom in which he was placed. The results were considered to be satisfactory. As a point of explanation, the graph depicted in figure 4–40 is considered to be an optimal one during treatment steps C–F in that there was a straight line progression of treatment effects. During treatment level G, there was some diminution in achievement digressing to 85 percent success. An optimal shaping program should move at 100 percent success or at least close to that level, so that the child does not experience failure. If one is unable to achieve that level of criterion performance, they should back up and reinstate at the previous step to achieve maximal performance from the child.

Teaching Troy to Attend to Academic Tasks and Teacher Instruction for Ten-Minute Intervals

Behavior Counted: Two forms of data were recorded for monitoring the success of this treatment program. In the baseline period, the teacher recorded the percent of time during five-minute blocks of instruction or academic work in which Troy was attending directly to the task or instruction. For the subsequent treatment intervals, B–H, and on a random sample schedule, the teacher recorded the percent of time occurring during the time interval in which he was attending appropriately to the academic task or instruction. Two clocks were used: one to record the total time being sampled, and the other to indicate the total time during that time block in which he was attending appropriately.

Treatment A: This treatment as depicted in figure 4–41, represents the baseline in which six samples were recorded of the percent time that Troy was attending to task or instruction within five-minute periods. The baseline conditions depicted in figure 4–41 show that the variance ranges between 60 and 80 percent of the sampled five-minute periods of instruction or work in which he would actually be attending to task. Recognizing the learning deficits demonstrated by this boy, it was desirable to accelerate his attention to task time for him to maximally profit from classroom instruction.

Treatment B–H: The treatment sequences for conditions B–H are shown on figure 4–41. This treatment sequence progressed from socially reinforcing Troy on a 100 percent schedule for attending at the criterion level, and also randomly reinforcing with cereal reinforcement for these successful trials. The treatment times progressed from ten seconds to ten minutes on task or attending directly to teacher instruction. During varying times during the school day the teacher reinforced him if he was attending at the criterion level. At more infrequent occasions, she sampled the percent of trials which were reinforceable at the criterion level to monitor the effectiveness of the program.

Results: The results were acceptable in teaching Troy to attend for ten minutes steadily on task or to teacher instruction in a group setting. This program was easily conveyed to the family and special class teacher in his local public school to maintain this level of atten-

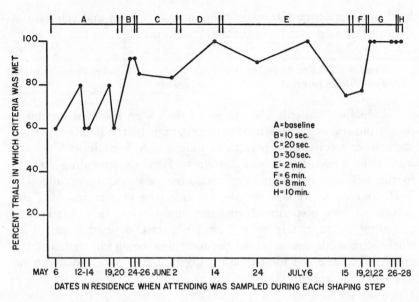

FIGURE 4-41 *Teaching Troy to Attend to Academic Task and Teacher Instruction*

tion to instruction. The cereal reinforcement was incipiently deleted from the program so that only social reinforcement was utilized to maintain this level of performance, with the latter being necessary for years after discharge.

Teaching Troy to Work Independently in the Classroom

Behavior Counted: Troy, with a group of three children, was trained to work independently for increasing periods of time in the classroom on academic materials. Formal data were not accumulated on this program except for occasional checks to determine if his progress was sufficient to advance to the next shaping step in the program. The data used to monitor this teaching sequence were: (1) counting the number of verbal distractions and "eyes off work" for five-minute samples; (2) the length of time he worked directly and independently on the task given him during that period; and (3) recording his attention (listening and watching) during a 1:1 program in a group storybook reading during a five-minute period.

Treatment A: In a series of time intervals in steps of five, ten, twenty, and finally, thirty minutes, Troy was praised for working independently for those time intervals. When the children were off task, they were redirected, told what they were doing wrong, and reinforced when the next time was successfully completed.

Results: Results were satisfactory in this shaping program since by the conclusion of his residency, Troy was able to work in the classroom for thirty minutes continuously without redirection from the teacher to remain on task.

Teaching Troy to Ask Appropriate Questions

Behavior Counted: On a designated sample day, staff counted the number of occasions Troy asked inappropriate questions. These data were accumulated for both baseline and treatment conditions, A and B, respectively.

Treatment A: The baseline of Treatment A was uncontrolled since staff acted however they wished to each time Troy asked them an inappropriate question. Questions were judged as inappropriate according to their judgment, which was based in part on discussions within the group. These inappropriate questions typically dealt with what was scheduled: immediately, in a few minutes, later on in the day, next week, etc., or irrelevant questions regarding the activity in which he was currently engaged. As for so many psychotic children, these questions centered around his daily structure. Troy would become obviously anxious when he was unaware of the exact schedule throughout the day. In the concrete type world which the psychotic child exists in, these kinds of questions are not unusual and quite understandable in that it is their attempt to provide some predictability to their myopic existence.

Treatment B: During this treatment condition, staff were required by a general management order for all days to make Troy substitute an appropriate question to replace each inappropriate one. Sampling was continued, and the effectiveness of this program is shown on figure 4–42. Social reinforcement was provided for his spontaneous appropriate questions as well as for those which he was required to rehearse to success which the staff could assist as much as necessary to elicit an appropriate response.

Results: The results were considered satisfactory regardless of the acceleration shown at the end of figure 4–42. This acceleration was attributed to his impending discharge to his home on a permanent basis with enrollment in the public school classroom. This was a

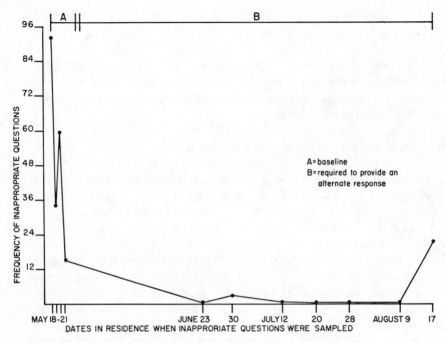

FIGURE 4–42 *Teaching Troy to Ask Appropriate Questions*

time in which he was facing massive schedule changes, which was an exacerbation of those conditions which historically triggered inappropriate questions. The treatment program was taught to parents and school teachers satisfactorily.

Teaching Troy to Speak Spontaneously and Appropriately

Behavior Counted: On the preselected sample days, the teacher recorded the instances in which Troy spoke spontaneously and appropriately to her and to his peers. Duration was not recorded in this program, but to receive a count the response had to be appropriate and at the language level which was currently expected for Troy. Thus, one statement usually received a count of "one," and a few seconds had to intervene between each statement to receive an additional count.

Treatment A: This treatment was held constant throughout the program. The program was conducted on a group basis in the classroom with the same management order maintained in the classroom. In either settings whenever he spoke spontaneously and appropriately to the staff or teacher, he received one token which was redeemable for the preferred snack at night time; he received two tokens for appropriate speech to peers. Greater reinforcement was given to peer interaction since he seemed to be least likely to speak to the other children.

Results: As shown in figure 4–43, during the course of training the sampled times in school decreased from ten minutes to five minutes, but there was still a definite acceleration of spontaneous speech. These results were considered satisfactory and indicated that a token combined with positive social reinforcement was helpful in facilitating Troy's spontaneous language production. Troy adapted to this program in his usual concrete fashion; he would speak and then hold out his hand in anticipation of forthcoming reinforcement from the teacher or staff member. It was recommended in his school placement that they attempt to diminish the reinforcement schedule to break up this stilted form of language. It is recommended with a similar child who responds in such a concrete manner to a language program that fading the reinforcement contingency be performed methodically—never when he holds his hand out for candy—and reserve the reward for occasions when his language is appropriate to the setting and elicits a response from another person.

There was certainly nothing very complex about this language program; in fact, most speech therapists would probably discredit it as being oversimplified. The simplicity of such an approach is that it may be implemented all day, by the teacher and family, which would

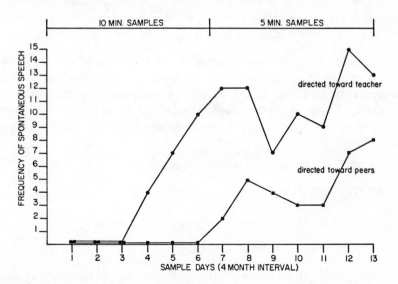

FIGURE 4–43 *Accelerating Troy's Spontaneous and Appropriate Speech*

probably be more effective than one or two hours of speech therapy per week. Furthermore, it enables the family to eventually be primarily responsible for the development of their child's language, which maintains the integrity of the family unit.

Acceleration of Troy's Spontaneous Conversation

Behavior Counted: Under general management order; not specifically monitored.

Treatment A: This treatment program was conducted in two fifteen-minute sessions each day by the cottage staff. This program was not baselined, but was assessed periodically in the school to determine if there was improvement in his conversational skills, and the information was relayed to the staff at the cottage. During these daily speech sessions which were on a 1:1 basis, staff took Troy for a walk or to some situation which was conducive to conversation. Staff initially asked Troy questions, but this was gradually reversed to requesting him to ask the questions and to be the instigator of the conversation. Gradually more complex replies and questions were expected of Troy, including, "Why," "How come," and "What makes" kinds of questions. The staff would require phrases and sentences in his responses. Since he was unable to provide an adequate and socially reinforceable response, they assisted him. If necessary, staff provided Troy the entire response to reiterate. Staff communicated with each other at shift break of their success so that those on the successive shift would be able to rehearse the error responses Troy previously incurred. He was reinforced socially during these sessions and throughout the day whenever he engaged in spontaneous conversations.

Results: Data was not accumulated for this particular program, which means that we could not scientifically assess how much this program contributed to his discharge language status. Clinically speaking, the change in communicative language was momentous. Four years after discharge, Troy is mainstreaming normal classes almost exclusively.

CASE STUDY: JEFF

Admission Age: 10 years, 3 months.

Duration of Residency: 4 months.

Diagnosis: It was difficult to conceptualize a formal diagnosis for Jeff, but diagnosis of childhood schizophrenia was questionably accepted. Jeff's birth history was normal, and he was a large baby, weighing 9 pounds, 7 ounces, with no reported history of birth trauma or prenatal difficulty. It was noted at an early age that Jeff was developmentally lagging. He did not walk until sixteen months of age, and he did not speak intelligibly until three years of age. Frequent neurological examinations and medical reports up to his admission yielded no abnormalities. However, he was not sufficiently compliant to take reliable intellectual testing during those years, he was difficult for the parents to handle, he did not play with other children, and he continued to develop as a withdrawn and isolated child whose play activities were not at the constructive or exploratory level expected for his age. There was never evidence of a reactive withdrawal on his behalf, but rather, as a child who was always behind his peers. He was out of step developmentally in comparison to his sibs, and he progressively acquired numerous strange behaviors which made him less adaptive to the school setting. Allowing for undetermined intellectual deficits, he was particularly unable to attend to instruction in a group setting to acquire the academic skills for the correct age-class placement. Available accounts of his classroom behavior prior to admission to the research group indicated that he engaged in masturbatory activity quite extensively, which was disruptive to the entire classroom. He demonstrated behaviors such as crouching and cupping his hands over his mouth and making monkey-like sounds, after which he jumped up and walked around in a hunched-over posture. Many of his behaviors were bizarre, such as crawling around on the bathroom floor among the toilets rather than going outside to recess. It was difficult for the teacher to control his behavior, which was seldom goal-directed, yet his behavior did not appear to be intended to simply obtain attention from others. It impressed us that Jeff preferred being by himself, and in his isolation he engaged in these strange behaviors which eventually prompted the referral diagnosis of childhood schizophrenia. He demonstrated numerous motor-mannerisms with his hands. He engaged in spinning certain objects and was occasionally aggressive with other children. Many of his vocalizations had a self-stimulating pattern rather than a communicative value with others. The parents' understanding of Jeff was understandably confused, because of their numerous contacts with professionals over the years which had resulted in blatantly inconsistent interpretations of Jeff's behavior. We were informed that Jeff was untestable, but the parents had been led to believe that he was potentially of average intelligence and would "grow out" of his difficulties. It had been variously speculated that he was emotionally disturbed, autistic or schizophrenic; the parents only concluded that he would mature out of this diagnostic puzzle and eventually bloom into a bright youngster like the remaining children in the family. Actually, no one knew what Jeff was—neither the parents, nor the professionals. And for this reason he was referred and accepted into the research group.

Admission IQ: Wechsler Intelligence Scale for Children: Verbal IQ, 84; Performance IQ, 72; Full Scale IQ, 76.

Discharge IQ: Wechsler Intelligence Scale for Children: Verbal, 72; Performance, 92; and Full Scale, 80.

Specified Referral Problems: Jeff could not be retained in a public school classroom, nor adapt optimally in his home and community for the following reasons: (1) inattention to instruction from other persons; (2) bizarre speech and mannerisms; (3) academic retardation; (4) failure to interact in play or cooperation with peers; (5) inappropriate eating behavior; and (6) bizarre and restricted language.

Accelerating Jeff's Compliance to Verbal Commands

Behavior Counted: The behavior counted was the number of commands delivered and number of times he complied; a correct compliance response was defined by his beginning that response within ten seconds after the command was delivered. The data was recorded on a hand-tally counter carried by the staff; it was accumulated both in the cottage and the school and entered in the data book as the percent of verbal commands to which he complied.

Treatment A: This treatment was a one-week baseline of compliance to verbal commands. During this baseline when commands were given, and after ten seconds had intervened with no compliance occurring, staff repeated the question. Usually the staff persisted in repeating the commands until compliance was achieved, although there were occasions in which they simply had to drop the command. Praise was not given for his eventual compliance to these commands during the baseline interval, which meant this was a controlled baseline because all staff responded the same.

Treatment B: During treatment, one-day-per-week samples were taken to assess the effectiveness of the program. A different day in each successive week was used for obtaining these samples of compliance and noncompliance. The management order was simple. He was allowed ten seconds to begin compliance, and if he did comply he received verbal praise from the staff member present. If he did not initiate compliance during that ten-second interval, he was given a two-minute time-out at that location. If he failed to take an appropriate time-out, he was taken to the quiet room where he received a three-minute time-out, which was the time-out training program for Jeff. Furthermore, there was a qualitative shift in this program in that the complexity of the commands were graduated from simple to more complex as the program progressed. These commands began very simply for all tasks and required less than one minute to perform. These tasks were presented all day in both cottage and school; as the program advanced, the commands required more behavioral steps to accomplish. The change in command complexity was communicated to the parents so that they could continue training at a comparable level on the weekends.

Results: Figure 4–44 shows the effect of this program. A special baseline interval reveals that he was compliant about 50 percent of the time. This was a moderately low level of compliance, particularly since the requests were at a very simple level; these same commands were also used at the beginning of the treatment phase. With a combined program of praise and time-out, there was a rather quick acceleration to about 80 percent compliance which continued to climb slightly above that level. It was concluded that he learned to become a more compliant child; the parents learned to perform this program

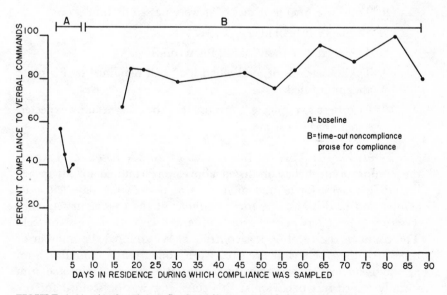

FIGURE 4-44 *Accelerating Jeff's Compliance to Verbal Commands*

without requiring constant supervision and were able to conduct the program on the weekends.

The parents were required to return data from the weekends to monitor the compliance program. Quite often they failed to provide this requested information, or more typically, had comments suggesting that he had been compliant the entire time, which was dubious. We suspected that their expectations had not progressed substantially, and they were making demands of him which they were certain that he would follow without opposition. The most important place for his compliant behavior to be maintained was in the classroom, and this seemed to generalize well at date of discharge. His teacher in the public school was trained in the conduct of this program so that she could maintain the discharge level of compliance.

Teaching Jeff to Control his Inappropriate Mealtime Behavior

Behavior Counted: Inappropriate behaviors which were counted during meals were as follows:

1. Back and shoulders hunched over table.
2. Lowering mouth to food rather than lifting food to mouth.
3. Using the wrong silverware.
4. Holding utensils incorrectly.
5. Smelling food as dishes of it were passed by him.
6. Touching food as dishes of it were passed by him.
7. Eating with his fingers.
8. Taking rather than asking for seconds.
9. Taking seconds of food when food still remained on his plate and unfinished.
10. Failure to say "please," "excuse me," or other usually expected social graces at a meal.

Treatment A: This treatment was a four-day baseline in which the inappropriate behaviors listed above were counted for all meals, including snacks, for a total of four meal periods per day. After accumulation of this baseline the remainder of the treatment sequence was sampled one day per week on a different day each successive week. The count of the baseline was controlled. We counted the number of times that these behaviors occurred while concurrently reminding him of the behavior he was demonstrating. We did not reinforce him socially for correct behavior at this time, nor was he scolded for the inappropriate response.

Treatment B: Throughout this interval, one-day-per-week samples of the above behaviors were monitored. The program was in effect for all meals and snacks; the parents were expected to perform it on the weekends. The treatment method required that at the beginning of each meal he was told by staff all the behaviors expected of him, i.e., not to do any of the above inappropriate behaviors, and a reiteration of appropriate table manners. For each occurrence of these inappropriate responses, he received a two-minute time-out on the bench outside of the dining room preceded by a reminder of the behavior which resulted in that time-out. He was allotted thirty minutes to complete each meal, including snacks, and the time in which he was on a time-out was deleted from this thirty-minute interval. The sample count at these times were the number of times he received time-outs, which was congruent with the same behaviors obtained in baseline; namely, the number of reminders he received for inappropriate behaviors. Social reinforcement was used variably during the meal for correct manners.

Results: The treatment effect was considered satisfactory. After the time interval contained on the graph, the management order was altered. As shown in figure 4–45, we succeeded in diminishing inappropriate table manners. However, he repeatedly demonstrated bizarre responses during his time-outs which would make him rather conspicuous when in public, as well as perpetuate those habits. The

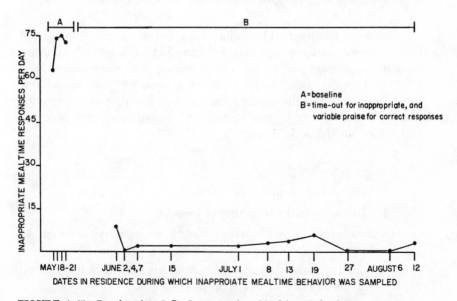

FIGURE 4–45 *Decelerating Jeff's Inappropriate Mealtime Behaviors*

management order was changed so that when he was taking his two-minute time-out for inappropriate behaviors, he concurrently exercised with calisthenics rather than just being seated. The rationale was to replace the bizarre behaviors with an incompatible behavior during the time-out interval. Jeff did not like to exercise, so in that respect it was making a punishment condition of the time-out. But, he was so compliant by this time that he performed these exercises during the time-out. This management order was retained in effect until his discharge with the exception of occasional samples to determine if bizarre responses had declined during time-outs when exercises were not required. Our clinical impression was that a deceleration occurred, but since there was no supporting data this remains purely conjecture. Also, as in the previous management order, he was variably praised for eating correctly and this reinforcement was diminished corresponding with the reduction of inappropriate behaviors. He was receiving fewer time-outs and less praise for appropriate table manners, but engaging in more conversation during the meals.

The parents were trained in performing this program at home. Their data was again sporadic and not sufficiently reliable for graphing. It seemed that they were having no complaints over his manners. This did not necessarily imply that his behaviors had generalized favorably to the home mealtimes, but rather the parents' expectancies may have been less than what we required at the Center.

Controlling Jeff's Inappropriate Sounds and Mannerisms

Behavior Counted: The behaviors grouped in this category of bizarre sounds and mannerisms were recorded by hand-tally counters both in the cottage and in the school during the entire sample days selected. Initially, two counts were taken, one for sounds and one for mannerisms, but these were later grouped together as a combined count. The following bizarre sounds and mannerisms were observed and tallied for the daily frequency.

Bizarre Sounds:
1. Whispering to fingers or silverware.
2. Mumbling and whispering to himself.
3. Loud yelling or "roaring" during an activity, or when by himself.
4. Giggling and hysterical laughter to himself, or out of context for the activity in which he was engaged.

Bizarre Mannerisms:

1. Posturing his mouth wide open without making a sound.
2. Changing the shape of his mouth by holding it open.
3. Contracting facial muscles in a grimace.
4. Crossing his eyes.
5. Smelling objects.
6. Protruding his tongue.
7. Flapping arms up and down.
8. Spreading and closing of his fingers in a rhythmical manner.
9. Holding head with hands and pulling at his face.
10. Clenching fists and knocking them together or placing them to his chin.
11. Effeminate prancing or skipping while flapping arms.
12. Banging objects together.
13. Sitting on a railing and posturing there.

Treatment A: This was a baseline frequency of these behaviors as observed over four consecutive days, both in the cottage and school. This was a controlled baseline in which all staff responded by ignoring the behavior and recording it as discreetly as possible so as not to accidentally reinforce the response by use of the counter.

Treatment B: The management order used was in effect for both the cottage and school. The data was obtained on one day per week, on a different day each successive week. Treatment B was a positive token program which was used as a reward system on an intermittent schedule. At various preselected times during the day—at least three times—he was observed. These observation times occurred at scheduled activities such as the swings, morning cartoons, meals, school, etc. The staff covertly observed him; if thirty seconds transpired with no occurrence of bizarre sounds and/or mannerisms, they praised him verbally and warmly, explained his correct behavior, and gave him a token. If during that thirty-second period of time he exhibited any of the above mentioned behaviors, the staff explained to Jeff that they had been watching him, and he would have earned a token if he had not demonstrated those responses. For those instances in which bizarre behavior did occur, he was required to positive practice that same time period without demonstrating the inappropriate behavior. He was socially reinforced for successful positive practice. For example, if he was watching TV and flapping his arms, he was asked to watch TV again for the same time interval without flapping, and he received social reinforcement and an explanation of his appropriate behavior. The tokens used for occurrences when he did not demonstrate these behaviors were different from those which he earned for cleaning up his room, and other daily chores. The program was initially a positive one based upon reinforcement and positive practice; he did not lose tokens he had obtained in the program. Each token was worth one minute of late night time, which was highly desired by Jeff. Ten tokens were exchangeable for a glass of chocolate milk during snacks if he wished. The left-hand vertical axis of figure 4–46 contains the baseline data against which the treatment effect is compared. That axis shows the total number of inappropriate sounds and mannerisms occurring during that period of time. The right-hand vertical axis shows the percent of observations occurring during treatment interval B in which he earned tokens. A stabilized effect occurred, so treatment C was initiated.

Treatment C: The program was altered to add a punishment aspect to control these inappropriate behaviors. The program required that at the conclusion of each meal, Jeff received twenty-five tokens. At the next meal he had to turn his tokens in without being instructed. If he did not, he did not eat until he had turned them in on his own

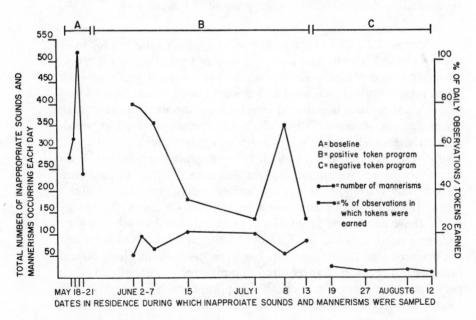

FIGURE 4–46 *Decelerating Jeff's Inappropriate Sounds and Mannerisms*

intention. He had to have ten tokens to earn the meal, and fifteen to have seconds. These tokens were removed from him for occurrences of observed bizarre sounds and mannerisms whenever he was in a public situation, exclusive of those times he was in his own room or in the bathroom. This program was arranged on a series of shaping steps which essentially "tightened down" the requirements, but this was performed in correspondence to the diminution of his bizarre behaviors.

The shaping steps were performed as follows:

1. Days 1–33, he received twenty-five tokens; he needed ten for the next meal and fifteen for seconds.

2. Days 34–41, he received eighteen tokens; he needed ten for the next meal, and fifteen for seconds.

3. Days 42–62, he received ten tokens; he needed five for the next meal, and eight for seconds.

4. Days 62–75, he received five tokens; he needed one for the next meal and three for seconds.

5. Days 76–discharge, he received three tokens; he needed one for the next meal, and two for seconds.

The data for this program are shown partially in treatment step C of figure 4–46, although these data were not shown in this graph since the preferred effect had become obvious. This program was a punishment program, perhaps to be construed as negative reinforcement, so that taking away the stimulus (tokens) accelerated the demonstrated appropriate mannerisms. Actually, it was taking away the stimulus to decelerate an inappropriate behavior. It may be construed as a punishment program in the sense that the desired tokens, which were redeemable for food, were removed for the presence of an abnormal mannerism or gesture that had to be decelerated.

Results: Figure 4–46 contains the data for this study and shows the frequency of mannerisms dropped precipitously from that plateau that had been occurring under the initial management order. The responses dropped to a very tolerable level where he always received his meals. The program was effective in the sense that he did not miss over three meals during the course of the entire shaping hierarchy in treatment C. The treatment effects were considered satisfactory, and were ones which the home could have been expected to employ, although we suspect that the family did not maintain this program very consistently at the home.

Results: The above programs were the ones for which data was formally accumulated on Jeff. Perhaps this may seem as a rather simplistic program for so disturbed a child—it was. There were a number of semi-formal programs which were also performed. These general management orders included such techniques as positive practicing inappropriate or bizarre language until it was communicative. Positive rehearsal was used extensively in his relationships with other children in which he was asked to repeat sequences of inappropriate behavior with direction and reinforcement until it was performed correctly. The school program was geared toward teaching him to be able to function in a large classroom with other children, both behaviorally and academically. Social and primary reinforcements were used extensively in that school program. The combined effect of all these programs was considered successful and he was able to be returned to the public school from which he had been ejected. He was able to be a part of the classroom setting, even though he still appeared as a strange youngster. Regardless, the acceptance for him was sufficient that he was voted as the "most popular child" at one time in his classroom, which was certainly saying something positive about Jeff's development and new ability to elicit sympathy from peers!

Parent training was considered successful, although the mother remained negative toward us throughout the program. Her anger stemmed primarily from our treatment-based prognosis for Jeff, which included his level of intellectual functioning and our prediction that he would never be able to aspire toward the higher education that she considered to be routine for all of her children. The father expressed his appreciation by donating money for the purchase of a tape recorder. Follow-up from the parents revealed that the mother was conducting the programs she was taught in the parent training sessions; she is primarily responsible for their implementation at home and she is maintaining liaison with the school. Yet, while she successfully uses what she has been trained, she still remains angry with us, which is an unusual circumstance to result from treatment. Usually the parent who remains angry does not maintain the programs after discharge.

When Jeff was admitted, referring agency personnel considered him to be a schizophrenic child on the basis of his bizarre behaviors, his aloofness from others, and his maladaptive social behaviors with peers and school. Now, instead of eating by himself, he eats at the table appropriately with other people. His language is not so bizarre, and can be corrected and rehearsed to success at home and at school. He is able to be retained in a public school classroom and to profit from that instruction. The diagnostic category of childhood schizophrenia is probably less applicable to Jeff now than it was before.

However, the basic deficiency, which predisposed Jeff to develop the kinds of behaviors which he demonstrated, probably still remains. His compensatory training was considered to be quite useful in this six-month program in which he was enrolled.

CASE STUDY: JERRY

Admission Age: 5 years, 1 month.

Duration of Residency: 6 months.

Diagnosis: Organic brain syndrome (petit mal and grand mal seizures), accompanied by mental retardation and severe behavioral problems.

Admission IQ: Stanford Binet Form L-M. Chronological age 5 years, 2 months; mental age 3 years 10 months; IQ = 71.

Discharge IQ: Stanford Binet Form L-M. Chronological age 5 years, 7 months; mental age 4 years, 5 months; IQ = 77.

Specified Referral Problems: Jerry had been exposed to numerous preschool and clinic experiences—none of which were able to control his behavior on an outpatient basis—and resulted in a variety of diagnoses ranging from brain damage to childhood psychosis. For 14 months prior to treatment he never had a bowel movement unassisted by either an enema or suppository. His petit mal seizures were high in frequency and grand mal had been controlled medically. Jerry was an angry, tantrumous, noncompliant child whose sparse language was incomprehensible to the unacquainted observer. His peer interactions were marred by aggression. The parents had been held responsible for his behavioral condition, but in consideration of his medical problems, retardation, and language handicap, it was our impression that any home would have experienced child-rearing problems. Primarily because of the parents' persistence with the parent training program, Jerry developed into such a smiling and compliant rascal that it is difficult to recollect what his behavior was really like.

Teaching Jerry to Acquire Eye Contact at Fifteen-Foot Distances from the Teacher for Five Consecutive Seconds

Behavior Counted: In order to teach Jerry understandable language, as well as preparing him for inclusion in a special classroom where he would undoubtedly be eventually placed, it was necessary to teach him to attend to the instructor. We selected fifteen feet from the instructor as the goal distance in the shaping sequence of training eye contact and to maintain that eye contact for five consecutive seconds. The behavior counted throughout the training sequence was the number of successful total trials which yielded a percent of successful eye contacts. Eye contact training was trained in sessions in the school.

Treatment A: This treatment, as shown on figure 4–47, represents baseline samples of his eye contact. The graph has to be inspected closely, since the data points are not connected by a line as they represent different steps which are trained later in the treatment sequence. The dots, numbered 1 through 5, represent respectively one-, three-, five-, ten-, and fifteen-foot distances of eye contact tested for one second. Ten samples were taken for each data point. Furthermore, ten samples were taken of each of these distances for one second during speech training which had begun at this time. The data shows that with increasing distance, his performance declined dramatically. Even at the one-foot distance he was able to maintain one-second eye contact for only 45 percent of all trials sampled. Jerry demonstrated zero

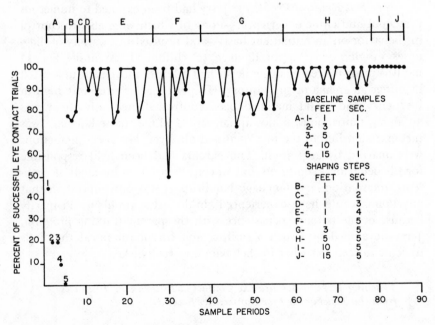

FIGURE 4–47   *Treatment Sequence for Teaching Jerry a Five-Second Eye Contact at Fifteen Feet in School*

percent success when the distance was increased to fifteen feet. Obviously, there was such a deficit in attention that he would not profit substantially in classroom placement where he would be seated at a distance from the teacher.

Treatment B: This treatment, as well as all remaining successive shaping steps of eye contact training, required that before he progressed to the next step in distance and time, he had to achieve at least 85 percent success on the training trials for several sessions. Treatment B represented teaching Jerry to maintain one-second eye contact at one foot. The general management order was held constant for the remaining shaping steps. The management order required scheduled training sessions at varying times during each day of school. During these training sessions he was seated at a desk facing the teacher who used his name as a command for attention, with correct responses being rewarded both with social and primary reinforcers in the form of preferred cereals and occasionally candies. The primary reinforcers were gradually deleted from the program, with social reinforcement retained as the dominant system by termination of the shaping steps.

Treatments C–J: The successive shaping steps for attention training are outlined in the following steps:

Shaping Step	Distance	Time
B	1 foot	1 second
C	1 foot	2 seconds
D	1 foot	3 seconds
E	1 foot	4 seconds
F	1 foot	5 seconds
G	3 feet	5 seconds
H	5 feet	5 seconds
I	10 feet	5 seconds
J	15 feet	5 seconds

Results: The shaping curriculum was successful in teaching Jerry to maintain five-second eye contact at fifteen-foot distance 100 percent of the time. By the last shaping step, his attention was maintained without the use of primary reinforcers in a group setting. Eye contact was assisted for generalization by having staff reinforce him socially numerous times throughout the day when he demonstrated eye contact at any distance for any period of time. There were also occasions in which they would "hold out" for the five-second time before reinforcement would be provided.

Five seconds may seem a long period of time for a child to turn and look at someone upon command and attend. However, for Jerry it was a necessary period of time to deliver speech trials and instructions for the kinds of tasks that he was learning at that time.

Teaching Jerry to Maintain Five-Second Eye Contact at Ten Feet while in the Cottage

Behavior Counted: The behavior counted in this shaping sequence was the number of successful training trials and the total number of trials in the training sessions administered throughout the day. The data yielded a percent of successful trials for each training session. When he attained 85 percent success on two successive training sessions he was advanced to the next shaping step.

Treatment A: Treatment A, as shown in figure 4–48, was the first step of teaching Jerry to maintain one-second eye contact at one-foot distances from the trainer. During this and successive sessions, there were four ten-minute training sessions each day with Jerry and one other child who was at a similar level of deficit in attending. They were seated at a chair across a table from the staff member providing the training. The cue was the child's name, and correct responses

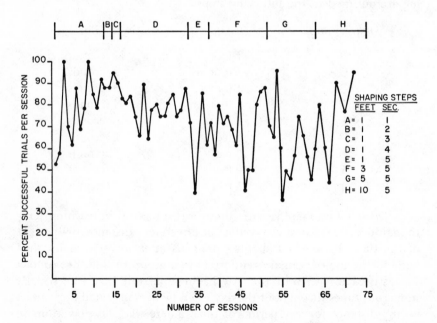

FIGURE 4–48 *Treatment Sequence for Teaching Jerry a Five-Second Eye Contact at Fifteen Feet in Cottage*

were reinforced socially and with a mixed primary reinforcer of raisins and preferred cereals. Several seconds intervened between trials.

Treatment B–F: The successive steps for this training sequence are listed below:

Shaping Step	Distance	Time
B	1 foot	2 seconds
C	1 foot	3 seconds
D	1 foot	4 seconds
E	1 foot	5 seconds
F	3 feet	5 seconds
G	5 feet	5 seconds
H	10 feet	5 seconds

Under treatment condition F, the program was running into difficulty. At this time we were having one training session in the cottage at this distance rather than the four that we had previously scheduled. It was also a time when his social behavior was becoming more complex, and he was beginning to be "testy" in many of the sessions. The primary reinforcement condition was maintained for correct responses during this time; however, error responses in treatment condition F were timed-out with a two-minute time-out period at that point. This was decided because it had become very apparent that he was capable of producing correct responses, and his incorrect responses were performed with an evasive grin, presumably to determine what would happen if he "refused." This was not necessarily a "bad" behavior since it represented a more complex social response for Jerry, but unfortunately, if this behavior was allowed to flourish, it might undermine the success we had achieved so far in cottage and school in teaching attention just prior to his being discharged back to home and school. A time-out condition was two minutes duration for error responses with primary social reinforcement being maintained for correct responses.

Results: The program was judged as satisfactory since in the cottage setting he was able to acquire five-second eye contact at ten feet, which was the goal behavior to be trained in that setting. There was greater variability in his performance in the cottage than in the school even though the programs were conducted concurrently. This was accounted for by the structure not being as "tight" as it was in school, which further substantiates the necessity for having a very concrete and structured training environment for a brain-damaged child such as Jerry. After the response had been reliably acquired, then generalization training could commence in a variety of situations with less structure. The variability in his performance in the more open setting of the cottage showed that there would be a greater likelihood of his retrieving inattentive behaviors in the out-of-school setting. This, in fact, was confirmed quite soon after his discharge when he became less attentive to parental instructions, yet was able to generalize quite well to the school setting. Several retraining sessions were necessary in the home to repair this deficit, and it is suspected that this program will have to be maintained for several years in the home before the preferred stability of the behavior is achieved.

Teaching Jerry to Take a Time-Out Which Would be Adaptable to a Public School Setting

Behavior Counted: During the course of Jerry's treatment programs a number of behaviors were being "timed-out" to decelerate their frequency. We intended to avoid the problem of discharging Jerry with a behavioral status that required use of a quiet room to maintain control of his deviant behaviors. Such a technique would not be available in the home, and less likely in the public school setting. We wished to train Jerry so that these behaviors could be controlled by the teacher or parents by their saying "Take a time-out," at which time he would go to some designated place and be seated quietly by himself, and when informed that the two minutes were over, return back to task. During the three steps of this training program, the staff recorded the number of successful and unsuccessful time-outs that he received for the number of behaviors that were being timed-out during the course of treatment. Thus, these data represent our teaching him to take an appropriate time-out for a variety of different behaviors which are not individually depicted on the graph shown in figure 4–49.

Treatment A: In this first step of the training program, he was told to take a two minute time-out in a place designated by the staff. The management order stipulated that the staff could take him there by his hand and sit him down. Unsuccessful time-outs were given an additional five-minute time-out in the quiet room when they occurred on this and later steps. An unsuccessful time-out was defined by his leaving that designated spot.

Treatment B: In treatment B, he was instructed to go unassisted to the place designated by staff for the two-minute time-out. After the time had transpired, he was told by staff to return to the activity and continue with the task he was working at prior to the time-out.

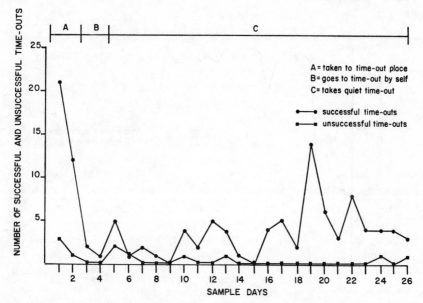

FIGURE 4–49   *Teaching Jerry to Take an Appropriate Time-Out*

Treatment C: In treatment step C, he was told the same instructions as in treatment B, but he had to be quiet when he took his timeout with no noise whatsoever. During treatment B, it was observed that he was going to the time-out place without assistance quite successfully, but was operating for various forms of attention by talking, etc.

Results: The results were satisfactory in that the number of unsuccessful time-outs were reduced close to zero. The successful time-outs were dominant throughout the course of this program. The line showing successful time-outs did vary at times due to the addition of new behaviors being decelerated. It should be noted that this graph represents a composite of all behaviors being timed-out during the course of treatment.

Teaching Jerry Compliance to Verbal Commands

Behavior Counted: The data logged for this program were the percent of commands given Jerry by staff in which he complied to that command within five seconds, as determined by staff counting silent to themselves, 1001, 1002, etc.

Treatment A: This treatment was an uncontrolled baseline in which staff would make requests of him with all staff reacting however

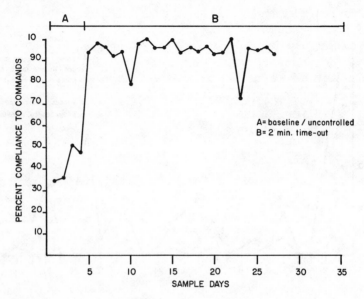

FIGURE 4–50 *Accelerating Jerry's Compliance to Verbal Commands*

they wished when he did not comply with the exception of never giving a time-out for his noncompliance. They counted the number of times they commanded him to do something, and the number of times he complied. The data for this is shown under condition A on figure 4–50.

Treatment B: Under treatment B, each time that Jerry failed to comply with a command given him by staff, he was given a two-minute time-out. This time-out was administered according to the time-out training condition in effect. Thus, in the earlier part of this program he may have been taken directly to the place for taking a time-out, but eventually he learned to take a time-out quietly and without supervision. During the treatment condition, if he did not begin to comply within five seconds, he was given a time-out. It was stipulated that if he stopped a task, staff were to re-issue the command and count it as a new trial. He was not given a time-out for having failed to complete the task after he had initiated it, since it was understood that his attention span was still delimited. However, if by the second trial he did not complete it, and he was known to be capable of doing so, he would be given a time-out. Considerable social praise was given for all compliance; primary reinforcements were not provided for this training program. For those tasks in which he was learning an entirely new behavior, such as certain aspects of manners, dressing, and eating, he was given very simple commands which divided the response into units which we knew he could perform. Thus, dressing may have been divided into a series of a dozen different commands for putting his trousers on, and later this was graduated so that he would eventually be expected to perform the entire task on command. In other words, the commands for compliance were at a level in which it was known he could succeed, but the demands were gradually increased so that he was learning to do more complex tasks with diminishing supervision. For example, if he began to eat with his fingers, or forgot to ask for something and simply grabbed it from the table, staff corrected him, such as, "Use your fork, Jerry," and that was counted as a compliance trial. If he then began to use his fork, it was a success and praised, whereas if he did not, it was a noncompliance for which he was timed-out.

Results: The results shown in figure 4–50 under condition B were considered to be unusually satisfactory. Jerry was a child who was most receptive to verbal praise, as evidenced by the grin on his face and the data shown in this figure. He was functioning at very close to a 95 percent level of compliance with the exception for one dip in the data just prior to his discharge which is typical for most cases. We were pleased with the results with this compliance program since it was apparent that with social reinforcement a minimum of time-outs, Jerry could readily be maintained in his home and school.

Training Jerry Normal Defecation

Behavior Counted: When Jerry was admitted, due to training and perhaps organic conditions unknown to us, he was a severely and chronically constipated child. His only defecation was with the assistance of suppositories, and even with such chemical assistance the results were unpredictable. He was a youngster who had to be taken to the physician quite frequently to interrupt impaction. Two kinds of data were recorded in this program of training the lower colon to defecate without chemical assistance. One kind of data, figure 4–51, was the number of stools which occurred during each sample day with the assistance of suppositories, and were diminished throughout the course of the program. The second form of data was the number of stools occurring per sample period without the assistance of suppository intervention.

Treatments A–P: The rationale for this shaping sequence was that since a suppository (Dulcolax) was sufficient in initiating the defecation, it may be possible to train this response with diminishing

amounts of suppositories, then substituting a nonchemical suppository
(glycerin) and finally deleting this mechanical suppository altogether.
This was a shaping program in which we were not only attempting to
train the lower colon to defecate on the diminishing stimulus of the
suppository, but also concurrently training the child to eat a diversity
of foods which would be likely to assist defecation. The data in figure
4–51 do not show the dietary changes for Jerry, but he was encouraged
and heavily reinforced socially for eating more roughage foods, as
well as using fruit as a reward in the other training programs in effect
during the six-month training program. In summary, the entire treatment picture was one of teaching Jerry to eat a more balanced diet,
using fruit and roughage foods as reinforcers as much as possible,
fading chemical assistance for defecation, and making toileting a
pleasant experience for him. Jerry, as well as similar children we have
worked with in the past on defecation problems, are often terrified of
the toilet because of the pain associated with defecation due to their
chronic constipation. No time-outs, negative reinforcement, or punishment were utilized in this program. It was entirely a positive shaping
program. The shaping steps A–P represents sixteen steps of shaving
off 1/16 of an inch from a one inch suppository, with advancement
to the next step contingent upon our ability to maintain defecation.

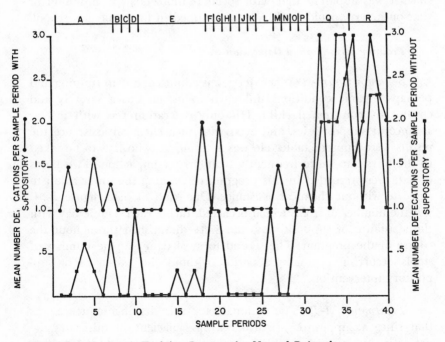

FIGURE 4–51 *Jerry's Training Program for Normal Defecation*

He was placed on the toilet several times each day and immediately after he received his suppository. After each meal he was placed on the toilet for at least five minutes.

The management order was simply that he was to receive a suppository each day and immediately placed on the toilet. The size of the suppository was to be decreased 1/16 of an inch each time it was administered, providing it was successful the day before in stimulating defecation. If he was unsuccessful in having a bowel movement after the suppository was administered, the size of the suppository on the next day reverted back to the previous level which was successful and retained there if necessary, or increased in size on successive days until success was again achieved. During the first half of this program, he would receive Colace each night to assist defecation. After every meal he was placed on the toilet and data was recorded if there was a bowel movement without the assistance of the suppository. This program was maintained by the parents on the weekend.

During conditions Q and R shown on figure 4–51, a glycerin suppository was used at a 1/16-inch length, and was successful in assisting defecation. This was dropped from the program during condition R exclusively, since he was able to defecate without the assistance of even that mechanical assistance. At this time he was discharged home and the glycerin suppository was used by the parents only if he did not have a bowel movement every two days. They were instructed to use ¼-inch or less length of the suppository.

Results: The results shown in figure 4–51 show that the average number of bowel movements occurring per sample period gradually increased, even though the suppositories were diminished in size by 1/16 of an inch for each successive shaping step. This data monitored the hypothesis that we were conditioning the lower colon to respond without chemical assistance. Furthermore, as shown in the right vertical axis in figure 4–51, the number of stools occurring per sample period without any suppository assistance was correspondingly increasing. Furthermore, by the termination of the program, as indicated by conditions Q and R, the suppository had been changed to glycerin, and even with 1/16 of an inch of glycerin, we were obtaining the same results as we had with the chemical intervention. By the conclusion of this program we were able to cease using the glycerin suppositories except on every third or fourth day at home if bowel movements did not occur. By the conclusion of the program we had a youngster who was going to the bathroom by himself and proudly showing staff what he had produced. The program was considered to be a success. It is doubtful if this would have been successful without the concurrent training of eating a greater variety of foods, including

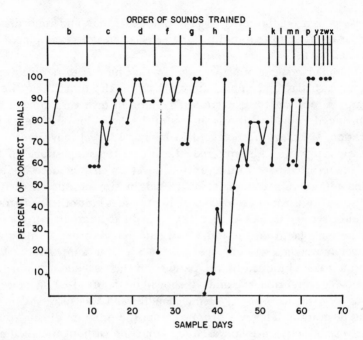

FIGURE 4-52 *Acquisition of Prerequisite Speech Sounds for Language Training*

roughage and fruits in the reinforcement program, which were recommended for continuation at home with Jerry.

Teaching Jerry Prerequisite Speech Sounds for Language Training

Behavior Counted: To monitor this program we recorded the percent of trials on the successive treatment steps in which Jerry was successful. Ninety percent accuracy on the sounds as sampled in school would be required before he was moved to the next speech sound.

Treatments A–E: The treatment program was the same both in the cottage and school for training articulation of sounds indicated in the treatment sequence shown in figure 4–52. Two ten-minute training sessions were required per day in the cottage and school. There was also a standing management order in which the sounds in training that occurred in his conversation with staff would be rehearsed to success. It was stipulated that before he moved on to the next sound that he be 90 percent successful at the frontal, terminal, and medial positions of sounds in words which had been trained up to that date. Figure 4–52 shows the data for the training sequence, and the table below includes the treatment sequence in which the sounds were trained.

Treatment Condition	Articulation Sound Trained	Treatment Condition	Articulation Sound Trained
A	B	I	L
B	C	J	M
C	D	K	N
D	F	L	P
E	G	M	Y
F	H	N	Z
G	J	O	W
H	K	P	X

In this session training program, primary reinforcers, composed primarily of fruits to assist the constipation program, were used in conjunction with social reinforcement. During the day, staff tried to stimulate the sounds currently under training from Jerry and reinforce him socially for correct articulation of the sound. At the termination of this program, Jerry was able to emit the sounds at least 90 percent accurately in their uses with words. Jerry will always be a retarded youngster whose speech content will remain delimited, and without much variability. However, he was now comprehensible, which was not the case when admitted. It was necessary for positive practice to remain in effect for his speech program, so that when he made error responses, he had to rehearse them to correction, for which he received social reinforcement. Thus, the articulation program was coordinated with the general speech program in which speech was stimulated and socially reinforced as much as possible throughout the day.

Results: The results were considered to be satisfactory in that he was able to emit the sounds being trained at a level which could be either understood, or he could be cued to rehearse the response he was trying to emit so that it was understood by the receiver. Error responses were always available to Jerry; it was necessary that positive practice be maintained at home and school. This training was given to the parents as well as to the speech therapist at his school.

CASE STUDY: KARL

Admission Age: 7 years, 1 month.

Duration of Residency: 6 months.

Diagnosis: Karl was referred with the diagnosis of childhood schizophrenia. His behavior was best described as entirely unpatterned.

He would run, stumble, and barge from one non-goal directed activity to another. The parents, clinic, and school personnel had been at a loss in controlling his behavior on various attempted outpatient programs. Our view of Karl was that of a severely retarded child with language acquisition handicaps that had rendered the child rearing practices of the home ineffectual. It was not our impression that the family was disturbed and the emotional relationships therein responsible for his behavior patterns. The diffuse label of autism was partially descriptive of Karl, but retardation was a more functional diagnosis.

Admission IQ: Untestable.

Discharge IQ: Stanford Binet Form L-M. Chronological age 7 years, 6 months; mental age 3 years, 3 months; IQ = 39.

Specified Referral Problems: The almost total absence of compliance, minimal eye contact, and reckless abandon of his hyperactivity made it impossible for community resources to provide services for Karl. His language was restricted to mimicking TV and radio commercials, and was otherwise totally non-functional. His eating was limited to a few highly preferred foods; he was not affectionate to other peers and adults, in fact, his social aloofness was of concern to the parents by age three-and-one-half.

Teaching Karl to Eat a Variety of Foods by Using Preferred Food as the Reinforcer for Eating Nonpreferred Foods

Behavior Counted: Karl was such a low-level autistic child that it was necessary to use foods as rewards for training a variety of prerequisite behaviors necessary for returning him to the home and public school. Unfortunately, as with many autistic children, food was not particularly reinforcing for Karl. He had free access to the food cupboards in his very uncontrolled existence at home. When the parents were not watching, he would race to the cupboard and snatch the preferred items which he wished, gobble them up, and then move on to some other more disoriented activities. Obtaining food was probably one of his most goal-directed behaviors. Considering this extent of motivation, we suspected that we would be able to use these preferred foods as reinforcers for training him to eat nonpreferred foods. The variety of foods offered at mealtimes would be used in general as reinforcers for other prerequisite behaviors in attention, compliance, and language training.

In this program, data were recorded on the number of trials during mealtime in which he was offered a variety of nonpreferred foods and the percent of those trials in which he took the nonpreferred food and was reinforced by receiving some preferred food. As the data approximated 100 percent reinforcement, new foods were added and offered on a round-robin basis.

Treatment A: A baseline was accumulated for two days, (six meals) in which we offered him meals on a free-choice basis to determine if there were any preferences in addition to those the parents had reported to us. It was found that very few items were actually preferred; most foods were rejected by him. Cereals and starches dominated his diet.

After accumulation of this baseline information, we used those foods identified as being most preferred to reinforce eating of other nonpreferred foods. The management order was held constant throughout the program and was as follows: On each trial he was given one-half teaspoon of food. If he ate this, he received one teaspoon of reinforcing food which also was held in front of him. Initially, we began with the most highly preferred reinforcement foods. As the food program progressed, we used foods which had acquired a reinforcement valence to reinforce eating new foods. We checked off on a menu those foods which were most reinforcing and least reinforcing and moved from reinforcing more preferred foods down to less preferred foods. The verbal cue before he was given the nonpreferred food was, "Karl, eat the _____." He was given each bite of the nonpreferred food on a teaspoon on a plate before him. He had to use the utensil himself to put the food into his mouth, but the staff presented the reinforcement food to him. During this program, primary reinforcement was not used for other programs; food was used exclusively in this program. The total mealtime was twenty minutes. This was sufficient for Karl to receive the majority of his meal yet managed to maintain some level of drive state. He was not allowed between-meal snacks. The initial reinforcers were composed of chocolate milk, ice-cream, potato chips, and certain kinds of cereal, the latter particularly being used at breakfast. As the program gradually progressed, we moved in the use of crackers, bacon, frosting, candy, and sugared cereal. Further into the program other acquired reinforcement foods were used to reinforce eating the remaining nonpreferred ones. This program was in effect for all meals every day of the week; the data are shown in figure 4–53. The successive meals were sampled over a period of forty-five days.

Results: The treatment goal was satisfied. Karl, in his very concrete way, learned to adapt to the program of eating food in a "round-robin" fashion throughout the meal. He began to like a much greater

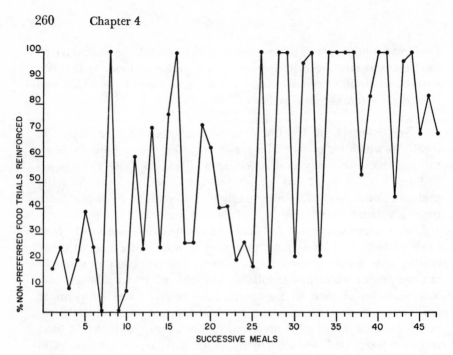

FIGURE 4–53 *Treatment Sequence for Teaching Karl to Eat a Greater Variety of Foods*

variety of foods; in fact, toward the termination of the program, we had a youngster who was gradually becoming overweight and was becoming very persistent in his rummaging about for all kinds of food. This may, in fact, be a detrimental aspect to this kind of program for certain autistic children in that they may become overtrained and food acquires too high a valence as a reinforcer for them and becomes an obsession in their daily routine. Caution should be advised in the implementation of such a program, particularly in that its use may be restricted in the home setting because of this problem.

Accelerating Karl's Spontaneous Speech in Both Cottage and School

Behavior Counted: Two kinds of data were accumulated for this study. First was the number of speech trials in which staff trained him according to the management orders listed below. This data was recorded to monitor that the program was being performed as scheduled. We learned that if staff are not required to record the training trials, that they gradually provide fewer trials until the language training is entirely ineffectual. Spontaneous speech was the second behavior counted in this program; staff counted on the designated sample days, the total frequency of his initiating spontaneous speech which was appropriate to the situation. It should be clarified that his speech was always limited in its complexity; quite often his language was relegated to simply labeling an item or making a very simple three- to four-word statement.

Treatment A: Karl's speech program required staff expanding on his responses to their cue, followed by his positive practicing the correct response. This was accomplished by scheduling speech training sessions each day. Each trial would begin by having a basic question such as, "What is this?" or "What is X person doing?" If he was able to give the correct response, it was affirm by saying, "Yes, Karl, this is a ball." Thus, for each response he gave he was reinforced and also given cues on how to expand his answer. We then positive practice with him the expanded phrase we gave back in response to his answer. Error responses were assisted with as many cues as possible to prompt him to provide a suitable answer. If he could not do this, we gave him the answer and had him rehearse it at least two times, followed by social and primary reinforcement. The special education teacher provided the graduated questions staff taught during the training program. When he reached 85 percent success on the question in training at any one time, as assessed by her testing him in the school situation, staff were given more advanced questions to teach him. The speech sessions occurred once in the morning and again in the evening and also at mealtimes, using food as a reinforcer. This program was conducted after food had acquired its reinforcement value as indicated in the previous program. At that stage, he was able to reinforce himself with the food when staff indicated that he made a correct response by reinforcing him socially, after which he took a bite of food. The reinforcement schedule for all trials was 1:1 social reinforcement successes, including hugs. When he was in session training, which included mealtimes after eye-contact had been established, he received the 1:1 social as well as 1:1 primaries. During the remainder of the day when a staff asked him a question in which he was to respond, he was given 1:1 social reinforcement only for correct responses. Sampling was recorded in the cottage on all-day counts on the designated days.

Results: As shown in figure 4–54, the number of speech trials dropped from greater than 180 down to 60 per day. The frequency of his spontaneous speech occurring outside of session time did accelerate from roughly 10 times daily to approximately 60 times per day. The quality of his speech was not sampled or demonstrated in this figure, but was represented in his language examinations of the pre- and post-test. The results were considered satisfactory in terms of accelerating his language and improving complexity slightly. It

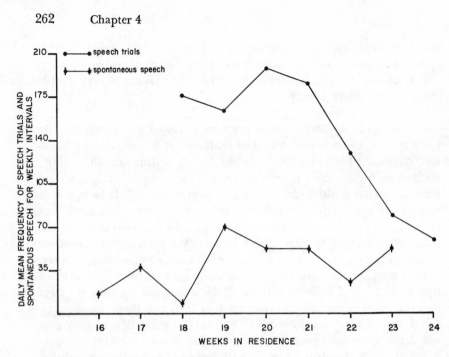

FIGURE 4-54 *Accelerating Karl's Spontaneous Speech in Both Cottage and School*

was apparent that to maintain the level of speech, as retarded as it was, did require considerable reinforcement and stimulation by other persons. It is predictable that without this constant programming, his speech would drop to that very simplistic and often inappropriate form apparent at date of admission.

Teaching Karl to Control his Darting Behavior

Behavior Counted: The behavior counted as shown in figure 4–55 was the number of times he ran away from a situation in which he was supposed to be occupied either by direct instruction or loose structure such as playing in the dayroom. However, during the baseline and treatment condition B, we counted the number of times he darted during two twenty-minute sessions occurring in the morning and evening, whereas under treatment condition C, it was a total all-day sample count. So, in treatment condition C there were more occasions for the occurrence of darting to occur, which perhaps was a more sensitive indicator of generalization of treatment effects.

Treatment A: This treatment was the baseline condition, two twenty-minute intervals; we counted each time Karl left the room in which he was occupied with a staff, or expected to remain on some task by himself, or by playing with other children. When he left the room, which usually was while running, staff would say, "Karl, come back to the room." If within five seconds, he did not return, they walked him back to the room. The dotted lines on the graph represent days when samples were not taken.

Treatment B: Under this treatment condition, a verbal cue was given Karl to return back to the situation each time he darted away. If he did not return within five seconds staff went to him, benignly, and walked him back. They then gave him the expectation of "Stay in your room." If he stayed there for several minutes (two or three minutes), they praised him for having done as they had requested. The purpose of this program was to praise the alternate behavior, and hopefully to teach him to respond to the verbal cue of returning. As shown in figure 4–55, this program was not sufficiently effective, since within the sample interval he darted at least twice. This would have certainly been an annoying behavior in a public school classroom if, within every twenty minutes, he ran out of the classroom two times. This was a program in which we had to have total control of the behavior. We then proceeded to treatment condition C.

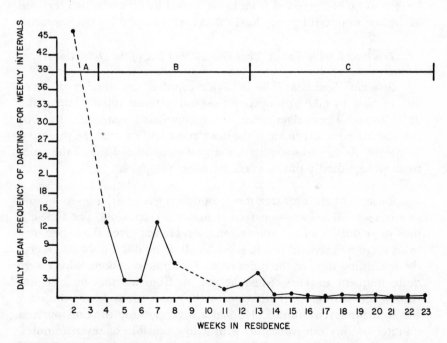

FIGURE 4–55 *Karl's Darting Responses in Both Cottage and School*

Treatment C: In treatment condition C, each time Karl darted from a situation he received a two-minute time-out with an explanation of why he received that time-out. He then was returned back to the situation, and after several minutes had transpired in which he was in that situation and not darting, he was praised socially, and variably given primary rewards of preferred cereals. The cereals were gradually eliminated from the program towards termination of treatment. This program was in effect during the remainder of his residency and also taught to his parents and public school teacher.

Results: The results were considered satisfactory after we had instigated the time-out condition. We surmised that the reason we were unable to achieve a complete elimination of the behavior was that his running away elicited reinforcement from us by simply chasing him. He seemed to maintain a stable rate of this darting behavior. Thus, this treatment condition of B was ineffectual in completely controlling the behavior because of these hypothesized inadvertent reinforcement properties of the procedure. The punishment program of the time-out was necessary to eliminate this response from his repertoire during his treatment residency. This was a difficult program for the family to maintain at home as well as for the public school teacher because of the long-standing duration of the sporadic reinforcement he had received from being chased by others, which was one of the few wonderful games Karl could exercise upon his environment.

Teaching Karl to Take a Time-Out without Use of the Quiet Room

Behavior Counted: The behavior counted was number of times he was able to take appropriate time-out without reliance upon the quiet room. These data were not accumulated systematically, but checked infrequently to see if the quiet room had effected the preferred treatment. As this was acquired, the time-out without use of the quiet room was gradually put in effect for other programs.

Treatment A: This treatment condition gave Karl a seven-minute time-out for all behaviors currently under deceleration. The time-out took place outside of the quiet-room door. He was given the expectancy to sit there quietly and not to move at all; if he did, he would receive the remaining time in the quiet room. On those occasions, which were quite frequent initially, when he got up from his time-out, he was then taken without verbalization to the quiet room where the door was shut for seven minutes. He had a total possible time of fourteen minutes on any one time-out, with a low possible of seven minutes. Gradually, as he succeeded in taking his time-out appropriately and not having to be placed in a quiet room, he was moved further and further away from the quiet room.

Results: The program was effective in that we were able to use a two-minute time-out for a variety of other programs in effect without having to rely upon the use of the quiet room to "back-up" his taking an appropriate time-out. This program was a necessity for the classroom and the home. It should be pointed out, however, that when he did return home he retrieved much of his darting behavior, and a quiet room had to be built into the classroom and in his home to back-up his taking appropriate time-outs. The program was considered effective at home eventually, since a later visit revealed that the quiet room we had constructed was being used as a cupboard for storage of food. Either they had given up on the use of a portable quiet room as necessary for the back-up or else Karl was getting considerable reinforcement for taking that quiet room time-out!

Teaching Karl to Control Frequency of Bizarre Sounds

Behavior Counted: Karl demonstrated a variety of whining, howling, and screaming sounds as well as other bizarre articulations which had no word value. Staff were to count the total frequency of these sounds, which were exclusive of communicative words. These were all-day counts taken on the assigned sample days.

Treatment A: This was a baseline condition in which all staff responded in a controlled manner of ignoring him and simply counting the total frequency of these bizarre sounds emitted by Karl. One-hundred fifty-five was the high count for the daily frequency of these sounds per day.

Treatment B: In treatment condition B, each time he emitted one of these sounds, staff told him, "Stop that noise." This was done in a negative manner, in a form of verbal social admonishment. Periodically during the day in cottage and in school, when Karl was not demonstrating the sounds, staff praised him socially for appropriate language usage, reflecting that he was not making a bizarre sound.

Results: The results in figure 4–56 show that the frequency of these behaviors was diminished, but not eliminated as preferred. Since his total program had an excesive number of time-outs, and was overloaded on the negative side, we felt that this response was more tolerable than the others currently on a time-out program, so we did not press for further deceleration. It was suspected that the stable rate

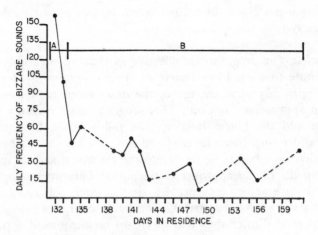

FIGURE 4-56 *Karl's Bizarre Sounds in the Cottage*

was occurring because of some reinforcement value in the social admonishment. We suspected that there was some reversed polarity of
his reinforcers which accounted for this unusual effect. This is not
unusual with some autistic children (Browning and Stover 1971).

Teaching Karl to Maintain Four-Second Eye Contact at Fifteen-feet in the Classroom and Cottage Setting

Behavior Counted: Staff counted the total number of trials in
which Karl was successful in maintaining eye contact criterion. Eye
contact was defined as his turning and looking and holding eye contact with the trainer for a specified time period.

Treatment A: This attention-shaping program was performed at
meals with staff seated across the table from Karl. Initially, primary
and social reinforcement were given on a 1:1 ratio with a staff feeding
Karl for maintaining eye contact at criterion. As shown in later steps,
this was changed to where he eventually fed himself for correct eye
contact. This was gradually changed to performing this program in
sessions outside of mealtime in which social reinforcement was used
on a 1:1 ratio for correct responses. Before moving on to successive
steps, he had to achieve at least 85 percent success. This is not reflected in the data since weekly averages are represented. But, at the
last training trial before moving to the next successive step, he received at least 85 percent success. We began at a one-second criterion
level which he initially could maintain for only about 15 percent

of all training trials. The program progressed from sitting right next to him to eventually a fifteen-foot distance. This criterion was considered to be acceptable for speech training and was all that we were able to effect during the six-month curriculum. Actually this was not a sufficient duration for public school room requirements in academic structure. The results of this program are shown in figure 4–57.

Treatment B: A 1:1 primary reinforcement schedule and social reinforcement program performed at meals requiring two-second eye contact for reward.

Treatment C: A 1:2 primary reinforcement schedule, with a 1:1 social reinforcement schedule was utilized to maintain two-second eye contact as trained during mealtimes.

Treatment D: A 1:2 primary reinforcement schedule with a 1:1 social reinforcement schedule for correct trials was established to maintain two-minute rest interval intervened between each set of five trials because we were expriencing fatigue effects with Karl and a diminution of performance.

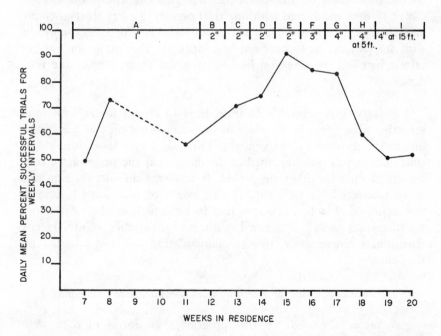

FIGURE 4–57 *Training Karl to Maintain a Four-Second Eye Contact at Fifteen Feet*

Treatment E: This program was the same as treatment Step D, with the exception that a one-minute rest interval occurred after each set of five trials.

Treatment F: This program was the same as treatment Step E, with the exception that three-second eye contact was demanded for the criterion response which would receive reinforcement on the 1:2 primary and a 1:1 social schedule.

Treatment G: This program was the same as treatment Step F with the exception that four-second eye contact was now required.

Treatment H: This was the same as treatment G, with the exception that the program was conducted at five feet from Karl, and he was allowed to reinforce himself with food as directed by staff for correct responses on a 1:2 primary reinforcement schedule and 1:1 social reinforcement schedule.

Treatment I: This was the same as treatment Step H, with the exception that we now trained with staff fifteen feet away from Karl. At the conclusion of this treatment step, two twenty-minute sessions each day were conducted with one trial occurring every thirty seconds at a distance of at least fifteen feet. A 1:1 social reinforcement schedule with no primary reinforcement was utilized. This program was retained in effect on a session basis during the remainder of the residency.

Results: We were able to train Karl to attend for at least four seconds to his name in a variety of situations—not only at mealtimes but in the dayroom, classroom, etc. This was a very short interval of time, and it was recommended at discharge that the program be continued to increase this time period. It was very difficult for him not to be distracted for time intervals in excess of four seconds, and it was expected that this program had to be kept into effect for many months, and always sustained with some variable reinforcement schedule. Unfortunately, this recommendation was not adopted by the school.

Treatment Sequence for Teaching Karl Compliance to Commands

Behavior Counted: In this program, two forms of data were accumulated as illustrated in figure 4–58. The primary data were that of the number of trials in compliance training and the number of times he responded appropriately and was reinforced. This provided us a daily mean percent compliance to verbal commands based on weekly intervals. Later in the program we sampled his attention during these sessions to determine if there was a relationship occurring between these responses.

Treatment A: As an introduction to this shaping program, there are several points which should be clarified. First, Karl was a very primitive child and we had to decide in advance the kinds of instructions we were going to teach him to respond to. These would be ones which would be expected in his home and in school. This program started at a very low-level, and it did not advance to very complex behavior. In a sense, we were training this very concrete child, who had difficulty generalizing, to respond to a very circumspect number of commands. Generalization was slight to other commands in the school setting. But in general, he learned by the conclusion of this program to respond to these and similar commands.

In treatment condition A, two fifteen-minute sessions per day were performed. These sessions were held fairly constant throughout the program. On days when more sessions could be conducted they were carried out. In treatment A, he was repeatedly given training on the command of, "Come here," for which on successful responses he received social and primary reinforcement on a 1:1 schedule. He was not shown the reinforcement when the command was being made. The commands were given first at five feet and gradually increased until it approximated that expected in the classroom, with twenty feet being the outside limits of most commands.

Treatment B: During this treatment condition the reinforcement contingency was entirely a social one on a 1:1 basis. He received this reinforcement for responding appropriately to the commands given in the two fifteen-minute daily sessions of: (1) come here, (2) sit down, (3) come in the day room, (4) hold my hand, and (5) pick up. . . . When he did not comply to these commands, he would receive a maximum fifteen-minute time-out for noncompliance. This time-out took place in the quiet room, but also was coordinated with the program of teaching him how to take a correct time-out. That is, if he took the time-out without using the quiet room it was acceptable, but if he could not, the quiet room was utilized.

Treatment C: At this stage, the time was decreased to a fourteen-minute time-out in the quiet room or an acceptable time-out beside the quiet room. The commands added at this point in his compliance training included: (6) take off, (7) put down, (8) walk, (9) stay in your room, and (10) sit up.

Treatment D: In this stage of the treatment sequence, time-outs for noncompliance to the commands being trained were a thirteen-minute time-out in the quiet room or an appropriate time-out beside the quiet room. As may be seen, we were diminishing time in the time-out while also adding a greater variety of commands. The new commands added to the list to be trained were as follows: (11) put "X" on "Y" (different educational objects), (12) put "X" in "Y" (different educational objects), (13) color, (14) walk to "X" place, and (15) point to object indicated.

Treatment E: At this stage, a twelve-minute time-out in the quiet room was used for noncompliance. We continued a 1:1 social reinforcement for compliance to the new commands added to the list which were: (16) stay in bed, (17) stand on "X" place, (18) walk beside me, and (19) stop whining.

Treatment F: At this and successive steps, the same commands described above were continued not just in sessions, but also at other times during the day. We were trying to expand generalization effects by training at various times and places so he would not be conditioned to just being compliant to these commands in various circumscribed conditions.

Treatment G: Ten minutes time in the quiet room for time-outs was used at this stage.

Treatment H: Nine minutes time in the quiet room for noncompliance was utilized; the rest of the program remained constant.

Treatment I: Eight minutes time in the quiet room was used for noncompliance, and the commands now also included response to simple questions for which we knew he had the available response. Treatment I was extended at its later stages to include a seven-minute time-out for noncompliance. This program was held in effect until we discontinued his residency.

Results: The results were considered satisfactory to the extent that we were able to teach this child a variety of very simple commands which would facilitate training in the classroom and at home. Social reinforcement was useful, although a seven-minute time-out was necessary to maintain the program. His adjustment was being maintained only at about 65 to 70 percent, which is not considered optimal. The extent of his attention during these trials is shown on figure 4–58. This was measured by the number of trials in which he

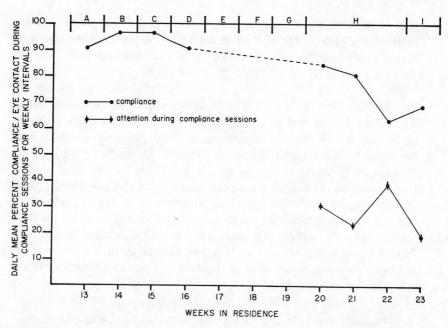

FIGURE 4-58 *Karl's Compliance to Verbal Requests*

gave eye contact to the commands given to him. As may be seen, this eye contact attention was very low, which probably accounted for some of his difficulty in maintaining the criterion level of 85 percent compliance which we anticipated. This also indicated that his attention training had not generalized to this situation, whereas it had been trained for language.

Controlling Karl's Pilfering other Children's Belongings, and in Offices

Behavior Counted: This program was not monitored for Karl but was placed on a general management order.

Treatment A: The treatment program was simply to give Karl a two-minute time-out outside of the room where the behavior occurred, or to be backed-up with the quiet room if he was unable to take that time-out appropriately. This time-out was given for each occasion in which he was stealing foods, pilfering other childrens' rooms, or rummaging through the nursing station or other offices when they were unattended. This was exploratory behavior and not really a malicious doing on his part whatsoever. It was one aspect of his intellectual deficit in which he was not really able to distinguish what was his or someone else's. In fact, it is questionable if he even realized the concept of ownership, beyond his own clothing and a few personal items in the form of toys. He was given a time-out using a rather low-level verbal reprimand for this behavior, if it was observed before it was actually completed.

Results: The treatment effect was considered to be useful at the Treatment Center but we were unable to monitor its effect at home or in the school setting. It was our general impression, which was conveyed to the home and school, that this program would have to be kept in effect for several years. Its generalized effect would be to train a rather controlled youngster who simply did not touch much of anything unless he were instructed to do so. Unfortunately, Karl did not have a program in which he was reinforced for using his own things correctly, which may have facilitated this discrimination for him. In retrospect, we felt we did not capitalize on his exploratory behavior sufficiently, but that presumes a normal child model, which was not the case for Karl.

Teaching Karl to Remain in his Seat for Periods of Ten Consecutive Minutes while in School

Behavior Counted: While in school and receiving instructions where he was expected to be in his seat, the teacher counted the number of times Karl was out of his seat, the length of time he was out of his seat, and the length of time of the instruction session. Being out of his seat was defined as his bottom not touching the chair and included partially lifting himself to wandering aimlessly about the room.

Treatment A: One of the reasons Karl was not eligible for placement in a special education classroom in his community was that it was impossible for him to be seated for any reasonable period of time in the classroom. He was constantly bounding, running about, and darting out of the room. Other teachers' attempts to keep him seated by admonishment or physically holding him there had been fruitless. The intent of this study was to train Karl to remain seated for at least ten-minute intervals of time. It was hypothesized that his wandering around and apparently "getting into things" was enjoyable and reinforcing activities for Karl, and seemed to typify most of his daily behavior. Being out of his seat and wandering around doing the things he wished, so long as it was not exceptionally disruptive to other children, was used as the reinforcer for learning to remain seated in his chair for increasing intervals of time. The program was graded on shaping steps in which he received a diminishing amount of out-of-seat time as the reinforcer allowed for increasing periods of time of being in his seat. We thus were using the inappropriate response to be the reinforcer for the preferred and acquired behavior. It should be pointed out that this kind of an approach, albeit often successful, is one which should be done with considerable thought. One does run the risk of using an abnormal response as a reinforcement when that response may be so disruptive it would put the child at a loss on his eventual return home. In this case, however, we were concurrently training Karl to be appropriate when he was out of his seat by not being disruptive to other children or destructive to property in the classroom.

The baseline data, shown in figure 4–59 under condition A, was controlled. Four thirty-minute sessions were recorded for Karl's out-of-seat behavior. When he left his chair, after the first thirty-seconds, he was asked to sit down; thereafter, the teacher ignored him, sat in a chair by his desk and looked and played with the task that she had been instructing prior to his leaving. When he returned to the chair, which he eventually would, they continued with the task, with no further comment about his leaving. He was not reinforced for sitting, or returning. If he got up and did something destructive, then the teacher got up and led him away from that activity with as little attention as possible and then left him. He was still expected to go back to the chair on his own during this baseline interval. Figure 4–59 shows that 80 percent of the time during these thirty-minute

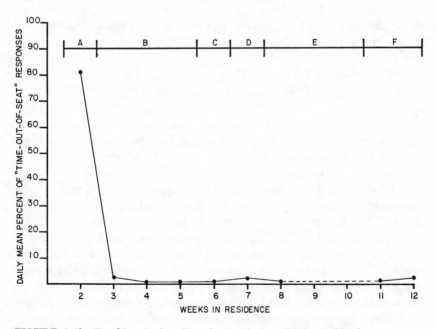

FIGURE 4–59 *Teaching Karl to Remain in His Seat While in School*

sessions, Karl was out of his seat and wandering around. Obviously, his behavior was problematic, even under such positive conditions.

Treatment B: The remaining treatment conditions were conducted throughout the time that Karl was in school under direct supervised instruction. A timer was used with a bell to ring after the completion of a set time interval. During condition B, the time was set for five minutes. When the timer rang, Karl was told he could get up and play for five minutes. If Karl got up and left his chair before the five minutes had transpired, the teacher got up and directed him back to the chair with as little physical and verbal interruption as possible. She would merely say, "Sit," and reinforce him socially and occasionally physically for sitting at that time. Also, throughout the five minutes in which he was seated, he was socially and physically reinforced by the teacher on a variable schedule set by herself. Ninety-five percent accuracy for four consecutive days was necessary before moving on to the next shaping step. This criterion was held throughout the course of the treatment program.

Treatment C: At this stage Karl had to remain seated for seven consecutive minutes, after which he was allowed three minutes of walking about the classroom.

Treatment D: At this stage Karl had to remain in his seat eight consecutive minutes; the reward was two minutes out-of-seat time to wandering around.

Treatment E: Karl now had to remain seated for nine consecutive minutes; the reward was two minutes out-of-seat time.

Treatment F: At this step, Karl had to remain seated for ten consecutive minutes, the reward was two minutes out-of-seat time to wander about the classroom.

Results: As shown in figure 4–59, the results were acceptable. By the conclusion of this program, which involved twelve weeks at the Center, he was working for ten minutes in his seat without leaving it. This program was maintained throughout the course of his residency. It was not performed as stringently during the remainder of the time, since it became apparent that he was gradually learning to be seated for longer intervals of time. However, it was seldom expected of him to remain in his seat working continuously for longer than fifteen minutes. This program was instructed to his teacher in the public school.

Improving Karl's Speech in School

Behavior Counted: This was a shaping program so the responses being reinforced on successive treatment steps were different. Thus, the behavior being monitored was the percent of successful trials on each successive step to ascertain if that step had been mastered sufficiently to progress to the next one. The data are shown in figure 4–60.

Treatment A: At this initial step, we were working on teaching him how to match Peabody language training picture cards with ones that were the same and conceptually the same. This involved matching two identical pictures out of a group, and progressed to matching ones which could be categorized the same such as food or animals, etc.

Treatment B: At this stage in training sessions during the day and in school, the picture cards were used as well as other objects about the room. He was asked a simple question, to which he was expected to give only a one-word response. The questions dealt with "what color," "how many," "what is 'x' doing," and a yes/no answer to a question. The trials were conducted at least six seconds apart. It was necessary to keep his training trials moving fairly consistently; otherwise, his attention tended to drift, particularly at this stage.

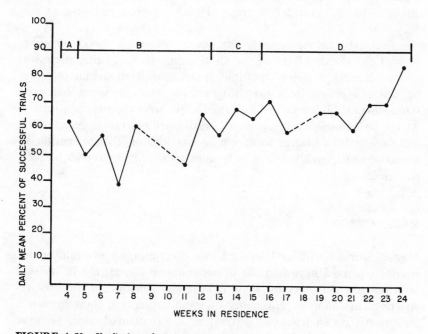

FIGURE 4–60 *Karl's Speech Program in School*

Treatment C: Treatment B was continued, with the addition of more complex questions that included "who" and "what" at trials five seconds apart. If an incorrect response was elicited, the teacher waited ten seconds and repeated the question. If an incorrect response was again given, she waited ten seconds and it was repeated, but this time with a correct answer for him to reply with. When he gave the correct answer, social and primary reinforcement were used for the correct responses. Error responses were ignored and correct responses were reinforced with social and primary reinforcement on a 1:1 ratio, as was the case for treatment B.

Treatment D: At this stage a 1:2 social and primary reinforcement schedule was used for the same training questions as in treatment C. Whenever he said anything spontaneously that was appropriate, he was reinforced initially with primary and social reinforcement; later it was only with social reinforcement. If there was something that he wished to have, we required that he use one word to indicate his need. Pronunciation was not emphasized at the initial stages of the program, but rather simply to accelerate verbalization. After he stated the one word indicating his wish, he was socially reinforced, and given that which he wanted. A list of words indicating things that he knew and did not know was maintained so that staff was aware of the available responses that he had, and those from which he would require "priming" in order to respond with a correct response.

Results: The results over the twenty-four-week speech program showed that at this level of speech training, he was being successful greater than 80 percent of the time. It was considered satisfactory since he had progressed from matching picture cards to using one-word statements to making known his needs which were socially appropriate. At the beginning of the program, he did demonstrate speech, but it was usually in a bizarre form, e.g., recitations of TV commentaries, advertisements, and words which were totally irrelevant to his current needs.

REFLECTIONS

Having worked with and studied this diverse group of children for fourteen years, I have had the opportunity to discern the behavioral requirements necessary for these children to function in the least restrictive environment. For many of these youngsters, their eventual, least restrictive environment is likely to be a structured group home at some point in their life, in contrast to the most restrictive environment of protracted residential care in a state operated facility. This protracted experience leads you to always think in terms of fifteen years ahead when you first interview that five-year-old handicapped child. You must consider from the very beginning what the community will tolerate in this child's behavior when he or she is an adult. You need not feel repulsed by a highly structured, and in fact restrictive, environment at a young age with a handicapped child. It is easy to move from that kind of programming to a less restrictive one. The child's development, his or her data, will allow you to make that discretion. However, if you err in having an unstructured environment and lack of control of the disruptive behaviors, those habits will only become more engrained, more impervious to extinction or replacement by alternate behaviors, and progressively diminish the likelihood of that child functioning in a community based program as an adult. In other words, you can easily progress from a tightly controlled behavioral program to a more open and free operant program if a child has the skills to cope with that kind of learning setting. But the converse is not likely to be the case; it is unlikely that you will have much success in rectifying behavior of a noncompliant, aggressive and bizarre adolescent. Even if you begin with a young preschool child, such as the autistic youngster, he or she is facing years of tightly controlled learning setting simply in order to acquire the prevocational skills necessary for functioning in a sheltered workshop. If you consider the prospects of competitive employment, you may be assured that employers will not tolerate disruptive or asocial behavior.

Quite often teachers only have the opportunity to work with a particular youngster for a year, or perhaps two or three at most. Seldom are they able to follow the same youngsters for a dozen years to determine what happens when there is supervision, as contrasted to the lack of it. Our experience has been to not believe that any of the disruptive behaviors will developmentally melt away. If there is a variety of bizarre behaviors, we have observed longitudinally that these may qualitatively change, but the same behavior patterns persist—sometimes in a different form. With some youngsters, the identical behaviors can be retrieved after even five or six years of work. This is not discouraging, it simply means that these children also have memories. You may almost bet that the very symptomatic autistic child with unchecked bizarre mannerisms at age five will progress into lethargic posturing by adolescence. You can almost be assured that the hyperactive, distractible, out-of-seat, brain-damaged child—if unchecked by adolescence—will be a drop out, if not already catalogued into an anti-social group of peers. If we are ever to achieve the goal of the handicapped child eventually functioning in a community, we must pay attention to the behavioral requirements in that community. The following are some of the behavioral requirements that are necessary for prevocational training, and the expectancies for functioning in a sheltered group home or apartment living environment.

If a young adult is to function in a sheltered workshop facility, there are a variety of prevocational skills which must be acquired. For example, the individual should be able to work from 9:00 A.M. to 3:00 P.M. and be in seat, on task and nondistractible for one hour intervals with five-minute breaks maximum and a forty-five-minute lunch break. The individual should be trained on match-to-sample tasks. Aggressive, bizarre, and disruptive behaviors of any kind must be nonexistent or very marginal. The individual must be able to function on a variety of transportation systems, either by taking public transit unescorted or riding without behavioral disruption in a handicab. They must be able to eat appropriately and independently without bothering their peers at that unstructured time. Their work and behavioral performance must function on an exceedingly thin reinforcement schedule with very infrequent redirects; time-outs must not be necessary—in fact they cannot depend upon point or token systems to sustain their behavior except by the end of each shift. Compliance to redirects back to task activity, or to cease some disruptive behavior, must be in excess of 95 percent expectancy. If the individual is to function in gainful employment, the behavioral requirements would even be steeper. At this point, one must consider dress, grooming, language, or facility with alternate forms of communication, and ability to tolerate extreme forms of frustration, such as rebuff from other peers on the job.

The behavioral requirements for functioning in sheltered apartment living, or in a group home environment include the above and more. Here the individual has to be able to handle money, or follow supervised budgeting. Self-care and hygiene must be almost entirely independent. The individual needs to be receptive of normal types of entertainment such as television and group games, and not disruptive of other person's participation. They must be tractable to following a group in community travel, if they are not able to do so independently by walking or using public transit. Toileting and eating obviously must be of no problem to the caretakers, in fact their table manners should be close to normal. Making beds, straightening their room, participating in cooking, setting the table, vacuuming rugs, washing hair, and complying within two seconds or less reaction time to adult commands or requests are all almost taken for granted.

These kinds of reflections represent our experiences. The recommended approach is for the parents and teachers of the children to visit the possible adult community facilities and to record the behavioral requirements in those programs. To observe and write down exactly what those adult participants do during the day, would be most beneficial in the future planning for a handicapped child of that family and teacher. We suggest making that kind of assessment when the child is five years of age. In fact, these are the kinds of educational goals which should be stipulated in the individualized educational plan for the elementary age child. The normal child has all of those goals stipulated, and it is understood that he or she can achieve those goals. This is seldom the case with the severely handicapped children; they end up with a year by year curriculum which does not embody the long term goals and continuous program which takes into consideration that they too need a consistent educational environment. Academics are secondary to behavioral goals for these handicapped children. For the normal child, two plus two is always four through basic addition, the multiplication tables, long division, and on to higher math in high school. For the autistic, psychotic and neurologically involved child, in some years aggressive behavior means time-out, other years it is tolerated, and other years it means expulsion from school. This kind of discontinuity is what assures a nonadaptive adult.

References

Akerley, M. A. "The Invulnerable Parent." *Journal of Autism and Childhood Schizophrenia* 5 (September 1975): 275–281.

Anthony, W. A.; Buell, G. J.; Sharratt, S.; and Acthoff, M. E. "Efficacy of Psychiatric Rehabilitation." *Psychological Bulletin* 78 (1972): 447–456.

Bartak, L., and Rutter, M. "Differences Between Mentally Retarded and Normal Intelligence Autistic Children." *Journal of Autism and Childhood Schizophrenia* 6 (June 1976): 109–120.

Bender, L. "A Longitudinal Study of Schizophrenic Children with Autism." *Hospital and Community Psychiatry* 8 (1969): 230–237.

Browning, E. *One Step at a Time.* Manuscript in press, 1979.

Browning, R. M., and Stover, D. O. *Behavior Modification in Child Treatment.* Chicago: Aldine-Atherton, 1971.

Cain, A. C. "Special 'Isolated' Abilities in Severely Psychotic Young Children." In S. Chess and A. Thomas, *Annual Progress in Child Psychiatry and Child Development.* New York: Brunner-Mazel, 1970.

Churchill, D. W. "The Relation of Infantile Autism and Early Childhood Schizophrenia to Developmental Language Disorders of Childhood." *Journal of Autism and Childhood Schizophrenia* 2 (1972): 182–197.

Darby, J. K. "Neuropathologic Aspects of Psychosis in Children." *Journal of Autism and Childhood Schizophrenia* 6 (December 1976): 339–352.

DeMeyer, M. K.; Churchill, D. W.; Pontius, W.; and Gilkey, K. M. "A Comparison of Five Diagnostic Systems for Childhood Schizophrenia and Infantile Autism." *Journal of Autism and Childhood Schizophrenia* 1 (1971): 1975–1189.

DeMeyer, M. K.; Pontius, W.; et al. "Parental Practices and Innate Activity in Normal, Autistic, and Brain-Damaged Infants." *Journal of Autism and Childhood Schizophrenia* 2 (1972): 49–66.

Dullaart-Pruyser, E. "Operant Conditioning with Autistic Children: A Survey of the Literature." *Nederlands Tijdschrift voor de Psychologic en haar Grensgebieden* 32 (July 1977): 307–332.

Goffman, E. *Asylums.* New York: Anchor Books, 1961.

Gold, S. "Further Investigation of a Possible Epileptogenic Factor in the Serum of Psychotic Children." *Australian and New Zealand Journal of Psychiatry* 1 (1967): 153–156.

Gollin, M., and Moody, L. "Review of Behavior Modification in Child Treatment." *Journal of Contemporary Psychology* 157 (1973).

Havelkova, M. "Follow-up Study of 71 Children Diagnosed as Psychotic in Preschool Age." *American Journal of Orthopsychiatry* 38 (1968): 846–857.

Hutt, C.; Hutt, S. J.; Lee, D.; and Ounsted, C. "Arousal and Childhood autism." *Nature* 204 (1964): 908–909.

Hutt, S. J.; Hutt, C.; Lee, D.; and Ounsted, C. "A Behavioral and Electroencephalographic Study of Autistic Children. *Journal of Psychiatric Research* 3 (1965): 181–197.

Kanner, L. "Follow-up Study of Eleven Autistic Children Originally Reported in 1943." *Journal of Autism and Childhood Schizophrenia* 1 (1971): 119–145.

Kanner, L. "Early Infantile Autism Revisited." *Journal of Autism and Childhood Schizophrenia* 2 (1972): 27–32.

Kehrer, H. E. "Behaviour Therapy in Childhood Autism." *Zeitschrift fur Kinder-und Jugend Psychiatric* 2 (1974): 233–247.

Lichstein, K. L., and Schreibman, L. "Employing Electric Shock with Autistic Children: A Review of the Side Effects." *Journal of Autism and Childhood Schizophrenia* 6 (June 1976): 163–173.

Lockyer, L., and Rutter, M. "A Five-to-Fifteen Year Follow-up Study of Infantile Psychosis." *British Journal of Psychiatry* 115 (1969): 865–882.

Lovaas, O. I. *The Autistic Child: Language Development Through Behavior Modification.* New York: Irvington, 1977.

Lovaas, O. I.; Schreibman, L.; Koegel, R. L.; and Rehm, J. "Selective Responding by Autistic Children to Multiple Sensory Input." *Journal of Abnormal Psychology* 77 (1971): 211–222.

Marr, J. N.; Miller, E. R.; and Straub, R. "Operant Conditioning of Attention with a Psychotic Girl." *Behavior Research and Therapy* 4 (1966): 85–87.

McConnell, O. L. "Control of Eye Contact in an Autistic Child." *Journal of Child Psychology and Psychiatry* 8 (1967): 249–255.

Mehegan, C. C. "Hyperlexia: A Study of Exceptional Reading Ability in Brain-Damaged Children." *Neurology* 19 (1969): 302.

Mulcahy, R. F. "Autism: Beautiful Children." *Mental Retardation Bulletin* 1 (1972–73): 73–77.

Ornitz, E. M.; Ritvo, E. R.; Panman, L. M.; Lee, V. H.; Carr, E. M.; and Walter, R. D. "The Auditory Evoked Response in Normal and Autistic

Children during Sleep. *Electroencephalographic and Clinical Neurophysiology* 25 (1968): 221–230.

Ornitz, E. M., and Ritvo, E. R. "Perceptual Inconstancy in Early Infantile Autism." *Archives of General Psychiatry* 18 (1968): 76–78.

Ornitz, E. M.; Ritvo, E. R.; Brown, M. B.; Lafranchi, S.; Parmelee, T.; and Walter, R. D. "The EEG and Rapid Eye Movements during REM Sleep in Normal and Autistic Children." *Electroencephalographic and Clinical Neurophysiology* 26 (1969): 167–175.

Premack, D. "Toward Empirical Behavior Laws: I. Positive Reinforcement." *Psychological Review* 66 (1959): 219–233.

Prior, M. R.; Gajzago, C. C.; and Knox, D. T. "An Epidemiological Study of Autistic and Psychotic Children in the Four Eastern States of Australia." *Australian and New Zealand Journal of Psychiatry* 10 (June 1976): 173–184.

Ricks, D. M.; and Wing, C. "Language, Communication and the use of Symbols in Normal and Autistic Children." *Journal of Autism and Childhood Schizophrenia* 5 (September 1975): 191–221.

Ritvo, E. R.; Freeman, B. S.; Ornitz, E. M.; and Tanquay, P. E., eds. *Autism: Diagnosis, Current Research and Management.* New York: Spectrum, 1976.

Seller, M. J., and Gold, S. "Seizures in Psychotic Children." *The Lancet* 1 (1964): 1325.

Simmons, J. O., and Lovaas, O. I. "Use of Pain and Punishment as Treatment Techniques with Childhood Schizophrenics." *American Journal of Psychotherapy* 23 (1969): 23–35.

Sullivan, R. C. "Hunches on Some Biological Factors in Autism." *Journal of Autism and Childhood Schizophrenia* 5 (June 1975): 177–184.

Tanquay, P. E.; Ornitz, E. M.; Forsythe, A. B.; and Ritvo, E. R. "Rapid Eye Movement (REM) Activity in Normal and Autistic Children during REM Sleep." *Journal of Autism and Childhood Schizophrenia* 6 (September 1976): 275–288.

Ullman, L. P. *Institution and Outcome.* Oxford: Pergamon Press, 1967.

White, P. T.; DeMeyer, W.; and DeMeyer, M. "EEG Abnormalities in Early Childhood Schizophrenia: A Double-Blind Study of Psychiatrically Disturbed and Normal Children during Promazine Sedation." *American Journal of Psychiatry* 120 (1964): 950–958.

Index